THE THINGS OUR FATHERS SAW

THE UNTOLD STORIES OF THE
WORLD WAR II GENERATION
FROM HOMETOWN, USA

VOLUME VII:
ACROSS THE RHINE

Matthew A. Rozell

WOODCHUCK HOLLOW PRESS

Hartford · New York

Copyright © 2021,2023 by Matthew A. Rozell. Version 3.28.24 LARGE PRINT. All rights reserved. No part of this publication may be reproduced, distributed, or transmitted in any form or by any means without the prior written permission of the publisher. Grateful acknowledgement is made for the credited use of various short quotations also appearing in other previously published sources. Please see author notes.

Information at matthewrozellbooks.com.

Maps by Susan Winchell. Cover design by Mary R. Rozell.

Front Cover: "Crossing the Rhine under enemy fire at St. Goar, March, 1945. 89th Infantry Division." US Army, Office of War Information. Public Domain Photographs, National Archives.

Back Cover: "Then came the big day when we marched into Germany-right through the Siegfried Line.", ca. 1945. Unknown photographer, United States Army. Office of War Information. National Archives, public domain.

Any additional photographs and descriptions sourced at Wikimedia Commons within terms of use, unless otherwise noted.

Publisher's Cataloging-in-Publication Data

Names: Rozell, Matthew A., 1961- author.
Title: Across the rhine : the things our fathers saw : the untold stories of the World War II generation, volume VII / Matthew A. Rozell.
Description: Hartford, NY : Matthew A. Rozell, 2021. | Series: The things our fathers saw, vol. 7. | Also available in audiobook format.
Identifiers: LCCN 2021922786 | ISBN 978-1-948155-49-6 large print pbk. | ISBN 978-1-948155-28-1 (hardcover) | ISBN 978-1-948155-14-4 (paperback) | ISBN 978-1-948155-26-7 (ebook)
Subjects: LCSH: World War, 1939-1945--Campaigns—Netherlands. | World War, 1939-1945--Campaigns--France--Normandy. | World War, 1939-1945--Campaigns—Belgium. | World War, 1939-1945--Campaigns—Germany. | World War, 1939-1945--Personal narratives, American. | Veterans--United States--Biography. | Military history, Modern--20th century. | BISAC: HISTORY / Military / World War II. | HISTORY / Military / Veterans. | BIOGRAPHY & AUTOBIOGRAPHY / Military.

matthewrozellbooks.com.

Created in the United States of America

*~To the memory of
The World War II Generation~
and
Tom Warner, Sr.
1931-2021*

***

'To survive ten months was to survive a hundred years. I could not even remember my former life. I was a fugitive from the law of averages.'

— U.S. TANK COMMANDER, RECOUNTING HIS BATTALION'S ADVANCE ACROSS THE RHINE

*

'Heroes are important—they exist, and can help you to know who and what you are. Tell the children that I was a warrior.'
— U.S. PARATROOPER, MOHAWK NATION, SIXTY YEARS AFTER THE WAR

THE THINGS OUR FATHERS SAW VII:

ACROSS THE RHINE

THE STORYTELLERS

(IN ORDER OF APPEARANCE):

NICHOLAS F. BUTRICO
ALBERT L. TARBELL
RICHARD M. MAROWITZ
TIMOTHY J. HORGAN
LAWRENCE E. BENNETT
AUGUSTINE J. DIFIORE
ROBERT C. BALDRIDGE
RUDOLF F. DRENICK
CHARLES J. ZAPPO
ALVIN M. COHEN
EMILIO J. DIPALMA
TONY HAYS
DOUGLAS VINK

THE THINGS OUR FATHERS SAW VII:

ACROSS THE RHINE

TABLE OF CONTENTS

PART ONE/THE ROAD TO THE REICH 19
TO LIBERATE A CONTINENT 23
THE RANGER 27
   'LOOK IN THE DEAD FILES' 30
   SHIPPING OUT 33
   COMMANDO TRAINING 34
   THE DAY OF DAYS 36
   POINTE DU HOC 39
   'NOT MADE TO TAKE CARE OF PRISONERS' 44
   'IT WENT RIGHT THROUGH MY LEGS' 48
   'LET'S GO TO PARIS' 52
   THE LAST MISSION 54
   THE ACCIDENT 62
   LOOTER NICK 66
   A CHANCE MEETING WITH GEN. PATTON 69
   THE LETTER 75
A BRIDGE TOO FAR 85

THE PARATROOPER I 91

INTO THE PARATROOPERS 98
ITALY 102
MARKET GARDEN 104
OUT THE DOOR 107
THE DUTCH UNDERGROUND 111
CROSSING THE WAAL 113
THE RAILROAD BRIDGE 116
'THEY'RE ZEROING IN!' 118
'LET'S HAVE THE INDIAN WORK ON HIM' 123
THE ROSARY BEADS 125
THE OLD CAT 127
THE OUTPOST 128

THE RECON MAN I 135

SHIPPING OVERSEAS 145
I&R MEN 148
ON THE ROAD 153

PART TWO/SETBACKS 165

THE CAVALRYMAN I 169

REPLACEMENT 173
THE BATTLE OF THE BULGE 176
PATROL DUTY 177
THE BOOBY TRAP 182

THE PARATROOPER II 187

    Moving Out 189
    'They Turned the Flak Guns on Us' 190
    The Priest 194
    Christmas Is Here 197
    'You're Going To Freeze to Death' 201
    'Be Good to Your New Commander' 206
    Annihilated 209

PART THREE/CROSSING OVER 213

'THE WAY IT WAS' 217

THE INFANTRY SERGEANT 221

    'They Had a Lot of Fight Left in Them' 227
    The German Soldier 230
    German Prisoners 232
    'A Hornet's Nest of SS' 235
    The General 239
    War's End 239
    'The Spirit Is There' 242
    Reflections 244

THE GIVER 247

    Harvard Man 252
    'A Little Lost Puppy' 256
    'We Ain't Taking No Prisoners' 259
    'We Were Supposed to Draw Fire' 263
    Seeing General Patton 266

- 'They Were Going to Hang That Kid' 267
- 'I'm A Giver' 271

THE FORWARD OBSERVER 275
- The Fire Direction Center 278
- The Guns 280
- Crossing the Rhine 282
- The New Jet Planes 284
- Nordhausen 286
- 'No Hero To Me' 289
- The Russians 290
- The Barter System 291
- 'I Can't Get Home!' 293

THE ROCKET MAN 297
- 'I Had a Grudge' 300
- The Secret Documents 302
- Operation Paperclip 303
- The End of the War 307

THE PARATROOPER III 311
- At Rest 312
- The Mark V 316
- 'It's Not My Time Yet' 320
- The Siegfried Line 323
- The Last Rhine Combat Patrol 328

THE CAVALRYMAN II 345

- Hitting the Rhine 345
- The Concentration Camp 347
- The Russians 349
- Rescuing the Lipizzaners 352
- Return to the Rhine 361

THE RECON MAN II 365
- The First Ones in Dachau 366
- 'I'm Throwing Her Down the Stairs!' 372
- 'These Things Come Naturally' 375

THE MEDIC 387
- 'A Horrible, Horrible Battle' 390
- 'A Horrible, Horrible Sight' 395
- Russians 399
- 'You Don't Realize How It Is Going to Affect You' 405

THE FALL OF BERLIN 409

THE PARATROOPER IV 411
- On To Berlin 411

JUDGMENT AT NUREMBERG 421

THE JEWISH GUARD KEEPER 425
- Overseas 429
- The Siegfried Line 431
- 'I'll Blow Your Goddamn Head Off' 433

- Pulling Guard Duty at Nuremberg 436
- 'Fresh Air Fanatics' 438
- 'How Do You Like Having a Jew Guard?' 441
- The Russian Delegation 444

THE COURTROOM SENTINEL 449

- Le Havre Replacements 453
- 'That's What You Call a Short Round' 456
- Crossing the River 459
- On The Run 461
- The Slave Laborers 464
- The Farm Raid 465
- 'They've Been Drinking with the Russians' . 467
- Nuremberg 469
- The Documents 470
- Sergeant of the Guard 471
- 'Goering and I, We Didn't get Along' 472
- The Return to Nuremberg 480
- 'I Think About Things Like That' 486

PART FOUR/LAST THOUGHTS 489

THE PARATROOPER V 491

- 'I Didn't Talk About the War' 497
- 'Tell the Children that I'm a Warrior' 498

DACHAU AND THE QUESTION 501

- Dachau Will Always Be with Us 505

WAR STORIES **517**
AMERICANS CAME TO LIBERATE **547**
ACKNOWLEDGEMENTS **565**

"Soldiers of the 55th Armored Infantry Battalion and a tank of the 22nd Tank Battalion move through a smoke-filled street. Wernberg, Germany."-Pvt. Joseph Scrippens, April 22, 1945. Source: National Archives, public domain.

Author's Note

I sat in the living room of the family of the eighty-year-old retired judge and former New York State Supreme Court justice, a reluctant but willing soldier who began his military career with the familiar letter from Uncle Sam, a ticket to picking up cigarette butts as a private at Fort Knox, then training in M4 Sherman tanks for what would become the invasion of France. He rocked in the chair and recounted hours of war stories, some funny, others that brought out the fluctuations between boredom and terror as his tank battalion moved from the beaches at Normandy to the Siegfried Line, the fortified dragon's teeth that demarked and viciously forbade entry upon German soil.

Some of his remarks at that conversation in the summer of 2001 struck me, and will be familiar to my longtime readers, as Judge Walsh became my friend—and my hero—in how he navigated his life with humility and concern for others, qualities that predisposed him to excel in his future occupation. As it was, in the summer and fall of 1944 he was just 23 years old.

Now actually I was kind of an old guy for the time; a lot of the infantry guys were eighteen, nineteen years old. Oh yeah, I was considered an old guy. Now let me tell you about the combat I was in. Like I said before, you couldn't remember what your mother looked like; you thought you had been there forever. I was in combat ten months straight. You have to realize that was a long time to be in combat and still be alive or not wounded! You just give up; you know there is no use to hoping that maybe you will get out tomorrow, you just are going to go on. You have that feeling and you just trot along; that's why we did [some] crazy stuff... Once we got to the Siegfried Line, then the Germans would tighten up. From October into December, it was bad. We were in Germany, the 743rd

Tank Battalion and 30th Division, north of Aachen, we even fought at Aachen. That was tough going—to survive ten months was to survive a hundred years! I could not even remember my former life. I was a fugitive from the law of averages, as it was.

A few years before our talk, as a high school history teacher I had begun inviting veterans into the classroom to share their experiences. As word got out and other students wished to join us, I began organizing morning, afternoon, and sometimes all-day symposiums on various topics related to World War II and the Holocaust. We began in the late nineties with local Pacific veterans. Near the 45th anniversary of the liberation of Dachau concentration camp, April 2000, and a year or so before my talk with Judge Walsh that would go on to change thousands of lives, three members of the local chapter of Veterans of the Battle of the Bulge made one of their first of many appearances at my high school, before a student audience of over 100 polite and respectful kids. Two of the three were Jewish; one had been present at the liberation of

Dachau forty-five years to the day, and the other, a guard at the Nuremberg War Trials after the war. Said one, in a later interview,

> There's three of us that have been going around to schools and churches and synagogues and so forth, talking to kids. They've got us running. That's been phenomenal. We each do about seven, eight minutes, a little bit of background of who we are and what we did in the Army and whatever. We ask for questions. We now book no less than two hours, and we go over time. The kids, the hands never go down, unbelievable.
>
> We did Hudson Falls High School. This was early on. We were only booking an hour and a half. We were supposed to talk from 1:00 to 2:30, and never got out until 4:00. Unbelievable. They're hungry. And the phenomenal part of the whole thing, the teacher wasn't even born yet.

That teacher was me. I was born sixteen years after the killing stopped; when I began my teaching career in the late 1980s, just forty years after the war, many veterans were still with us and newly retired—about the age I am now. Some felt ready to share their stories, and all who visited the classrooms across America were refreshed, energized, with a renewed sense of purpose after engaging with the future generations. As most of my readers with parents who lived through World War II can attest, most did not talk about it after the war. For many, it was only when they realized that people did not know about World War II, or worse, denied that the Holocaust had taken place, that they felt another duty to speak out. Teachers like me gave them the space and time to do that; I went on to create my own oral history project, and we were honored to ask the questions, listen to the answers, and provide the platform for a forum, a bridge between generations of Americans. The New York State Military Museum's Veterans Oral History Project came into being shortly after that; we gave our 200+ interviews to them and gleaned more from the interviews found there that were conducted at the same time we were doing our work. I knew I was doing something important, but it started with the spark of wonderment forty plus years ago, as the veterans of the European campaign returned to Normandy for the 40th anniversary of D-Day in 1984.

A lot of these guys lived with the trauma of war and witnessing the Holocaust for the rest of their lives. And because of Judge Walsh's interview, I went on to become a Holocaust educator as well (as detailed in my 2016 book and teacher memoir, *A Train Near Magdeburg*).

Our Dachau liberator told the kids,

> It was [the concentration camp] Dachau that we had smelled miles before we got there. And yet, people in the village who were right next to the camps said they didn't know what was going on; people in Munich, which was actually only nine miles from Dachau, didn't know what was going on. Now if you want to believe that, the Brooklyn Bridge is still for sale. But when you looked around some of these tough soldiers were throwing up and crying all over the place. It is not possible to

really describe the number of feelings you get when you walk into something like that, because, well, first of all, nobody told us about the camp! We had no idea what a concentration camp was! We were going to Dachau, period. It was just another village as far as we were concerned. That's kind of a shock to get all at one time.

He continued, to his later interviewer,

> Every now and then they go, 'Gee, this stuff is not in the books.' I said to the kids, 'Now look at what you've learned today. You'll never find it in a book anyplace.'

Until now. The book you are reading is the seventh volume of my oral history series, with several more projected. Thank you for reading, and for remembering with me.

Matthew Rozell, November 11, 2021
Washington County, NY

PART ONE

THE ROAD TO THE REICH

'We're sitting there, and we're just bullshitting—there was really nothing in the town—and this command car comes up and it's his car! The command cars are wide, you know, because it has the flag and the three stars there, and he went right past us, and [the driver] squeezed the brakes and stopped, and he had the driver back up. We were sitting there; we weren't getting up for shit—we were still sitting there. General Patton looked down on us and then we realized who he was, *but we still didn't get up, and he saluted us and he left; he never said a word. He must have seen the patches on our shoulders. He didn't say a word!'*

—US Army Ranger, somewhere in Europe

Gen. Dwight D. Eisenhower speaks with men of Company E of the 502nd Parachute Infantry Regiment, 101st Airborne Division in England on the evening of June 5, 1944, as they prepare for the Battle of Normandy. Credit: U.S. Army photograph, public domain.

CHAPTER ONE

To Liberate a Continent

The first Allied troops to land in occupied Europe in 1944 were tasked with the final push to free the continent from under the heel of the Nazi jackboot, an undertaking that would not be completed in that long year. While optimistic, no military planner had a crystal ball; no one could foresee the setbacks and brutality of almost an entire year before finally crossing the Rhine River for good in the spring of 1945. Suffering through cold, fatigue, hunger, and other punishing conditions, many a soldier wondered just what it was all about, and would question just what they were fighting for.

Later, almost every GI who finally set foot on German soil would get the opportunity to witness for themselves the things that would never leave them, and, in some cases, haunt and hound them for the rest of their lives.

They would have the answer to their question.

Nicholas Butrico holds up a copy of his famous D-Day letter
as reprinted in a magazine. Source: NYS Military Museum.

CHAPTER TWO

The Ranger

Comfortable on his couch in his New York home, Nick Butrico gives a lively talk about his time in the 5th Ranger Battalion in Europe, from the D-Day landings and participation in the assault on the German fortified gun position at the formidable cliffs of Pointe Du Hoc, to spearheading into German territory at night, using, as he called it, rope boats to pull themselves across. To the astonishment of later D-Day historians, he even wrote a description of the scenes he encountered on June 6, 1944, a few days after D-Day, on the back of Eisenhower's famous Order of the Day letter to invasion servicemen, ending it with a supplication to God to keep him safe thereafter, his first dramatic day of combat.

Speaking quickly and gesturing emphatically, he has a lot to say about his experiences in the war, even to the point of turning the military acronym SNAFU into a verb.[1] He sat for this interview in February 2003 when he had just turned 81; he entered the service as a twenty-year-old Italian kid from New York. Like many of our World War II veterans, he had his medals and citations in a shadowbox display, which he described to his interviewers.

'This is the original dog tag that we first got when we first went in the service, but they were taken away when we went overseas. But I kept mine because your address is on here—where you lived, and they didn't want that to get in German hands. Now we come over here—This is the Bronze Star. That's for gallantry, I don't know how I got it.

Now this is the Purple Heart, and that little thing in there is the oak leaf cluster, which means you were hit twice. They don't give you a medal every time you get hit; they gave you a cluster. And this right down here is

---

[1] *military acronym SNAFU-*"Sarcastic expression 'Situation Normal: All Fucked Up.' The original military acronym stood for 'Status Nominal: All Fucked Up,' but also bowdlerized to 'all fouled up.' It means that the situation is bad, but that this is a normal state of affairs. The acronym is believed to have originated in the United States Marine Corps during World War II." Source: Wikipedia.

the Presidential Citation with an oak leaf cluster. It's equivalent to the Medal of Honor, only in a unit. We got a cluster—one was for Normandy, the other cluster was for Zeef [my last mission, in Germany].

I'll tell you about the guy that jumped off the boat in Normandy; he held on then, his name was Sergeant Walters, he was the nicest guy, he had two kids, I don't know what the hell he was doing in the Rangers with two kids! Well, another sergeant, he wanted a cup of coffee, but somebody had to stay in this foxhole.

Walters said, 'Go ahead, I'll go in your hole. You go for the coffee.' Now while he went for the coffee, the Germans were throwing artillery and one goes right into the foxhole and killed Walters. And I always said to the guys when I got back, 'He could have just as well died on the beach.'

The war was almost over; this was March. He went through all this, and he had to die that way! The guy that he covered the hole for went berserk. They put him in the bunker. He went berserk, you know.'

Nicholas F. Butrico

I was born in New York. I was born January 29, 1922. I only went to high school, that's all. In those days, not many people went to college.

[When I heard the news of Pearl Harbor], I was upstairs. I'm not sure about the time; it might have been the afternoon, I don't remember. I was [listening to] the football game, the Giants were playing, and they interrupted, 'Pearl Harbor was bombed.' I don't remember who was there with me, but I said, 'Where the hell is Pearl Harbor?' Hell, I never heard of it. I didn't realize it was our country being bombed. Then I went downstairs, and I met the rest of the fellas and they're talking, 'You know the United States is bombed and we're going to go to war.' I didn't realize at that time. So that's how I really found out that Pearl Harbor belonged to America.

'Look in the Dead Files'

I was drafted, but then again, maybe I enlisted. While I was home, all my buddies were gone. I had a few of the younger fellas [I was hanging around with]; I was considered 1A, [fit for military service]. I still have that stuff hanging around. And I went back to the local board, and I asked them, 'How come I didn't get called?'

He said, 'What's your name?' and then he said, 'We have no record of you.'

So I said, 'Look in the dead files.'

So he looked in the dead files, and my name comes up in the dead files! Now if I hadn't gone back there, I probably wouldn't have gone through the whole war! Then two weeks later I got the notice, went to Governors Island, and that's where I went for my physical. That's the preliminary—they want to see if you have two arms, two legs, you don't have a heart condition. That's not a real physical; the real physical came later on.

In October '42, I was drafted, and I remember going to Fort Dix, and Fort Dix shipped me out to Breckenridge, Kentucky. I was with the 98th Infantry Division. A funny story about that is, the 98th Infantry Division was a New York division—Iroquois. Every time I went out on [patrols with them], we used to get lost! So, I had another buddy—he passed away a few years ago—I said to him, 'You know, if we go out to combat with these guys, we're going to get ourselves killed.'

He said, 'Yes, I know. Every time we go out, we get lost.'

Well, we couldn't get out. I tried to get in the Air Corps, but they wouldn't take me because I'm colorblind. Later on, they were looking for guys [regardless of if you were colorblind], but they wouldn't take me. Then a general order came down—it was on the bulletin board. They were looking for volunteers for the Rangers. So, I said to my friend, 'What can we lose? At least maybe we get a better outfit. And it's not a big outfit.'

'Okay!'

Twenty-five-hundred men took the physical right there at Camp Breckenridge and only about two hundred passed. I was one of them. All these guys failed—either they were colorblind or something—and I was colorblind, but I was a little smarter. I was in the line and when I got up there, I had been to the back guy where they had [colored] cotton on the floor and they'd tell you, 'Pick the red one out,' and I was memorizing. So, when I got up there and the guy says, 'Pick the red one out…' They could have changed it and I wouldn't have known. [*Laughs*]

And then the 98th Division was going on maneuvers in Tennessee, and me and my buddy and a few other guys were pulled out and we were sent to the 5th Ranger Battalion in Camp Forest, Tennessee, with the 2nd Ranger Battalion. Both battalions were there. We trained there for a while and then from there we went to Fort Pierce, Florida, and we did a little amphibious training. I said, 'Hey, we're going to go to Japan, you know, they're teaching us how to use the rubber boats and stuff. Okay, we're going to Japan.'

But from there I came up to Fort Dix for about two months, just training and all this. The next thing I know, we're in Camp Kilmer, that's an embarkation point, and of course Camp Shanks is right down the corner from here. The 2nd Ranger came out of Camp Shanks, but we came out of Kilmer.

Shipping Out

We got on this ship, the *Mauritania*. We were going unescorted because the *Mauritania* was a big ship and it was fast; some probably couldn't catch up to it. Right out of the harbor, a tanker hit us in the front! Our boat didn't sink, but it shook it, and I said, 'Are we getting bombed already—

torpedoes?' Then we found out we were going back to port, to 42nd Street to one of those piers, and pulling in there. Right away all the GIs—you know there were a lot of GIs on the ship—the rumors started. 'The war was over, that's why they brought us back to 42nd Street!' Then we got the news they were repairing that cut and they probably could have made the trip, but to play it safe they worked all day, and the next day when I woke up all I saw was water; we had pulled out.

Commando Training

I ended up in Liverpool. It only took us six days. We went to Liverpool and from there we were shipped to Wales. We only stayed there to do little problems, then they shipped us up to Dundee, Scotland—British Commando School. Most of our teachers were British commandos, and the training was tough there. A lot of guys were pulled out—couldn't make it—they'd fall out of marches. Every time we'd do anything it was live ammunition, no simulation, everything was live ammunition, and we had to climb cliffs up and down—from the top down and climb up. They showed us how to do it. I remember, we used to put [the line] through our legs, and you could do good down, but it was up that bothered us. We had a lot of forced marches; we had a march—I think nine miles—and we had to do it in at least an hour. You try force marching with your feet starting to get you and if you didn't stay in, out you went—in other words, they'd ship you back to the infantry outfit or wherever.

We made it all through and after we got through with Dundee, I ended up down in the Isle of Wight, right down in the southern part of England, and then we did a little more training with boats coming in and we ended up on Weymouth. And we got on the ship on Weymouth and that's where we got this letter that I showed you inside. But you know, I didn't think anything of it. But we knew now—this was June 4—we knew where the invasion was coming, but we didn't know exactly what day. We knew where it was because we were getting maps from the Air Corps every time they'd come back from a bomb run, they'd come back [to us]—Pointe du Hoc, that's what our objective was. They'd take pictures; no sooner than they landed, we'd have them in less than an hour on our tables—where this was, and where that was, and where the guns were supposed to be. While we were doing this, we weren't allowed out. They had us guarded—here we were, barbed wire all around, British soldiers guarding us, and then they had another [perimeter] rim—American soldiers guarding the British soldiers, and if anybody in our outfit tried to get through the barbed wire, they'd shoot to kill them, because we knew too much, even though we didn't know the date, but we knew too much—we knew where it was coming. I'm on the ship there; the next thing you know, through the night—the boat—they'd pull out. This is about June 5. I don't know, they'd stayed in the harbor—we lay in that Weymouth Harbor for two, three days eating British food. All they'd ever give you was greasy lamb and stuff like that. We used to have to eat that.

The Day of Days

We landed in Normandy with the British LCAs they called them—very low in the water. You've heard of the Higgins boat? You've seen the movies where they'd come down—the doors opened in the front? We were on this ship and the next thing I know it was the 5th and they told us it wasn't going to happen because the weather was bad. Then on June 6, as far as we knew—I found out after—June 6 was better, but it wasn't any better because I was seasick. You know we didn't have to climb down the ropes like you see in the movies to get on the [landing craft], we just stepped right on as if we were going on a lifeboat. See, they used to lie right along the ship and used to drag us down into the water. We'd get on there, about five or six boats for the whole battalion, and then we'd circle around the ship and the *USS Texas*—big cruiser out there, big warship out there—was firing, 'Boom, boom.' Every time they fired the whole boat shook, you know, the little boat we were on shook! And as we were going into shore, the water was so rough, we started to sink. So, the limey there, the British coxswain, said, 'Hey you Yanks, you better start bailing out or we're not going to make it!'

Okay, so now everybody took their helmets off. And me, I was so sick my rifle was lying on the bottom of the water. I wasn't worried about bailing out so we could get the ship out, but we finally got it out because a couple of them did go down. And we made it to shore, but this is where I really found out what war was like.

As soon as we got there, there was this Chester—he came from Brooklyn—he said to me, 'Nick,' you know, he was one of my buddies, he said, 'Nick, I don't know how to swim.' I figured, well, you have a life jacket; it's got to be a piece of cake. Well, as soon as we got in, the coxswain opened the doors. My friend and Sergeant Walters were the first two off. Now when they went off, they went right down. There was a shell hole there from the Air Corps, and it was deep. The sergeant held onto the door, but the kid, he was only seventeen or eighteen, didn't hold onto the door so he just jumped out, and a big wave—the water was so rough—just came over right on top of him. And I found out a few days later from headquarters that they found him on the beach. He died and I felt bad, and then I knew what war was like.

*

Once I hit the land, I didn't even know I was seasick anymore, I was worried about my ass. I hit this dune. I stood there a while and I saw what was going on, and I saw the 29th Division and the 1st Division coming in, and some of these shells that the Germans were throwing out—88s or mortars, one of them hit. They had these big ships, these LSTs, with ramps on the side that you walked down. Well one of those shells—while the guys were coming down—hit that ramp. Everybody flying all over the place and I said, 'Jesus Christ, what the hell am I doing here?'

Pointe du Hoc

Now our objective that day, we landed on Omaha, but our objective was to go into the Pointe. Now we had three companies and the 2nd Rangers went right into the Pointe—the 5th Ranger Battalion and three companies of 2nd Rangers landed with us. We were attached to the 29th Division. Now our job was to get up to the road and head to Pointe du Hoc, which was about five miles away, and capture these guns from the rear. Everything was so snafued that the original guys who were going to Pointe du Hoc were about three miles off course, so they had to bypass along the shore to get to the Pointe, and the Germans were shooting at them as they went by. Well, they made it to the Pointe, and we had Colonel Snyder go into Omaha with the 29th, get up to the draw and meet on the top—get to the Pointe. That was his job. Get to the Pointe, Pointe du Hoc.

Okay, so when I hit that sand dune, I looked out there and said, 'Jesus Christ, what the hell am I doing here?' There were a few other guys and we turned around and the whole countryside was burning. So, we had to put on the gas masks to get up to the top. I finally got up to the top; everything was disorganized. I finally happened to see my captain and he said, 'Nick, what are you doing?'

I said, 'I don't know, there are only three of us here!' We picked up a few more Rangers; we ended up picking up twenty-three [in total], because they were scattered all over the place. So, twenty-three Rangers—and the captain, he got a DSC for this—he said, 'Let's go to the Pointe.' Actually, we were supposed to meet the whole battalion and then go to it, but we went to the Pointe. Twenty-three men and the captain were the only ones on D-Day that got to the Pointe Du Hoc on

June 6—it's in all the books—the rest of the battalion got there three days later, because the 29th was taking a hell of a beating; they were getting counterattacked. Pointe du Hoc was a big thing—in fact, we had artillery support. The *USS Texas* and the *Arizona* were our personal artillery support because they bombed the shit out of that place.² In fact, they even saved the guys [going up]. They threw so many shells into that cliff, it was practically going up this way! [*Moves left arm to indicate steep upward slope, instead of vertical climb*] But when the 2nd Ranger Battalion got to the top, there were no guns there—the Germans had moved them. They had like telephone poles for guns, but they moved them back about a mile.

And it just happened—Len would know, I see him so often—he and Sergeant Coon—who just passed away—were going with a few men up to this road, because they see heavy tracks, and there were the guns all ready to shoot ammunition all over the place, but there was nobody there!³ About

---

² *The Arizona*- Mr. Butrico probably refers to *USS Arkansas* (BB-33), which provided support at Omaha Beach with the *USS Texas* on D-Day.
³ *Len would know*- Mr. Butrico almost certainly refers to 24-year-old Sgt. Len 'Bud' Lomell (1920-2011), a fellow Ranger of the 2nd Battalion born in New York and raised in New Jersey, not far from Mr. Butrico. Praised by historian

a hundred yards away, there were about one hundred Germans. They were talking and eating, and they were getting ready to do something, so what

---

Stephen Ambrose as only second to Eisenhower for the critical success of D-Day, Mr. Lomell was already wounded before reaching the beach and scaling the cliffs.
'I was the first one wounded,' he recalled in a 2009 interview with Charlie Rose. He stepped off the ramp at the front and immediately found himself in water over his head. 'When I bopped up, my guys grabbed me and pulled me up,' he remembered. 'And then we hit the beach.'
Lomell said the wound burned a little, but hadn't hit anything vital, and they rushed to the cliffs, where the rocket-propped grappling hooks were launched, trailing long lengths of climbing ropes. Loaded with gear and explosives, they began scaling the sheer wall, hand-over-hand, while the Germans on top were desperately trying to cut the ropes or shoot them.
Those on the ropes couldn't shoot back because they were climbing, hoping only for covering fire from the ground. Many were hit and killed or wounded. Others fell to their deaths. Those who finally were able to reach the top overwhelmed the Germans and found a surprise waiting. The guns had secretly been moved. The artillery barrels that appeared so clearly on U.S. reconnaissance photos were nothing more than telephone poles set at an angle to disguise the real location of the weapons.
Lomell said it was critical to find the missing guns. As the battle raged below on the beaches, he and two other Rangers followed a set of tracks leading inland from the cliff, where they found all five carefully hidden in an apple orchard, left unguarded. Using grenades and other explosives, Lomell and the others managed to disable them, eluding discovery and rendering the coastal defense guns useless. It's a story that's been well documented in books and films. Historians recount it as one of the most important keys to Allied success that day. But for Lomell, it was less a day of heroics than one of loss.
'There was a lot of death,' he said in a 2007 interview with *The Star-Ledger*. 'I lost half my guys. What more is there to know?' Source: Spoto, Mary Ann. *Leonard Lomell, World War II hero from Toms River, dies at 91.* March 2, 2011. NJ.com. www.nj.com/news/2011/03/leonard_lomell_d-day_hero_from.
Mr. Lomell was also featured in Tom Brokaw's 1998 book, *The Greatest Generation*.

he did was, he got in there and he had a thermite grenade and threw it into the breach, into the barrel, and you know what that did—it melted everything. He only had two, but there were six guns there, so he had to knock out the other four, so he came back. He got a couple from the other guys in the back, and they knocked out all the guns, because these guns were facing Utah Beach. They could have been traversed to Omaha; that's why they wanted Pointe du Hoc captured, because those guns could fire on the *Texas*, they could fire on the *Arizona*, they could fire on the whole damn front. General Bradley had said, and it's in most of your books, 'The Rangers had the worst objective in the whole Normandy invasion—those guns,' but they didn't realize they weren't there. The French did find that they weren't there, but it was too late to get us because we were on our way. But the guns had been moved.

When we got there, they still had to hold on to a crossroad there so the Germans would not [counterattack]. But Pointe du Hoc was between Utah and Omaha, and they wanted a linkup and we were in the middle—Pointe du Hoc was in the middle there. They wanted us to protect the road, so the Germans wouldn't come in there. They wanted to keep us separated. But it never happened, they held on, so that's the story.

When they knew we had the Pointe secured, [we were told], 'Stay with the 29th Division and give them a hand,' so they were supposed to come to the Pointe too; that's what happened.

And from there I was okay—I didn't get a scratch, not a scratch. I was pretty lucky—I could see what was going on. We stood at about D+10, maybe 13—I don't remember the date—that's when I wrote the letter, and they took us off the line.

'Not Made to Take Care of Prisoners'

Cherbourg had fallen. They made us take care of prisoners, prisoners of war—take them down to the beach. We were about three or four miles out, and they had the thing lit up like Times Square. I suppose the Germans knew that it was a prisoner of war camp, so they didn't strafe it or bomb it, and there was another one right down on the beach. But this was about D+15 or somewhere around there, and we used to get one hundred prisoners and we got Italian prisoners, German prisoners, Polacks, everything, and we'd take them down to the stockade right on the beach, and then they would put them on ships to England or America or wherever they were going. And we did that for—I think we only lasted two days on the job. We weren't made to take care of prisoners.

We used to take the one hundred prisoners, and there were a lot of ships—we had a big storm there, and it blew a lot of these big ships right onto the beach, and every time we'd take them down to the beach, we'd run them along the [ship]. The five of us, we'd line them up; that's where they got us, because when they were in the stockade they were interrogated, they would leave them with their watches and stuff like that. [So before they would go in], we used to line them up and we used to clean them out, in other words, the Germans have watches—there was one German who didn't want to give up his watch. I'm struggling with this guy, and so I just took the bayonet out, and he got an idea of what I was talking about. 'Okay, you can have it.' So, [he took something else out of his pocket], and I thought it was going to be the valuable watch he was [holding back on]—it was a glass eye! I was so mad I felt like shooting him! I took the eye, and I threw it right in the ocean. I said, 'You made me do all this for a glass eye? Don't worry about it, when you go to America, they'll probably give you another one.'

When you get to the beach, the Navy's in charge. The Navy put in a complaint that the Rangers weren't following the Geneva rules because we had one hundred prisoners, but when we got to the stockade we had ninety-eight or ninety-six. What happened to the rest, well, we know they didn't run away; we had a lot of nuts in the outfit. But one incident—and nobody ever believes me, but this is the God's honest truth; whenever I say this story people just laugh—they don't believe it. Going down to the beach—now you try to walk in sand, it's tough, and we used to speed march, because the quicker we got to the other stockade, we'd go get a truck, a lot of trucks were going by— and we'd get a break. We didn't have to dig a foxhole because it was light, and the Germans knew it was there. Anyway, we were walking down to the beach, and we had a couple of older Germans, and so my sergeant came to me and said, 'Nick, these guys are holding us up. Take these two guys, with the medics, tell them to walk slowly and we'll meet you at the stockade.'

I said, 'Okay,' and it was dark because this was at nighttime. We were walking and I fell in a shell hole; there were a lot of shell holes there and when I fell, I lost the rifle. I had the rifle and it fell out of my hand—right into the sand it went!—and these two Germans and the medics jumped in the same hole with me and right away something went through my head, and I thought, 'This is it. [I'm dead.]'

The Germans grabbed me, they picked me up, they started wiping all the sand off my clothes. They picked the rifle up, they cleaned it, and they handed it back to me. Every time I tell that story, nobody believes me, but that is the truth! Then I figured, maybe they thought they were through, where were they going to go? The front line was maybe six, seven miles away. What were they going to do—escape so they could go fight again? They were smart, they didn't want to fight. In fact, most of the Germans didn't want to fight. They thought, 'What the hell are we going to fight for?'

From there, they threw us off that detail, I think we lasted two or three days. Those were some of the reasons why we weren't made to take care of prisoners.

'It Went Right Through My Legs'

I ended up in Brest. We had to get new men, or sometimes [guys were] coming back who had been wounded, and we had to train them again—they didn't get the same training we got, but they got some of it. Now in Brest, I got stuck with the 29th Division again. The 29th Division, the 8th Division—now people don't know this, I don't know if I should say this—but the 8th Division ran. They had sent us up there to Brest with the 2nd Ranger Battalion and the 5th for support to protect their flanks, because the flanks are the weakest part of anything. The Germans come in on the flanks—they wouldn't come this way [*motions towards himself with two arms directly in front*], they'd come this way. [*Motions towards himself with two arms spread to the sides*] The 29th Division used to go up about three miles and we used to just wait behind there to go right up there—we didn't have any firing to do or anything. We stopped right alongside the division. The Germans made a counterattack, and they pulled back, but they didn't tell us. We were stuck out there by ourselves. We had a colonel—an Irishman, his name was Sullivan—because the other one we had went back to the States. He said, 'I'm not giving up. I got here and I'm not going to [go back]. We stay until they come back!' And then a couple of days later [the 29th], they counterattacked and they came back again.

Now in Brest, there were twenty-six objectives. Now, mind you, there were two divisions there, I think three, the 8th Division, the 29th Division, which we were attached to—I think the 2nd Ranger Battalion was attached to the 8th—and we had a couple of armored divisions there, and there were other personnel. There were twenty-six objectives in the whole battalion, and we weren't supposed to do any fighting. Out of twenty-six objectives, we took twenty-four. And we were only four hundred fifty men, that's all. We weren't a big unit. You know a division has eighteen thousand men, and we took twenty-four objectives, which they were supposed to take. They only took two.

Brest was submarine base for the Germans. [The brass] wanted Brest very badly because it was a big port, but the Germans wrecked it; when we got there, they had wrecked it. And then we had this guy—I'll show you the book inside—this Sergeant Elms with eight guys went in there. He talked to the [German] colonel and he had the colonel believing that they were surrounded—he had eight men—so he told everybody to throw their arms down and go out the front door. Eight hundred, there were just eight guys who captured them. He got a DSC and I think he got the Silver; he got two awards for that.

While I was in Brest, I lost my hearing. We were making one of the objectives that we were going after for the 29th. We were running across this field—now this was July, and it was hot—and the Germans opened up. I was with two other guys, and we hit the dirt—there was a dead cow and the cow blows up like a balloon, you know lying dead in the hot sun, and they stink. So at least it was cover, but I said to the others, 'If we stay here, we're going to die. Either we're going to get shot or we'll die of the stink.' The smell was terrific. We got up and we started to run through a little hedge there, and as we were running the Germans threw up—they had forty-millimeter mortars—and I could see it coming right at me and I just froze. It went right through my legs and didn't even touch me, and exploded in back of me and killed the two guys behind me. All I got was a concussion, I was on the ground. The next thing I know I found myself at an aid station. I said, 'What am I doing here?'

They said, 'You have a concussion. You didn't realize it—that the shell had knocked you out.'

But I didn't get anything on me. Pretty lucky, but right after that I started having problems with my hearing. The guys said, 'Hey Nick, can't you hear what we're talking about?' And they always had to holler, and as the years went by, it got worse and worse. If I took this hearing aid off, I'm dead; I'm so bad—the hearing is so bad—but then the old age too, that doesn't help.

'Let's Go to Paris'

From there, I remember I came back to the outfit a couple of days later; they sent me back. They put us on a train—just a company, one section, the guard train. The French—the 'frogs,' we used to call them—were stealing the rations off the trains. Every time the train stopped, they'd steal the rations. We had this train, maybe one hundred cars, we were the last in the caboose in the back, and every time the train stopped, we had to jump off, some on this side, look up the line and see the French stealing the B-rations. The guys driving the trains, they probably were in cahoots, that was why they stopped. The Americans were losing a lot of stuff that way. But we took some of the B-rations, which was good stuff, like peaches and stuff like that; it was all good rations. What the hell, we always [got stuck] with K-rations, you know, a box of crackers. That's what we had. When we got to one of these boxcars there and took a box and there were peaches in a can—a big can—and other good food, eggs, powdered eggs, we took that to a town called Chars, but when we got there, the town was flattened. There was nothing there but just a train depot. We turned the train over to some outfit waiting for us; they took over. Now we were about six guys, so what do we do now? Our colonel was supposed to pick us up there. The rest of the battalion went on to Arlon, Belgium; Paris had fallen by then.

I said, 'What do we do now?'

The Irish sergeant said, 'Let's go to Paris.'

We weren't that far from Paris. We knew Paris was off limits at that time, but we got to Paris, we got in. There were a few Air Corps men there—they put us up in the Grand Hotel, a beautiful hotel in France. We stayed there, but we had a lot of trouble—the MPs grabbed us—we had our sergeant and another guy fighting with the MPs. They wanted to go out [on the town] and scout around and see what they could find. The captain from the MPs came up to this sergeant and ordered something. We happened to be upstairs—the MPs had locked the doors on us, they didn't want us to go downstairs. But these two guys—they both were sergeants—this captain from the MPs comes over and he must have said something, and this guy just hauls off and flattened the captain, right on the floor! That's a court-martial-able offense. They arrested him. Now finally our colonel comes to Paris: 'Weren't we supposed to be in Chars? What are you doing here in Paris?'

'Well, there's nothing there, so we decided to come here.'

He said, 'Where's the two sergeants?' We told him. He went down to the MPs.

'They're in the stockade there.' He got them out of the stockade, but they never were court-martialed. He just took them right out—I don't know, maybe he threatened them—and we went to Arlon, Belgium. We stayed there—a little training there—we got some new men.

The Last Mission

There are some parts [of the war] that I just don't remember, but the last mission we were on was Zeef, it was called Zeef. Patton had gone to the Bulge, left us down at the Bulge... [*claps hands together*] We were told they wanted the battalion to go over the Sauer River; we had to go by rope boats because the 94th Division had a piece of it on the other side. [*Gestures with hand-over-hand horizontal pulling motion*] We would go through them, eleven miles into enemy territory, and sit in secret—at the Zeef crossroads—and all they wanted us to do was to stop anything that came through there, tanks, anything. Well, I got a break on there; maybe I wouldn't have made it out of there.

The battalion was spread out, a company here, a company there. So, we were going to get all together at night—was about twelve o'clock at night, pitch black—and we were going to go eleven miles behind enemy lines. As we were going in, the Germans just happened to throw up harassing fire, which just happened to land right in the middle of us. [*Gestures to indicate artillery or mortar fire*] A lot of guys got killed; a lot of guys got wounded. I helped one guy up—he was hit in the stomach. I remember his name; it was Anderson. An ambulance pulled up and I put him in the ambulance. He was, 'Oh, oh.' He finally died. And then when I got out, the doctor in the ambulance or the medic said, 'Where are you going?'

I said, 'I'm going back to the outfit before they go over there.'

He said, 'You're not going anywhere. Don't you know you're hit?' I didn't know I was hit. I was hit right above the eye.

'You're lucky it didn't come down an inch. You'd have lost an eye!'

I was hit right about here. [*Points above right eye*] A small piece of shrapnel, but I didn't even know it. And it was bleeding, but I thought it was from the guy I was helping. And I kept... [*wipes eye repeatedly with back of his hand*] I must have felt relieved I didn't have to go. They took me back and checked it out and they said, 'You're all right, it didn't affect your eyes.'

Now, I couldn't get back to the battalion anymore; they had gone eleven miles into German territory and sat there. They were supposed to be relieved in three days—the 94th Division and Patton made this big push to the Rhine. We were supposed to see that the Germans didn't bring up tanks or anything. Well, I heard this from the other guys, because I wasn't there. A car pulls up, a German car; it's got the little lights in the headlight. They stop him. A funny story. A major of the

German army and two medics, and our guys said, 'You are our prisoners.'

And he said, 'It can't be—the frontlines are about ten miles away!' He said, 'What are you doing here?' The Germans didn't even know we were there yet. And we took them prisoners. We captured a bunker, and we were kind of using it for headquarters. When the Germans found out we were there, oh, Jesus Christ, they kept making counterattacks. They'd go through our lines; we'd send in our own artillery on our positions to get rid of them. They were calling, 'Goddamn Yankees, Yankee bums go home.' But the thing is, I wasn't there—I missed all this, but then again, I could have gotten killed too, because we lost a lot of men there. I'll tell you about the guy that jumped off the boat in Normandy; he held on, his name was Sergeant Walters, he was the nicest guy, he had two kids, I don't know what the hell he was doing in the Rangers with two kids! Well, another sergeant—and he just passed away—he wanted a cup of coffee, but somebody had to stay in this foxhole. Walters said, 'Go ahead, I'll go in your hole. You go for the coffee.' Now while he went for the coffee, the Germans were throwing artillery and one goes right into the foxhole and killed Walters. And I always said to the guys when I got back, 'He could have just as well died on the beach.'

The war was almost over; this was March. He went through all this, and he had to die that way! The guy that he covered the hole for went berserk. They put him in the bunker. He went berserk, you know. He passed away a few years back; he was an alcoholic; I don't know if that caused it, or what.

The Germans were dead all over the place. We had so many Germans dead that we had the German prisoners stack them in a barn. You could barely close the door—they had them all stacked in there. Every time they came up the road, we'd blast at them, kill them. They were all over the place; the place looked like west Normandy, only they were Germans. The German wounded—and we had a lot of German wounded—they were brought back to the bunker. Now our colonel turned around to the major, the German doctor, and he said, 'We have our medics and a doctor taking care of ours; you have free [rein] in the bunker, take care of your men with your two guys.'

The doctor said, 'Yes.' Well one thing about it, it turned out our colonel shook his hand when he left. The German worked on Americans and Germans—the ones who were wounded. He was a doctor even in Germany. Not all Germans were Nazis; not all Germans even wanted to fight—they would rather give up.

And from there we stayed eleven days—it was supposed to be three days—before they got to us, running out of ammunition, and I wasn't there all this time. I'm telling you the story of what's happening—the guys told me when I finally got back. Eleven days, the ammunition was low, the food was practically gone, they were eating German stuff! Our colonel was going to throw in the towel, there were only three other Ranger battalions that gave up to the Germans because they were surrounded, and that was at Anzio, and he said, 'We'll be the fourth.' But as it turned out, he said, 'We'll hold on.' They held on. They said, 'We'll send in some Piper Cubs and send you in supplies.' Just like the Army, they snafued it anyway. They sent in the Piper Cubs and threw ammunition and food down; most of it, the Germans got. All our buddies got was the ammunition; but most of the ammunition—you know, machine gun ammunition comes in belts; they were sending it down and it came in clips! So, we had to do it by hand. You ever try putting it in by hand? We didn't have a machine. We were putting these bullets in, then they started giving us belts. Finally, after eleven days, they held out, the 94th and I think the 10th Armored finally got to us. And they passed us up, and then we were pulled back.

*

I went back to the outfit and the doctor called me in the office and he said, 'Nick,'—everybody was 'Nick,' none of this… [*makes a saluting motion*]. We didn't salute—none of this saluting—nobody saluted anybody. Our captain—you never saluted him. We used to call him Ace; he never carried bars on his shoulder because the Germans would shoot [for the] bars. 'Don't salute; I don't want you to salute me.' Well this captain, he came back, and he called me in the office, and he said, 'Nick, we've reclassified you.'

I said, 'What does that mean?' I thought maybe they were going to send me home.

'No, you are going on limited service.' The war was almost over, it ended about a month later. This was March, and it ended in April. He said, 'We're going to send you back to another outfit.'

They sent me back to Compiègne. I was in limited service—Compiègne, France. That's where in the First World War they signed the [armistice ending the fighting with Germany] and Hitler took the train back out of there.[4] I went there. There were six of us. Pretty quiet—there was no war going on. We took care of Italian prisoners. They had their own kitchen. We didn't have a kitchen. We used to eat with some platoon outfit there; their food stunk. We had a captain—he was reclassified—so he said, 'Let's go to the Italians.' Now, they were prisoners, and they were eating better than we were! He set it up where they would feed us, we would give them the stuff. They made spaghetti. We couldn't eat that other stuff those guys were giving us! We were only six guys; they would serve us; they had a table all set; we had a tablecloth. We ate like kings! I was there until the

---

[4] *Hitler took the train back out of there*-Hitler insisted that the defeated French sign the Armistice of June 22, 1940, in the same rail carriage at Compiègne that German forces had capitulated to the victors in World War I.

war—I would have come home—they had a [point] system; I was going to come home under the [point] system. Even though the war was going on, I was going to get discharged, but I had no priority. The war was still going on with Japan—even when the Germans surrendered, I still had no status to go home, so I stuck with the [prisoner detail]. They finally repatriated all the Italians back to Italy.

The Accident

Now I remember a couple of days before we were going; I had a big GMC. We were driving. It was about seven o'clock in the morning. I had two Italian prisoners and myself; they did the driving. I said, 'Come on, pull over.' The roads are narrow in France. So, they pulled over because the roads are narrow.

We went in this café and had a cup of coffee; even though the coffee stunk, it was coffee. While we were inside, some dopey frog, you know what a frog is; he was on a motorcycle coming up that road. I don't know if he saw the truck—he hit the truck right in the middle and went right through the windshield and he got killed; he died. The MPs came and asked, 'What are you parked here for?'

We told them, 'We got a cup of coffee.'

Okay, we drove back—the two Italians and me. The two Italians couldn't go back to Italy; they had to get charged and I was charged with manslaughter, and they were charged with manslaughter. But the captain says to me, 'Oh, don't worry, this is a technicality. The reason that they do this is if you or these two prisoners decided to stay in France after the war, their family might sue you, press charges against you. We don't want that. And if we put you on trial, whatever comes out—you won't get anything.'

I was busted down to a private, and what did I care—I was going home, and a carton of cigarettes, that was the fine. And the Italians too—they finally went home. I got on the ship. I remember I was at Camp Lucky Strike.

*

I got on a Liberty ship to come home. This is from Le Havre. The name of the Liberty ship was the *Colonel Darby*.[5] You know who Colonel Darby

---

[5] *Colonel Darby*-William O. Darby (1911-1945) was regarded as 'the father of the modern Army Rangers,' leading his men in battles in North Africa, Sicily,

was? He started the 1st Ranger Battalion, and all the 5th Rangers were under his command. That ship took eleven days to go from Le Havre to Brooklyn. Eleven days, and that ship bounced all over the place! It was November. Bouncing up and down; bouncing up and down—I thought the ship was going to split in half, it was so bad! I remember we took it out when it was a blue, calm day. I looked out—the *Rex*—the Italians had a big ship named the *Rex*. It wasn't as big as the *Queen Mary*, but it was named the *Rex*. We passed it while it was docked in England. We had been out in the water maybe three or four days and it passed us; you could see it passing us. I said, 'Why don't they put us on that ship?' They put us on this thing even though it is called the *Darby*. Well that ship, every time it went up it came down, boom, it hit the water, and the whole ship [*makes a shuddering motion*]—Jesus Christ! 'I hope this thing holds up!' We finally got home, and then I got discharged. And while I was getting discharged—they give you a physical—the doctor said to me, 'You're losing your hearing, you know.'

---

and Italy. He was killed a week before the war in Europe ended. See more about him in Vol. 4 of this series, *Up The Bloody Boot*.

I said, 'Yes, I noticed that. The guys were talking to me.'

'That's probably because you were shot, the firepower—that's what could cause it.' He said, 'I'm just letting you know; tell them to put it down.'

Later on, I went back and said, 'I want this put on the records that I'm losing my hearing,' because if I hadn't done it, I wouldn't be compensated for my hearing because I get a pension for this. I wouldn't be getting compensation and I wouldn't be getting hearing aids for free or anything because it's not service connected. But today they do give it to you even if it's not service connected. But they wouldn't give it to me. These two hearing aids I have, this one is broken [*points to left ear*]–you know how much these cost? Six thousand dollars. You're paying for it, and you're paying for it. Three thousand each, and I'm getting new ones tomorrow and I don't know what they cost. Because I got these—every two years they give me new ones, these are two years old and then they take them back and they give you another two.

[*Phone rings in background*] That woman's husband [*points to phone*]—4th Ranger Battalion—we get together every so often. The funny part of it is I picked him up—we always go to the reunions and that's where I made friends with him, but I picked up something on the internet on Ben, he lives right in Queens. He was from the 4th Ranger Battalion; this guy's name is Black, his second name. His son put on there, 'My father was a 4th Ranger and he's looking for so and so. Fifty years ago, they were in a hospital together in Anzio and they came home together during the war and he's looking for this guy.' Right away [*points to head*], [I knew]. So, I wrote his son, 'Yeah, he lives in Clifton. Yeah, I know the guy.' I wrote back and I gave him the [information]. He finally came to the Ranger reunion in Atlantic City and they met after fifty-six years, and I was responsible for that. That's his wife that just called, because they call us every so often.

Looter Nick

Now I am going to tell you this—I was known as 'Looter Nick.' Every place I went—I don't care if it was a French house, Norwegian house, I don't care—I looked for loot. They used to call me Looter Nick. One time I went into a German house, and I always wanted a grandfather clock. I took it out of there, but the thing is, how would I get it home—how do I get this thing home? When I go up on the front line, what do I do? I knew a lot of guys in the kitchen because wherever we went, the kitchen went. It wasn't like the infantry where the kitchen was way back somewhere. But our kitchen—always when we moved, they moved. In other words, if we needed them, they'd tell them, 'Drop your aprons,' and they'd give them a rifle and they'd get out there because they were trained like we were. I said, 'Do me a favor. I have a grandfather clock and I've got to get it home some way or other.' I said, 'Would you put it on the truck?'

He said, 'Yes, I'll leave it on the back of the truck, and we'll move. But [moving it] on and off—it finally got damaged, and I told the guy to forget about it, leave it somewhere. But I did take a cuckoo clock; the Germans are good for cuckoo clocks. The cuckoo clock I got home because, you see, it wasn't as big. I put it in a box, and I shipped it home, but one of the weights was lost through the mail. My mother treasured that clock so much she finally went down and got a weight to keep time. I had that clock for years but I finally gave it to some guy because the cuckoo didn't cuckoo anymore because the lambskin inside dried up, but it kept pretty good time. I finally gave it away to somebody. I don't remember what I did with it.

That's why they called me Looter Nick. Every time I went into a German house, I opened all the drawers. I used to curse them because they must have taken all the good stuff with them; they left the sheets—who the hell wants sheets? A lot of things I didn't do—what I know now if I knew then, I'd be in a lot of money.

I remember I was in a repple depple, you know what a repple depple is?[6] I got into a repple depple after coming out of the hospital—they could not send me out as a replacement to the infantry like the 3rd or whoever they needed. They had to keep me there until our colonel picked us up because they weren't going to send me to the regular infantry. So, the guy that was in charge said, 'Listen, you guys are going to be here a while.' We were in a German camp. He said, 'Look around the camp and see if you can find some stuff.' The troops that

---

[6] *repple depple*-replacement depot

were coming through had a day room where they could play. So, okay, so we went down there, and we went into one of these empty buildings. I go into the cellar and what do you think I find down there? German loot! Pictures, big, framed pictures, and I looked at the date—1600.

I said to the other guys, 'What the hell? Who wants these old pictures?' What the hell did I know? If I knew, I'd have cut them out, rolled them up, and taken them home. But I didn't know. There were so many pictures there, I said, 'Who the hell would want these here?' And we went back, and I told him, 'There's a lot of pictures.'

He said, 'Where?' So, he went down there and the next thing I know, there's a couple of trucks backing in and taking it all out! But I didn't know. Like I said, if I knew then what I know now, I probably would have taken a couple, but I didn't. I said, 'What the hell am I going to do with these pictures—they're too old.'

A Chance Meeting with Gen. Patton

I saw Patton one time. I don't remember exactly where—it was someplace in Germany or in France.

Three of us were sitting on the curb. We're sitting there, and we're just bullshitting—there was really nothing in the town—and this command car comes up and it's his car! The command cars are wide, you know, because it has the flag and the three stars there, and he went right past us, and [the driver] squeezed the brakes and stopped, and he had the driver back up. We were sitting there; we weren't getting up for shit—we were still sitting there. General Patton looked down on us and then we realized who he was, but we still didn't get up, and he went like this [*salutes with right hand*] and he left; he never said a word. He must have seen the patches on our shoulders. He didn't say a word! He figured the infantry, you know, he was more infantry than—he respected the infantry more than he did the army [brass]. That's the only time I really saw Patton. Other times, I read in the papers where he slapped this guy in the face. I read that in *Stars and Stripes*.

*

I don't remember too well when President Roosevelt died. I might have said, 'Gee, the President died,' and then it got around to everybody—the president is dead. And I think I said, 'Who's this Truman? Who is this guy—I never heard of him.' Personally, I think he was the best president we ever had; we need more like him, because I worked in the post office, and he was a man that came up from haberdashery—worked his way up. Whenever the post office was looking for a raise—in those days the post office could never get anything until now, recently it's not so bad—but in those days, you couldn't get anything. Every time they gave us a raise, they gave us a big two percent, maybe about three bucks a year. Well, Truman came out with something different. We got two raises under him—four hundred dollars across the board a year for all government workers! And the big guys up there, they didn't like that because if it was a percentage raise, they'd get more. So, we all got four hundred. We loved this guy!

And then we had Eisenhower; he was another one—he vetoed everything. Then we had Nixon—that's when we went on strike. After that, the pay in the post office today is good. But I can't see these post offices—the kids today don't want to work anymore! You know how much you start at in the post office? We have a letter carrier, a nice guy, he's an Indian—he took the job. Americans don't want to work! You know how Americans are—they want to start at the top, but that's an unskilled job. Sixteen dollars an hour, twenty-four days' vacation, you get paid all holidays and you get hospitalization—now you pay a little, but it's cheap. I'm still paying it today.

When I retired from the post office in '77, I got a job right here in town. It was a pretty good job, pretty good salary I was getting there. I was in charge of the shipping. We used to make machines to make the chips for the computers we have today, and I worked there for ten years. I had no Social Security. When I got out in '77 we never paid Social Security. Now they do. You had Reagan calling us people who were getting two pensions double-dippers. You son of a bitch—he was triple-dipping! He was collecting Social Security, he was collecting from the theater guild's pension, and he was collecting, I think, for the presidency, and he's calling me a double-dipper? I might be a double-dipper, but he's a triple-dipper! Well, that's Reagan.

I worked there for nine years, and I finally built up my Social Security. I don't get much, but it's better than nothing. I retired from there at 64, going on 65; they gave me a buyout and I took it. That was a good company to work for. Boy, I wish I had that now, I was 100 percent dental. You see all this bridge here [*points in mouth*], they paid for everything, and they paid the hospitals, I was getting hospitalization free, it didn't cost me anything. The company finally went under. They sold it to the Japs—Sony—and then, I had to get out after that. They gave us a buyout and I took it.

I used the GI Bill when I got out of the service—at that time I wasn't married. I said, 'I'm not going to work.' I was one of the record holders [for the '52-20 Club']—a whole year.[7] I was getting twenty dollars a week and that was a lot of money. I was keeping it and I was getting a pension for my hearing and my mother used to keep that. But the funny thing about it was we used to have to report—today you don't, you send a letter that you're

---

[7] *the '52-20 Club'*-The Servicemen's Readjustment Act of 1944, or the G.I. Bill, included a provision for servicemen to apply for a twenty-dollar payment a week for up to a year as they re-integrated into the workforce seeking employment.

not working, and they send you a check. In those days, you had to report once a week, and they had a special line for veterans. So, the other line was for people who had worked and had gotten laid off. And every time you went there, there was always a line. I had to be there at 1:00 in the afternoon, but I used to go at maybe 9:00, because the guys got together—we had an old, beat-up car and we went to Jones Beach, swimming, [in the afternoon].

Mr. Butrico brings out and displays a magazine on the opening of the National D-Day Museum New Orleans and commences to read from it.

'Nicholas Butrico, a Private in the 5th Ranger Battalion, received the Order of the Day issued by General Eisenhower to all the troops heading into France; he scribbled a brief prayer at the top. Shortly after D-Day he wrote his memories of landing on the back. Years later, he talked about what had happened to the 'buddy' he mentioned. "We were on the landing craft. His name was Chester, and he was standing next to me, and he says, 'Nick, I'm afraid I can't swim.'

I said, 'Don't worry about it; this boat will go right up to the land.' But a sailor dropped the ramp too early, and my buddy happened to be the first one out, and as soon as he went out, a big wave caught the craft and pushed it right over his body. A few days later I heard from headquarters that he was found on the beach."

The Letter

I think this is from when they opened the D-Day Museum down in New Orleans a couple of years ago, I don't remember the date.[8] When you go into the museum, they have a Higgins boat, they have a P-51 hanging up, and if you go, they have a lot of things about D-Day, and on the third floor, it was more dedicated to the Rangers. Now, I never knew I had this [on display]. I didn't know they did this. But when you go on the third floor—they had this

---

[8] *D-Day Museum in New Orleans*-The brainchild of author Stephen Ambrose, the D-Day Museum opened its doors on June 6, 2000. Three years later, Congress officially designated it as the United States' official National WWII Museum, changing the name to reflect that. New Orleans had been the home of the Higgins boat, the shallow draft invasion LCVP made famous on many D-Days that was based on boats made for operating in the area's marshes and swamps.

letter copied; you could see this picture [*shows the picture of young Nicholas Butrico in uniform*]. The picture was taken in Camp Breckenridge, Kentucky, in 1942, around there. There are a lot of [copies of Eisenhower's D-Day Order of the Day] around—but this is the only one that has a letter written on the back. Nobody else had it; see, I had it in my pocket. I didn't realize it—if you notice it on the top, June 4—now that's two days before the invasion, and if you'll notice on the back of the letter, June 6, but I didn't write the letter on June 6. I just put down what I saw on June 6, and I mention that on the bottom.

Would you like me to read it? It's a prayer, more or less. [*Begins reading*]

'June 6. Landed one hour before D-Day, H-Hour. It was my first combat. As I turned around, I could see hundreds of bodies lying on the beach, not one moving. Some tried to move, and some were drowning. I'd never prayed before, but I really prayed that day. I lost somebody but I made it and we took our objective.

'That day I'll never forget—we landed on the worst beach of the invasion—Omaha. At night Jerry planes would come and try to knock us out and we held out. We had to or all the plans would go haywire. All I thought of was, if anything happened to me, [I hope] my family wouldn't take it too bad, but I'm glad I made it for my family's sake. I thought of the boys that didn't make it, and how their families would feel. I lost my best buddy on the beach. He never got to shore—just a kid of eighteen. He came from Brooklyn, and he was Italian. All I can say is I am thankful that I made it. Please protect me for whatever lies ahead for me! I thank you, Lord.'

Now this is the only one; there is no other one. This is what they were interested in, asking me if they could copy that. The next thing you know I got a phone call from somebody from Virginia telling me they would like to have it. I said, 'Well, I don't know—my kids don't want me to give it up.'

They said, 'No, you send it to us. The copy that you sent to the Eisenhower Museum is just a copy.

We want to make a copy the way we want to copy it.' They sent me a box, Federal Express, prepaid. They said, 'Put the letter inside, seal it, and if you notice it's insured for $1500.' So I sent it. I think a week later I got it back, then a couple of days later I got a call from California. A woman got on and she said, 'We saw your letter.' I don't know how they saw it, they must have seen it somewhere; it was in a *Forbes* magazine—I remember getting that, I was sitting in here. My wife says, 'Here— brown envelope,' and I open it up and see the magazine. So, I opened it up, in the first few pages, there is the letter, big—and it tells the story. And I call my wife, and my daughter-in-law got all excited, and the next thing you know, she's in the store buying all these magazines. Then a few days later, I get this call from California. They'd like to interview me for the D-Day Museum opening. I said sure, why not. I was on Channel 7; I was on Channel 2; I've been on all these channels. I've got a lot of newspapers I've been on around in this neighborhood. In fact, some friends of mine just went to New Orleans, they went on a senior citizens tour, and they asked me, 'Nick, tell us where it is!'

I said, 'It's on the third floor,' but they couldn't find it, and they finally did find it, and then they're telling these people—this was only a couple of weeks ago—'This fellow comes from our own hometown, Congers!'

[When I got that call], they said, 'You just sit still. We'll send a limousine to your house, pick you up and take you to 52nd Street and 5th Avenue, up in a big studio. We want to tape.' Big cameras there and they put a wire on my neck.

The limousine picked us up and I talked to the guy. I said, 'Is this limousine you are using only for celebrities?'

He was telling me, 'I've taken President Nixon in this limousine, and I've taken big movie stars. We don't cater to college proms.' He said, 'It costs you a lot of money to use it.'

So, I asked him how much would it cost because my nephew is Jewish and he's getting barmitzvahed at Tavern on the Green and we're all invited, so I asked, 'How much would it cost us to rent this to take us one way and then back—that would be 57th Street right off Central Park?'

He said, '$1800.' One trip! That's what they charge.

I said, 'Forget about it.'

He took us to the city, and they took me to this room, and they asked me all kinds of questions. I must have been up there for two hours, and the guy said to me, 'I'm talking to you, and you will not hear it. We'll just hear your voice.' Now when it came onto the History Channel, they cut it, they just took the parts that fit into the [narrative] because there were other people on there.

When I was in New Orleans, I was treated like a king, and then I was on the podium—I was sitting there, and guess who's sitting next to me, on both sides? Tom Hanks and Stephen Spielberg. Because Stephen Spielberg made *Private Ryan*. [I saw it, but] even the beginning—it's ridiculous—the guy running around with his [severed] arm [*raises left arm overhead*]—that's overdoing it—and another guy running around with his guts hanging out. That's overdoing it. He's hollering, 'Mama, Mama.' Well, I heard guys hollering, 'Mama,' but this guy has his guts out; he's not going to be living. A lot of the Rangers—we go to reunions, and we talk about [that film]. Well, the Army would never have taken one section out of the Rangers to go look for one guy to get him home because the Rangers, when we landed in Omaha, we had one objective, Pointe du Hoc.

*

Now I will tell you a story about Dinah Shore, which I never told. We were just outside Saint-Lô. I tell you the truth, in all the time I was in the service, in combat, overseas, I never saw a USO show. We always said, 'If you are in the Air Corps, you see it.' You don't see it, maybe if you're in the hospital. The rear echelon always saw it. But it just happened this jeep pulled up, and Dinah Shore was in it with two captains or something and she was going to entertain us. This was just before we were going into Saint-Lô and they were pushing towards Paris. So, we got there and that's just before we went to Brest; she got on the jeep and no sooner had she sat on the jeep, [we were told], 'All right, get your stuff ready, we're pulling out!' But she's sitting on the jeep and the two captains are mushing her up like mad, [acting a bit randy]. She said, 'Now behave yourselves, boys!' [*Laughs*] You know how she was.

Jesus Christ, that's the only time I ever got close to [a show]. John Garfield came to the USO—I heard this from a guy up in the 4th because he was there—so he went there to entertain the troops.[9] Just to show you how this government of ours works, when he got out [on stage], he said, 'First of all, ladies and gentlemen, before I start, all you people in the front, colonels, generals, you know, all brass, I will not entertain while you people are sitting there up front, and all the GIs and wounded veterans are all back there! Have them come up here, and you go back there.' The next day they shipped him back to the States. [*Laughs*]

---

[9] John Garfield (1913-1952), remembered as the 'Jewish Brando' after his death, was an American actor who played tough, working-class characters who didn't mince words, preceding the likes of Brando, James Dean, and others. From *Body and Soul,* a 1947 film noir sports drama, in which he played an up-and-coming Jewish boxer facing bad choices and moral dilemmas: *"In Europe, the Nazis are killing people like us just because of their religion. But here, Charlie Davis is champion, and we are proud."* Garfield was attacked by the House Committee on Un-American Activities and denied communist affiliation and refused to give the committee 'names,' for which he was blacklisted, ending his career. Hounded by investigators, he died at age 39 from a heart attack. The HUAC then closed its investigation without charges, which cleared his name.

Well, that's the story. I hope it was interesting.

In 2005, Nicholas Butrico got to attend the 50th year anniversary of D-Day ceremony in Normandy along with his comrades in arms. He passed the following year on August 6 at the age of 77. Today, a memorial plaque in his honor is displayed at the WWII Museum in New Orleans, a testament and tribute to the twenty-two-year-old Italian kid from New York who prayed to God to keep him safe, and for the friends whom he lost on the beach, and their families.

Operation Market Garden. Map by Susan Winchell.

CHAPTER THREE

A Bridge Too Far

Following the success of the Normandy landings and the breakout in France and across Belgium, the Allied armies were moving so quickly that the supply lines simply could not keep up as the reconstruction and further expansion of the significant coastal ports could not happen overnight. The Red Ball Express, manned by mostly African-American servicemen and operating literally around the clock, moved about 12,500 tons of supplies a day at its peak, but more ports had to be opened, including the port of Antwerp in Belgium, which in the near future would also be the coveted objective of Hitler's push through the Ardennes Forest in December 1944.[1]

Two different proposals competed for the attention of Allied logistics planning and supplies in the drive to cross the Siegfried Line and Rhine River in the push to Berlin. Omar Bradley, Commanding General of the 12th U.S. Army Group (including the First, Third, Ninth, and Fifteenth Armies, 1.3 million men strong) and British Field Marshal Bernard Law Montgomery had different ideas. In simple terms, the Eisenhower and Bradley camp advocated for keeping the pressure on Germany in a 'broad front' approach, while Montgomery was convinced of his 'single thrust' strategy that would concentrate resources specifically targeting the industrial Ruhr Valley and the Rhine River, driving a dagger into the heart of the Reich.

Antwerp had fallen on September 4 to the British 11th Armored (the same outfit that would be stunned to the core at the capture of the Bergen-Belsen concentration camp the following spring, with its 60,000 sick, emaciated, and dying prisoners), but with the Germans controlling 60 miles of the Scheldt River's tidal estuary, it could be of no use until the waterway was opened.

Given that roadblock, and the fact that the Germans were still launching hundreds of V-1 and V-2 buzz bombs a week toward England and elsewhere from the occupied Netherlands, Monty proposed crossing the Rhine in the north, in the Netherlands, and outflanking much of the fortified Siegfried Line. The way to do it, he argued, was to allow him command of the First Allied Airborne Army (which included the British 1st Airborne Division, the Polish 1st Independent Parachute Brigade, and the United States' 101st and 82nd Airborne Divisions), pairing it with the ground operation of the British Second Army. In order to reach the lower Rhine at Arnhem, four rivers and three canals would have to be breached. It was imperative that the airborne troops capture the bridges intact, if possible (as it would be equally important to the 9th and 10th SS Panzer Division to hold the bridges at all costs to facilitate control and counteroffensive measures, once the attack began). The bridges would be seized and defended at key locations while awaiting ground reinforcements; the last bridge to be taken by the British Red Devils in Arnhem was a daunting 65 miles distant from the start of the British Second Army ground offensive. It was a bold plan, and one that Eisenhower had his misgivings about, but something had to be done; it was approved in early August in a concession to circumstances, to the dismay of General Patton and other American commanders, as it would siphon men and materiel from their own drives.[2] Still, Ike may have seen Operation Market Garden as a side 'theater' of the broad thrust into Germany plan. It would go on as planned, but plans, especially military ones, don't always come off the way they are expected to.

Sgt. Albert Tarbell, 504th Parachute Infantry Regiment, 82nd Airborne Division, World War II.
Source: Albert Tarbell.

CHAPTER FOUR

The Paratrooper I

On the morning of September 17, 1944, 4,700 aircraft carrying more than 35,000 men began leaving England in the largest airborne operation in the history of the world.³ Between 1 and 1:30 in the afternoon, the C-47s began the approaches to the drop zone; the first hours were considered a success, with the majority of men landing near their assigned targets. Not every paratrooper, however, was that fortunate, although twenty-one-year-old Albert Tarbell hit the Dutch drop zone successfully.

Albert L. Tarbell was of Mohawk descent, born at St. Regis Reservation in northern New York in the late summer of 1923. The Mohawk people were traditionally the 'Keepers of the Eastern

Door,' the most easterly of the five original nations of the Iroquois, the fierce guardians on the eastern frontier of the indigenous confederation, a power to be reckoned with by European interlopers for over 200 years. In the early 20th century, many of the Mohawk established a reputation for bridge and high-rise building construction, particularly in a burgeoning New York City, over 300 miles down the Hudson from their traditional settlement area along the border with Canada. Colloquially called 'skywalkers' for their prowess and fearlessness in working at dizzying heights, and renowned for their ironworking abilities, these Mohawk men took pride in doing jobs that most would shy away from; in 1931, they helped complete a project that became emblematic of the Empire State, an eminence that would be, like the Statue of Liberty, one to welcome home returning soldiers in 1945—New York's iconic Empire State Building. At 1,454 feet tall, it would be the tallest building in the world until 1970, when the twin towers of the World Trade Center were completed. Following the horrific attacks in 2001, it reassumed its title, only to be surpassed once more in 2012 with the completion of New York's Freedom Tower at One World Trade Center in Lower Manhattan. Notably, fully ten percent of the iron workers on that deliberate, painstaking—and defiantly proud—rebirth of sorts were Mohawk.

Imbued with this incredible Mohawk work ethic, Albert spent his life creating and building, bringing good into the world and retiring after 34 years in ironworking and related work. Like many of his peers witnessing Pearl Harbor unfolding, the young man of eighteen was anxious to join up and defend his nation—but like several northern New Yorkers, he was already serving a hitch in the Canadian army. Released from that obligation, he would meet up with Canadian armed forces again, in a land he probably never dreamed of going to, thousands of miles away and years on the horizon.

In 2003, Mr. Tarbell sat for this interview in Syracuse, New York, recalling his participation in the war as the very first Mohawk Indian paratrooper to qualify and be accepted into the legendary 82nd Airborne Division. Now eighty years old, spry, and with a twinkle in his eye and a subtle self-effacing chuckle punctuating some of his humorous incidents, he also grew serious in recounting the harrowing nature of his combat experience and remembering the friends he lost, buddies sometimes right next to him, or worse—someone who had momentarily taken his place on the line.

In this first part of his nearly three-hour-long epic storytelling, he recalled his paratrooper training, his first combat experience in Italy at Anzio, and his part in the largest airborne operation in the history of the world with the 82nd Airborne's 504th Parachute Infantry Regiment, soon to acquire the enemy nickname the 'Devils in Baggy Pants.'

In 1977, the film epic based on Cornelius Ryan's book *A Bridge Too Far* was released to great fanfare. In a memorable scene, actor Robert Redford, portraying the 504th Parachute Infantry Regiment's 3rd Battalion commander Col. Julius Cook, leads a daring daylight river crossing to assault the northern end of a bridge over the Waal River in the Netherlands; in real life, Mr. Tarbell was right there with Julius Cook.

'We got out in the river just a little way, and it was just like [it was starting to] rain! The Germans opened

up with machine guns on us and the water was rippled just like rain was falling on it! They threw machine gun [fire]. They threw mortars. They threw 88s. You name it, they [threw it at us].

Out of the twenty-six assault boats we had, there were only eleven that were still in service when we got to the other side. Most of them were either sunk or the guys were all killed; we lost half our company there. The boat right next to me took a direct hit; I could still see the guys [who were in it] as I was turning and paddling, I was trying to call cadence with these guys [for the paddling] ... trying to keep it together at the same time.

About midway across there, I looked [to] the side, and I see my buddy stand up. Then he just looked at me like as if he'd given up... I turned, and he was gone. I can still see that look on his face, you know—his eyes, his eye contact with me. They never found his body until, I think, after the war. They found it up alongside the bank further down the Waal River.'

Albert L. Tarbell

I was born on the St. Regis Indian Mohawk Reservation in Hogansburg, New York, August the

24th, 1923. When I went in the service, I had two and a half years of high school, and it was not until after the war that I got a full high school diploma from the Fort Covington High School.

[In late 1941], I was attached to the Stormont, Dundas, and Glengarry Highlanders in the Canadian Army, and when we heard about Pearl Harbor, we knew that the United States was going to war. There were quite a few of us in that area there that were from the American side that were in the Canadian Army. [I joined the Canadian Army] after I dropped out of high school. I see all these parades in Cornwall and this and that, and I guess, next thing you know, my cousin and I joined, and then we were really too young to go overseas, and so I ended up being a corporal in the training staff—but when I heard about Pearl Harbor, I knew then that eventually I would probably be going back to the States. I left Ottawa, I think it was around March. It was a bitter cold winter, and I had a slight cold. I got home and I caught pneumonia when I was home on furlough, and my father and mother discouraged me from going back. They said, 'If they can't take care of you, you should not go back.' So I stayed home, and I worked on a farm, and then I went to work in the spring in Massena; I ended up working as an apprentice lineman. To make a long story short, I ended up in Syracuse, New York, and then this is where our union hall was and I worked around the States for a while, in New York State, Buffalo and mostly in Syracuse, doing repair work for Niagara Mohawk. That was all through the union, Local 1249 of the International Brotherhood of Electrical Workers.

I was drafted and I got my call to report in February of 1943; I entered the service in March 1943. We went for induction through Utica, New York, and then from Utica went to Fort Niagara. From Fort Niagara, they took us by train to Camp Swift, Texas, which was a new camp outside of Bastrop, Texas; I think it's northeast of Austin, Texas. There was a new camp there. The 97th Infantry Division was being formed there and mostly all us guys from the north were sent down there. We had eight to 12 weeks of training there, basic training. I ended up in the communications section. Being out of the union, they figured I had something to do with linework, so I ended up doing my basic training in that. They were much more strict in the Canadian Army. Our corporal was just as high as a master sergeant there. He had a lot of authority. And in the States, it was a little more lenient. It wasn't as strict. I found the training not as hard at all.

Into the Paratroopers

Before I was drafted, I had gotten married, and my wife came down to visit me for a while in Texas. And then when my furlough came, I came back to Syracuse, and then after my furlough, I noticed this guy prancing up and down on the train here, with some outfit he was in, and we couldn't figure out what outfit he was with. He had a cocked hat on, you know, and he had boots on with a blouse. Man, he looked terrific! When he told me he was getting $50 a month more than me as a private, I said, 'Well, I think I'm going to look into that.' So when I got back to Texas, I put in for my transfer.

And in the outfit that I was in, being in communications, I could only go into the Air Force or the paratroops, so the paratroops like that, so I joined the paratroops. About a month later, around August the 13th, at 1300 hours, 13 of us left Camp Swift, Texas, for Fort Benning, Georgia, and then I had to start training all over again. And this was basic communication training, airborne. And it was not until around November that we got into jump school, and all that summer, we trained, physical training, airborne infantry training, shooting different weapons and stuff like that.

It had taken four weeks to go through jump school and we received our wings, I think it was around December 2. We were given 14-day furloughs to come home after our graduation. We had had a little baby born while I was in jump school. I couldn't come home because I couldn't interrupt my training there; they wouldn't let me go. So, I met my baby, and we went up north to visit for a few days and then we came back home. Meanwhile, this buddy of mine from Rochester who rode back with me asked me, 'Did you get a notice to come back to camp?'

'No,' I said, 'did you?'

He said, 'Yeah, I got a telegram, but I was only home a couple of days.' So I thought he was just kidding. When we did get back to camp, there was nobody there! They had moved out to the Alabama area and were getting ready to ship away from Fort Benning! And the first thing my company commander said when he saw me, when I reported back to the camp, was, 'Did you get the telegram to come home to report?'

I said, 'No.'

He just smiled a little bit, you know, and said, 'You sure?'

I said, 'Well, sure!' It wasn't until years later, when I got out of the service, I asked my dad, 'Did I ever get a telegram?'

'Yeah,' he said, 'the telegram came in about two days after you were home.' He said, 'Heck, I tore it up. You just got here, and they wanted you to report back to camp!' So right after New Year's we moved out of Fort Benning to Fort Meade, Maryland. Meanwhile, my wife came to Baltimore. My mother was living there at that time, and I was able to get a pass every night while I was in Meade. And then, around about the 15th of January, I could not go out on pass anymore and I was told that we were going to be getting ready to move out. [The commander] said, 'Tell your wife that you won't be seeing her for a while.' So, we ended up at Hampton Roads, Norfolk, Virginia, and I ended up on the Victory ship *John Hart Benton*. Two hundred and fifty of us got on that ship in the afternoon and we heard this band playing music. We looked down the street and we could see some soldiers marching up there, and we saw these guards on the side with shotguns and we ended up with 250 'shotgun volunteers' with us on that ship to go ship overseas. These guys were out of the stockade, and they marched them right out to the Victory ship. They posted those guards on there until we got ready to pull out, but we got along great with the prisoners. I was made acting corporal, I had charge of the KP on the ship, and I made sure that the guys all reported for work duty on the KP work roster, and we just had no problems with them. Three miles out, I never saw so many pistols show up on these guys, I don't know where they got them from, but they had them in underarm holsters! And one of them was Rita Hayworth's brother, and he said that he was not part of those guys, but he got on the ship with them, though he said he had nothing to do with those guys. [*Laughs*] We lost track of them when we got to Casablanca.

Italy

We had joined the convoy, and about three days later, we woke up one morning and we were all alone—the convoy had left us, and we had gone in a different area, different direction. And it took us eighteen days, and we ended up in Casablanca, French Morocco, where we stayed a couple weeks, and then we went by train from there to Algiers, Algeria. There was a camp outside there near an airbase. About a week or so later, we went by plane to Naples, Italy, and then from there I ended up in Venafro. I was attached to the H Company, [3rd Battalion], 504th Parachute Infantry Regiment, 82nd Airborne Division. When we joined the outfit, we came back to Naples Harbor, and we got on LCIs and went to Anzio beachhead as replacements for the 504th Parachute Infantry Regiment.

It was in the latter part of February when we got there, and we stayed there until the latter part of April. We left Easter Sunday on the *Capetown Castle* to go to England. We left Naples on April 11,

1944, and we arrived in Liverpool, England, on April 22.

We did extensive training there in England for the Normandy invasion. We did all their problem jumping, and we did anything to do with dispersal areas and flight formations for the planes and this and that. We usually jumped in mass jumps, we jumped two men to a plane, and all different things like that; we had to [try to experiment] for all those problems they figured they would encounter in the Normandy invasion. We did not make Normandy, because the big boss figured that our men were all so new—they had lost most of their men in [the fight at] Anzio. So the two other outfits took our place, the 507th and the 508th Parachute Infantry Regiments took our place, and they went into the 82nd for the Normandy deal. So we stayed in England training, and then we started training for more missions; there was always training, airborne training, jumping. I did a lot of jumps in England, practice jumps. We had about four or five different alarms to go on a mission, and they were canceled each time, because the army was moving so fast in France.

Market Garden

Around about the 15th of September, we went back to [RAF] Spanhoe Airfield and we were closeted in, and we couldn't leave or nothing, you know. And we were just stuck in that camp, and we knew something was coming up; we were getting lectures from intelligence and stuff like that, [so] we definitely knew we were going on a mission, we were going in the Netherlands, Holland. We started getting our equipment ready, more or less honing up for our mission.

We left Spanhoe Airfield Sunday morning, September 17, about ten o'clock, and jumped about sixty-five miles behind the German lines around 1:15. We landed in Grave, Holland. On our way over, it was quite a sight to see all those planes—in fact, this was the first daylight mission in American airborne history. We had planes like, my God, when we were jumping in Holland, they were still leaving the airfield in England! And it seemed like you could just walk on the planes, you're glad you saw so many planes in the air, and we had fighter escorts. As we hit the mainland, we got some artillery flak from flak stations. And the fighter planes went right to work on them, knocked them right out.

As we were going in, you could see the people sitting on the roofs, they're waving to us, they knew something big was coming on. Being Sunday, everybody was home, and not working. And then when we got near, oh, just two miles inland, my company commander and I looked out the window, I was sitting next to him by the door.

I said, 'Jeepers!' I said, 'We're not at the DZ yet, these guys are starting to jump!' We noticed the plane next to us was on fire, the bottom was all on fire; guys were jumping through it! And they had shot another one of the planes down, and we could see it go down, but we lost track of it—it was right next to ours.

All of my buddies were in that plane [with the hole in the floor]. One that I chummed around with quite a while [was also in it], and I met him again 34 years later, [after] he had retired from the CIA. He verified what happened; it was that they had taken [flak] fire, and underneath the plane, these equipment bundles which contained Composition C-4 [plastic explosives] caught on fire, and it melted the bottom of the plane, so they just fell right through; they hooked on their static lines and fell right through. Most of them were captured, I think an exception of two guys showed up about a month later; they rejoined our outfit, they hid in with the Dutch underground.

Now we were still going in, and a little while later we were talking to first sergeant about the plane, what happened. And we were leaning in, talking to each other, and all at once, he flew up in the air and landed right in the middle of the C-47, middle of the aisle. I looked around, and I said, 'What the heck's going on here,' you know. One of the guys looked at where [Sergeant McHogan] had been sitting; there was a bullet hole right where he was sitting. It missed him, and the bullet went right up his shoe—the impact sent him flying right up to the middle of the floor! So it wasn't long after that that we got to our [drop zone], and we were starting to get flak from the bridges there, Grave Bridge. And when we got up to get ready to check our equipment and hook up, the company commander told him, he said, 'First Sergeant

McHogan.' He said, 'Mike, you don't have to jump that chute. You can go back to England.'

The first sergeant said, 'Like hell I am. I'm getting the hell off this plane right now!' [*Chuckles*] We made our jump; so he jumped the chute, and he was all right.

Out the Door

I had a radar bag with a radio in it and rope. When we left the plane, I let loose of the static line, you know, and it broke. I think shrapnel cut it, because we were getting shrapnel from the bridge, flak shrapnel. They were aiming for the door; I think it cut my line. Anyway the radio went one way, and I went the other. Coming down, the first sergeant hollered over and I could hear him, you know. I was looking around for a few seconds. He said, 'There's a guy behind that barn, that building, watch out!' So when I come in, I come in backwards and I landed on an apple tree. I had all my weight and the weight of all my gear, and it just put me right to the ground nice and easy, no problem. I took my chute off, grabbed my Tommy gun, and I got ahold of this guy, he was just a young kid standing there. He was watching us jumping, wondering what was going on, you know.

So I motioned to him, there was a wheelbarrow near the barn door, and I said, 'Bring her over.' We loaded our gear on there, and he took it up to the main road for us. The first sergeant and I, we brought our stuff, and [the kid] wheeled it out for us. First thing I saw when I got there was a priest was there, and there were a lot of kids and parents in the road, and every one of them had orange on—the girls had orange ribbons, the men had orange lapels or something orange in their suit jacket there, to show that meant that they were going to help us. They would be our friends. They were always Queen Wilhelmina's colors, orange. We were told by the intelligence then that whoever had that on would be helpers, be willing to help the Allies. So that was about the first day of the jump.

We didn't receive too much opposition on the ground. We more or less saw we had part of our regiment there. One company jumped on the south side of the bridge; the rest of the battalion came in from the north side. We had our mission accomplished before five o'clock that night! From then on, it was mostly going from village to village, town to town, and capturing other small bridges. We had to take these bridges for the British armor to go through, to go into Arnhem, where the main British force jumped the bridge in Arnhem. Ten thousand men jumped there; the 101st jumped in Eindhoven. We jumped next. We jumped in Nijmegen area. Our area was the Grave Bridge outside of Nijmegen. We had to get all of those bridges to make a direct link to Arnhem and then the 30th Armored could go right through into Germany or the Ruhr River Valley, or wherever they were going to go. That was the idea. [But] I think that if the British had gone through like they were supposed to do, we could have had that problem, [but the British armor was slowing down]. As it was, we ended up, on the 18th, we got resupplied; the gliders come in and I was there on the ground. I had to meet our company driver, he came in, and I had to lead him back to our area. So that was quite an experience there, being in the field when the gliders came in. They didn't have no brakes, you know. They just plowed right along the field until they stopped, they stopped—and I never wanted [to be in] one, either. [When my driver got me there], I found out from the, I guess it would be the landing officer in the field there, he said, 'Stand right here. Your friend will be somewhere here in this area.'

And sure enough, just a few feet away from where this glider came in, he was on that. They opened a side up, and when he got off that glider, the front opened up and he drove his jeep out and he hollered over, said, 'Tarbell, run over here!', and I run over there and he threw his hat on the ground and said, 'Tarbell, that was the last damn time I'm ever going to ride in them things!' I guess he had quite a ride coming over. [*Chuckles*] But anyway, then we got supplied by B-24s, and years later I found out one of the guys resupplying us was a rear gunner on a B-24, a guy from up home that I knew very well, John Cook was his name. It was a small world. Here I'm on the ground helping [in retrieving and] receiving the supplies, and he's up there in a plane delivering them, you know. We never found that out until about forty years later.

The Dutch Underground

We got all our mission pretty well done. Mostly we worked with the Dutch Underground for a while here and there, from village to village and this and that. We were accepted with everybody, all the Dutch people; the Underground cooperated one hundred percent. Everybody was just so happy to see us, willing to help! First mission, we went out on this little town. We went out with one truck, we came back with [German] motorcycles. We came back with a [captured] truck, another car, you name it—and we even met the Dutch Underground there, they drove us around looking for pockets of Germans! Just unbelievable, you know. We'd never seen anybody help us like that, you know, [in] the other places that we've been. We never got that cooperation from any other country as we did in Holland.

Around about the 18th, the 19th, the British showed up at the bridge; we heard early in the morning that they were coming in, so I went out early in the morning with some of the other guys. We sat on the bridge waiting for them to come in. We're just sitting there, waiting and [walking] around, smoking and talking. One of the civilians comes up and he said, 'You know they had an office down there.' He pointed down at the valley below the bridge. Three of the guys run down to it, and I went down with them. By the time I got down there, they had everything all cleared off, they had taken the mementos off the table. All there was left was a flag behind the desk, so I took that and I folded that up and put it aside; I still have that flag from that bridge. It was from the guard staff who had their office there.

We stayed there for I think it was that afternoon, that was the 19th, and we got back to the area where we were staying. We had to move out towards the city of Nijmegen, which was just a few miles, but we moved on and I don't remember if we got trucked out there or not. Of course, at that time, we didn't know that they were having such a hard time at the Nijmegen Bridge on the Waal River. They were trying to get the assault in, [the bridge was] heavily fortified. They were able to get part of the railroad bridge, but on the main bridge, they were having a fierce fight at both ends. The SS were there, you know—the 9th and the 10th SS

Panzer Divisions were stationed there. Bittrich was the commanding general there, General Bittrich of the SS, and they said that they'd have to make a river crossing and get in the north end of the bridges in order to take over the bridge. So they told us finally the following day, the 20th early in the morning, we found out we were going to make a river crossing. We were told there was an assault boat coming up that we're going to use, so we got ready for the river crossing. I was on the first wave of H Company; H and I Company were to be ready to make the first wave.

Crossing the Waal

We kept waiting all morning for those boats, and finally round about three o'clock, they showed up. They were the [portable] canvas boats with plywood bottoms, and they had sticks that you turned counterclockwise to spread them out like an accordion, to open them up to make it stable. God, they were just nothing but canvas, I don't know how many paddles they were supposed to have had, but we ended up with sixteen men; thirteen men to each boat, and then three engineers to help navigate the boat. They had little bitty motors on them, they weren't worth a crap! You know, you're getting sixteen people on that boat, and you've got over ten-mile-an-hour currents, and they didn't figure on that.

Anyway, when we started down, I was right behind my company commander, and we grabbed the boat; we took it on each side, and we ran down the bank. All at once, the CO took all his gear off, and he dove right into the river! One of the guys on the other side had fallen in and he was drowning with all his equipment on. Our company commander just threw his gear off, dove in, and got him up to shore, and then we helped him back up! Then we jumped in whatever boats we could; it was just a fiasco. When we first started out, the boat was going one way and then the other, the guys were not used to paddling the boat—I don't think that some of them had ever even been on a river or something like that, you know, with a boat! We had quite a time navigating. Finally, we got somewhere near a decent [stroke]; we got out in the river just a little way, and it was just like [it was starting to] rain! The Germans opened up with machine guns on us and the water was rippled just like rain was falling on it! They threw machine gun [fire]. They threw mortars. They threw 88s. You name it, they [threw it at us].

Out of the twenty-six assault boats we had, there were only eleven that were still in service when we got to the other side. Most of them were either sunk or the guys were all killed, and this and that. We lost half our company there. The boat right next to me took a direct hit; I could still see the guys [who were in it] as I was turning and paddling, I was trying to call cadence with these guys [for the paddling]… trying to keep it together at the same time. About midway across there, I looked on the side, and I see my buddy stand up. Then he just looked at me like as if he'd given up… I turned, and he was gone. I can still see that look on his face, you know—his eyes, his eye contact with me. They never found his body until, I think, after the war. They found it up alongside the bank further down the Waal River.

We finally did get to the other side, and we fought our way up to the canal. At one time I ended up with the colonel, Colonel Cook, and

Captain Kep. We were fighting wherever we could; we were all kind of mixed up, you know; there were so many casualties and things that went on. We tried to regroup as we went inland towards the bridges. One of my buddies came by and he said, 'Hey, look, I got another Purple Heart!' He had his thumb shot off. Just a few minutes later there I see his body on the other side of the building. He was killed, so he got two Purple Hearts that day.

The Railroad Bridge

We ended up on a railroad bridge. My company commander was there, and the executive officer was there; at each port hole, they were there, and we were passing grenades to them. We had a lot of Germans trapped in the middle of the bridge; the guys that were shooting at us as we were crossing the river. [We were using] Gammon grenades, composition C2, C4, C2. We made them up ourselves; pound and a half pound, whatever. They're concussion grenades. When you would throw that, it's got a little metal belt on it. You throw that and it had a lead weight on the end. When it's in the air, that belt comes off, and it pulls that pin out and that's going to go off. We did quite a job with that. We used up all that with our Gammon grenades because they would rush us. As they would rush us, we would throw the Gammon grenades at them. They had quite a few casualties there on that bridge; the Germans did. They had over 264 on the bridge and I don't know how many jumped over on the side.

They had those bridges loaded on the girders [*glances upward to indicate explosives above*] and every place else. They really ambushed us coming across [the river], but we caught them when we got to the bridge, because we sealed the north end off. By that time, the south end was sealed off by the 505th Parachute Infantry Regiment. Then finally, towards evening, we ended up to the north end of the main bridge; the railroad bridge was where we fought at first. The main bridge, where the tanks would come across, was where we ended up that evening. Then, when the British took over that area there, the I Company was there, the I Company commander and some of our platoons took it over. We ended up all up there and the rest of H Company. We seen the tanks come across and they didn't go any further than just to the end of the bridge. One of the tanks got hit, so they said, 'Well, that's all right. Keep on going.' One of the officers said, 'We'll knock that tank gun out for you. Keep on going to Arnhem.'

The reason that we were doing this was that the British Airborne was being annihilated in Arnhem. There were 10,000 of them there, and they had run right on top of a nest of panzers; they came and they were fighting for that bridge but the rest of them were being isolated on the other side of the river.

The tanks that they had to get there to help them to fight to get that bridge, and to relieve those guys there, [but] they stopped right at Nijmegen. They didn't go any further than there.

'They're Zeroing In!'

The next morning, we fanned out. We set up a CP; I think it was the 21st or the 22nd. I had my SCR300 radio.[10] That was my job, I was an

---

[10] *SCR300 radio-* backpack-mounted radio transceiver used in World War II, the first radio unit to be nicknamed a 'walkie-talkie.'

SCR300 communication man. As a sergeant, my job was to make sure that we had company communications from company to platoons and to outposts. I'd make sure that we had that. We had the SCR300 for battalion communication. The following morning there, we were trying to see how many casualties we had at the CP we were at. The company clerk and I were on a call with a bunch of others. When the battalion called, I would [set up] contact with my radio and then I was using the phone line to contact the different platoons and see what their casualties were. We were writing the guys' names on the list; Sheldon, the company clerk, was writing the names of the guys. Then we started getting shells, which were getting closer and closer to our CP. The first sergeant was downstairs in this building. He said, 'Tarbell, they better bring that radio down here. I think they're zeroing in on your radio set! They're getting closer and closer to us!' We bent over to pick up the radio, Sheldon and I, and our heads were together and a shell came into the courtyard, right behind us. Shrapnel came through the window, missed me, hit Sheldon in the forehead and killed him instantly; blew his head off and the back of his head out.

We had three other guys on the other end of the building. There was Rosser, I think it was Keith, and Zimmerman. They all got just slightly wounded. It never touched me. I mean, I don't know how it missed me. [*Shrugs slightly, looks down, shakes head*] Then first sergeant came up. The worst part of that deal was having to put Sheldon's name on that list that he was making out. We had fifty-four men down; when we ended up, it was a fifty-fifty casualty [rate] from our company for those two days. The hardest part was putting Sheldon's name on that list that he had started... [*Pauses reflectively*]

I got downstairs and company commander said, 'Call the medic over. Give him something to calm him down,' because I was just about ready to do... [*shakes head*] ... something. I went right to sleep. The medic said, 'Lay down here and rest.' I went right to sleep. I slept finally. I slept until it was just about getting dark and the company commander woke me up and said, 'Grab your Tommy gun.

Let's go and check the positions.' So, that felt good. I felt better then, you know.

We stayed there a couple days. A day or so later, we pulled back out and those tanks and those guys were still in the same area north of the bridge. They had never moved. We didn't [accept] that too well. We figured they'd be all the way over in Arnhem or some place, but we lost all those men for nothing, really.

So we came back and walked across the bridge and then we got on to some ducks over there, amphibious trucks, and they trucked us back to division reserve, and then after that we had a lot of fighting in different defensive setups.[11] For what was supposed to have been a two-day mission, we fought [for almost two months]; we ended up getting relieved on the 12th of November. We were there from September 17 to the 12th of November until we were relieved by the Canadian army. You know, between that time, we lost a lot of men from

---

[11] *ducks*- six-wheel-drive amphibious modification of the 2 1/2-ton CCKW trucks used by the U.S. military during World War II and the Korean War; the DUKW was colloquially known as the Duck. Source: Wikipedia

shrapnel, or from mines and from artillery barrages, mortars, being out on patrols.

A lot of things happened in that time there. One time we had an outpost way out in the Den Heuvel Woods, and we had a fierce SS counterattack there against us; there was a lot of fighting there. Because we had the outpost way out there and we had lost our communications, I had to go out that night, and I had to feel the line. I didn't know where [the outpost] was; I had to find my way out there by following the lines. As I got near this building, a barn, I found the break in the line, and every time I tried to fix it, I would get shocked, if you know what trying to fix a communication wire is like.

It was thirty years later, when I found my buddy [who had been back at the CP], and he said, 'Lieutenant was on the floor there, just grinding away at that crank!' I was getting shocked...[*Chuckles*] Finally, I was able to repair it, but meanwhile the Germans crossed the side of the road and started shooting at me, and some of our men started shooting back, and here I'm between the devil and the deep blue sea. Finally I got the line fixed, and the sergeant came out—Rosencrantz was his name—and he said, 'Tarbell, come on in, it's all right now!' They quit shooting, our guys quit shooting, so the Germans stopped, too.

I went in, he said, 'Come on in, have a cup of coffee.'

I said, 'I'm getting the hell out of here!' So that's the last time I saw Rosie. He got killed the following day. We lost a few guys there.

'Let's Have the Indian Work on Him'

I think it was the following night, they sent a patrol out, and they wanted to get a prisoner. They went up to this one building there, in a barn, or some building, this lieutenant was coming out to take a leak, and they grabbed him, German lieutenant or captain. I think he was a first lieutenant.

Now that time in our area there was a grenade fight in one of the buildings, and one of the guys got killed. Rice was his name, Sergeant Rice, and I think it was Private Byer. They would throw hand grenades in there and watch for each other's back. The Germans would throw them back out. Finally somebody threw one grenade, it landed behind

Rice's back, and it blew up and killed them. So we heard about it, and the commander went out there, and we saw him, his body right there on a stretcher beside the building. He was pretty broken up about it, the commander, because [Rice] was a well-liked kid, a well-liked guy.

Just then, who comes in? The patrol came in with this German lieutenant, and the commander said, 'Tarbell, let's get this guy out of here before he gets killed here!' We needed [this prisoner] for interrogation. So we took him back to battalion, and there was an interpreter there, he was with the intelligence, interrogated him, kept him. Colonel Cook was there, and Captain Kep and myself, and the guy couldn't speak English. He couldn't understand nothing, he couldn't understand nothing.

So Captain Kep said, 'Colonel, let's all go in the other room, and let's have the Indian work on him!' He then turns around to me, loud so everyone could hear, and he said, 'Tarbell, get him in the guts! Work on him in the guts!'

God, he was surprised by how that guy spoke such good English right after that, and let me tell you, I was too. [*Laughter*] He said, 'Let the Indian work on him,' but I was one happy Indian myself, that he could speak English. I would have had to do it, but oh my God, that would have been awful if I had to, so I was sure happy he spoke good English. He gave up some machine gun positions and stuff like that. Years later, he met Lieutenant Carmichael, and he said, 'You guys accused me and my men of killing that sergeant, that was not my patrol. That was an entirely different patrol that had the fight there,' but they were going to kill him. Rice's men would have killed him if we had left him.

The Rosary Beads

So anyway, it's like that, you know, you go out on combat patrol, and you get guys wounded, and you get guys killed. It was just trench warfare. There was another funny instance that happened one time [when we were on patrol duty there]. There was a Dutch family that was supposed to be moved to Belgium, but instead of moving them to Belgium, they moved them up towards [what would become] the front lines where we were fighting. So this family was staying in a barn, and whenever we came off the front line to come back to the rear, I used to stop in and visit these people; there was a bunch of kids, and we got to be very friendly with them. They were the Smollers family—in fact, I'm still in contact with them right to this day—but anyway, one day I didn't come in there, and they said, 'Where's Tarbell? Where's Tarbell?'

One of the guys from another company, I guess, said, 'Albert? He got killed last night on patrol,' but there was another Albert, you know. [*Laughs*] So I went there the following day to say hello to the kids—they were just little kids. There were two boys grown up, there were [a couple] 14 or 15-year-old girls, and then the little kids. There were about five or six of them at the end, and they were saying a rosary for my demise, but I walked in and all hell broke loose! [*Laughs harder*] Oh, they were so happy to see me that they gave me silver rosary beads! I still got those rosary beads; I carried them all the way through.

The Old Cat

Then another time we were in a bivouac area in a big circle, and we went to the center of that circle because we had troops all the way around; in an airborne operation, that's how you do it. We were getting shot at by these nebelwerfers, God, and they would call them 'screaming mimis.' I think they're light barrel mortars and they would fall over the place, here, there, and everywhere, but they made the weirdest sounds coming in. Well, I noticed this old cat that came around. I love strays. I would give them milk or whatever I could find, I would give them bits of my food. He was always sitting inside our dugout; we had a good dugout where we were staying. He was inside there, and finally one day Clark Fuller said, 'Let's watch that cat. I think he knows something about them nebelwerfers.' The cat's ears were all ripped up and he was deaf, yet he could hear those nebelwerfers before they'd [start screaming], before they landed! All at once, his tail went straight up, and he made a beeline for a foxhole and we followed him! After that, I'd holler, 'Incoming mail, let's go!', and everybody would scatter. [*Laughter*] The nebelwerfers came in after we were [safe] inside; that was a comical thing. [*Chuckles*] I don't know what happened to that cat, but we sure took good care of him there. The nice thing is you think about it afterwards, you live to talk about that happening, and that's just one of those experiences you talk about afterward that makes you feel good.

*

We were supposed to be relieved the 11th of November by the Canadians. And at 11:00, the company commander said, 'Let's shoot all that extra ammo out. Let's shoot it towards the German line.' We were shooting it towards the German line, and I asked the captain, 'What if they decide not to relieve us tonight?'

'Yeah,' he said, 'that's a possibility. Call them back, tell them to cut it out.' So we got hold of the platoon and they stopped, but we ended up getting relieved the following day.

The Outpost

We got relieved on the 12th. We headed right through Belgium, right into France on the trucks to a French army barracks, licking our wounds, getting replacements and stuff. We had a lot of replacements to do. Most of our company was wiped out and we had different activities to do, and they were sending some guys, the old guys on leave to Paris, some of the older men. They were going to Paris. See, I was their replacement; there were guys older than me from Sicily [invasion jumps]. I had nice duty, though. You see, in combat, I was a communications sergeant. Three of us sergeants in the company, we manned the switchboards, and we did any line communication and voice communication by radio, and we [escorted] the company commander, when we were not on [switchboard] duty; he worked us like bodyguards—wherever he went, you went.

That's what our job consisted of. It was Sergeant Brick, myself, and Sergeant Photowell. He had a rank of buck sergeant, and Clackford was our media sergeant, he was a staff sergeant. When I went to the outpost, they were having a cover attack on those Den Heuvel Woods, and everybody was on edge because there was such fierce fighting that everybody was involved. There was, during the day, an AT [rocket] gun that got set up just across the road from us. It was, I think, [manned by] five guys, and it was a 57-millimeter. The first sergeant watched them set up across the road from our CP. And all at once we saw, they got one shot off and a few seconds later they had a direct hit from a German self-propelled gun. We went over there to check the guys, and all five of them were dead. It was just a direct hit, killed all of them. We figured, well, they're gone, let's see if we can at least get the wristwatches. Even the wristwatches—the glass was all busted in that, too. It's just no good. So, we started back and between the gun position and our CP there was a haystack. And meanwhile, with all of this fighting going on, we had foxholes dug around in case we got overran. We could fight from there. Well, that self-propelled gun [crew] saw us walk away from that gun position and go towards the haystack. They must have figured we had another gun set up near there. And all at once, we could hear that shot coming and we dove behind that haystack, right into that. And we had about seven or eight shots fired at us—and you're talking about being shot at point blank by an 88. That's an awful weird feeling. You could hear that shot and then you could hear that crack when it sort of hit—just like a rifle. Man, I'm telling you, I never hugged that ground so fast. I dove down to that ground, and who the hell did I find underneath there but my first sergeant, all six foot four of him, underneath me already. We stayed there and they just tore it up. They just abrogated that haystack.

When I came back that night, from the outpost, I got into my sleeping bag, and after I reported to my sergeant what happened, about being at the outpost, and a guy shooting at me and Germans shooting back. So, I was just falling asleep in a sleeping bag, and I heard the first sergeant say, 'Lieutenant, don't go out there. You'll get shot! Don't go out there. Leave those guys alone. They're okay.' This little lieutenant, a new lieutenant who joined not too long before we were coming from Holland, he wanted to check the guard outside, and the first sergeant kept telling him, 'Lieutenant, you're going to get shot!' Sure enough, he had to go check the guard. Sure enough, he went out there and he got shot and he died about three days later. He got shot by one of the guards. Just very on edge.

Unfortunately, history would record over 15,000 Allied troops as being killed, wounded, and captured during Operation Market Garden, while German loss estimates range between a half to two-thirds of that figure. In not accomplishing the taking of the bridge at Arnhem, the operation failed to achieve the intended mission.
The Rhine would not be crossed in 1944.
The war would not be over by Christmas.

Mr. Tarbell's story will continue.

Nineteen-year-old Richard Marowitz (behind driver's left shoulder) and men of his Intelligence & Reconnaissance platoon.
Source: Richard Marowitz

CHAPTER FIVE

The Recon Man I

I met Richard Marowitz when I invited a trio from the Hudson Valley (NY) Chapter of the Veterans of the Battle of the Bulge to come up to the high school for a presentation on April 28, 2000. Now retired, he was busier than ever, and with a quick sense of humor that served him all of his life, he was quick to point out the funny things of his World War II experience.

'There's three of us that have been going around to schools and churches and synagogues and so forth talking to kids. They've got us running. That's been phenomenal. The kids, we each do about seven, eight minutes, a little bit of background of who we are and what we did in the Army and whatever. We ask for

questions. We now book no less than two hours, and we go over time. The kids, the hands never go down, unbelievable. We did Hudson Falls High School; we were only booking an hour and a half. We were supposed to talk from 1:00 to 2:30, and never got out until 4:00. Unbelievable. They're hungry. And the phenomenal part of the whole thing, the teachers weren't born yet. Every now and then they go, 'Gee, this stuff is not in the books.' I said, 'Of course not. What you have in the books came off of the front page of The New York Times back in 1944.'

He took a more serious tone when discussing a traumatic experience that happened to him on a spring afternoon like the day he was speaking to students—in fact, just one day shy of the 55th anniversary of the notorious event. As part of a well-oiled intelligence and reconnaissance task force, Rich and his friends were frequently the first Americans into enemy territory. Now only twelve miles away from the objective of the German city of Munich on that sunny spring day, they were assaulted by the overpowering stench of death—but while not uncommon in wartime, something even more sinister lay ahead, something that would register shock in soldiers not even out of their teenage years.

'We all thought the same thing. We never talked about it, but later on afterwards, after the fact, we realized that we all thought the same thing—we figured we're coming to another bombed-out farm with a bunch of dead animals. That's what we thought! Nobody ever told us it was a concentration camp! There is a village of Dachau. So, on the map, we saw a village of Dachau.
We were going to take the village. That's all we knew.'

Richard M. Marowitz

I was born in Middletown, New York, February 6, 1926. I grew up in Middletown. I went to public school and junior high, and then we moved to Brooklyn, the home of the Brooklyn Dodgers, and I was walking distance from Ebbets Field. I went to one game, and the team was great, but the fans were the worst fans I ever saw in my life, throwing bottles on the field. I said, 'Well to hell with this. I'm taking the subway to The Bronx and I'm going to go to Yankee Stadium,' and I became a Yankee fan. When the war broke out, I was on Broadway with my father, and the Times Square [scrolling news bulletin ticker] that was going around, that's the first place I saw it. I couldn't believe it. I didn't know; then, of course, I was [just fifteen].

[At that time, in high school], I actually played the trumpet. I was a little ahead of my time with that too; I joined the union when I was sixteen, doing club dates around New York, and if they had known how old I was, I never would have made it. I went on the road with a band actually, a couple of bands, and I turned eighteen in Dallas, Texas; I was playing at a club in Dallas, Texas. I went into a draft board in Dallas and signed up for the draft. I knew it was going to happen, so I had the address of the Brooklyn draft board, and I had him transfer it there. They finally caught up with me. I got a call from my sister to come home for the physical, and I was in so fast. I weighed 124 pounds. I was dead white from working all night and sleeping all day, and these big guys were stamping them rejected, rejected, rejected, and this skinny bag of bones walks up there, and was accepted. I said, 'What are you, blind?' But I don't really regret it.

I went to Camp Croft, South Carolina. At that point in time, it had slipped to third place. What I mean is, it's a gorgeous little camp in Spartanburg, South Carolina, but it had the reputation for years of being the toughest infantry camp in the country, believe it or not. They got a new commander in there that wanted to bring it back up to first place. The training was so tough he was burning guys out, guys were going to the hospital. It was awful. They finally got a new commander in. It was tough. My problem was that I was going to a specialist side of camp, so seventeen weeks of basic. So, the first seven weeks, I was supposed to do everything that the other regular straight rifle guys were getting in fourteen weeks, so they had us go night and day.

I couldn't get into a band, so they said, 'How about being a bugler?' I said, 'Great.' Well, I didn't know a bugler in the Army at that time was the scout and message runner. So, I didn't make out too well with that. I was getting all this special training, for the next seven weeks, we're supposed to go to school, learn the code converter [for the bugle]. About a week into school, they said, 'Well, they need the straight riflemen overseas. We don't know what to do with you so we're going to run the first seven weeks over again.' So, we did the first seven weeks over again, and two weeks of maneuvers and testing, and we were out of there. But I don't regret it. That training paid off later on.

South Carolina, Spartanburg, was a village, and it was all bars. The Army took over the town. It was ridiculous. It was totally ridiculous. I wasn't used to the black and white. Everything was marked black and white. That really teed me off, discrimination, oh yeah. You couldn't avoid it back in those days. I got on the bus one day—I always liked to ride in the back of the bus. I went right straight to the back of the bus, and the bus stops. Everybody is looking at me, and the bus driver said, 'Get up in front of that white line.' There's a white line on the aisle floor.

I said, 'Why?'

He said, 'You can't sit back there.'

I said, 'Did I give you my dime?'

He said, 'Yeah.'

I said, 'I'll sit where I want.'

The bus ain't moving. Now, I see all of these rednecks looking at me.

I said, 'Open the door.' I got off of the bus. I'm not dealing with these idiots.

So basic ends, and I had an 11-day delay en route to go to Camp Gruber, Oklahoma, to join the Rainbow Division. The first thing that happened to me walking down the street after I checked in, they put me right into Headquarters Company, 222. Great regiment. They put me in there, and I didn't know what I was there for. I didn't know what I was supposed to do, but I was still listed as bugler. So, every day, I went over to the rec hall because Corporal Stipple was in charge of the drum and bugle call. They gave me this plastic bugle. I'm double tugging and triple tugging, and doing all this crazy stuff on the bugle, and it blew his mind. I had brought my own mouthpiece; I had my horn with me. It just blew his mind. So, he said, 'How did you learn how to play a bugle like this?' Used to go to the rec hall and jam with the guys, and then I found out what I was doing there. The bugler that the Headquarters Company had was unfit for his duty, so I was taking his place. That's what I was doing there.

Then I helped them pack to go overseas. I didn't really know a heck of a lot; I was busy. I'm a workaholic kind of a nut anyway. The captain took me up to the motor pool and he gave me the clipboard. He said, 'These are the numbers that go on those crates, and you supervise.' He told me what to do. He said, 'Somebody will be here in eight hours to relieve you,' and nobody showed up.

I went to this lieutenant, and I said, 'Somebody is supposed to take my place.'

He said, 'Well, just keep doing it and I'll find out about it.' I never saw him again. Another eight hours went by, and the same thing happened.

So, the following morning, Captain McLaughlin, my company commander, walked in. He said, 'What are you doing?'

I said, 'I never left.'

'You've been here 24 hours?'

I said, 'You see all those crates? I could have my name on them.'

'Get in my jeep.'

We went over, and he balled the hell out of one of his second lieutenants. He took me back into his office, and he told the first sergeant, 'This guy is going to sleep. When he wakes up and when he feels like it, you just tell the mess sergeant to give him whatever he wants. And after that, forget the quarantine crap.'

He said, 'Give him a pass and let him go to town for two, three days. Doesn't make any difference.'

I said, 'Gee, that's pretty good, Captain.'

He said, 'You earned it.' That was it.

Captain McLaughlin probably turned out to be one of the nicest and best officers I ever had. This followed through in everything. His wife lived in town. He would go over and say, 'You going to town?'

'Yeah.'

'Take my car.' He gave me his wife's address, where his wife was living.

'Drop it off at the house, would you?' No problem. Then he'd take us all home, drunk or sober. It didn't make any difference when he found us, but he was a great guy. He didn't have to holler, and he didn't have to scream, although he could have. He was a big, tall, very handsome Irishman from Los Angeles. He was kind of a guy you just had to like. He liked action, but he wasn't getting it because theoretically one of his jobs was to find the next CP. If we were in this little village, and the regiment moved up, then he would find a suitable CP in the next village or whatever. But that wasn't good enough. He wanted action. To give an example of what kind of a guy he was, they used to get a liquor ration every month. His liquor ration came in, because we didn't know what he was getting and what he liked. He said, 'You guys come and see.' So, we went in, and he went into his little room that he had for an office, and the desk or the table, whatever it was at the time, was loaded with booze. He said, 'Okay, you guys, take whatever you want.'

'Captain, what did you say?'

'Take whatever you want.'

I said, 'And what is this for?'

He said, 'I have your necks out where they're not supposed to be.' We split the whiskey ration every month. I don't know if you know any officers like that, but I never met another one like that. That's the kind of a guy he was.

Shipping Overseas

I don't remember the exact day [we left to go overseas], but we left in November of '44. We landed in Marseille, France, at the end of November, around Thanksgiving, the hellhole of the world. Three infantry regiments went over, and it was called Task Force Linden because General Linden was in charge. This is what screws up the records. Actually, the rest of the 42nd Division didn't come over until February of 1945. So, we didn't have any support. So, we were being attached to the 86th or the 101st. There's a list. One of my buddies, Al Cohen, who was one of our [later classroom visiting veteran] trio, he got this list from somewhere, it lists every division, and how many days they were in combat, how many were killed, how many were wounded, percentages, and all that stuff. The Rainbow is listed as coming over on February 17, 1945—only a little bit of combat and not much action. It's totally wrong! I'm now a past president of the Veterans of the

Battle of the Bulge. Now, the Battle of the Bulge people do not have the 42nd Division as having been in the Battle of the Bulge because it wasn't, but Task Force Linden was in the Battle of the Bulge for a short time, [because] they needed bodies as fast as they could get them. So, they sent over the three infantry regiments to get the bodies over as fast as possible, then everybody else dragged in later when all the fun was over.

[The first camp area we set up] was a big, huge, windswept, ice-cold sea of mud in the middle of the night. You found a buddy. If he was alive, he got to have a tent. We pitched tents. We went to sleep. In the morning, we got up, and naturally the tents were everywhere. The officers were as green as we were, and they were still going by the book. The book was never ready for wartime. It was written for peacetime. The first thing they did was get these tents [re-set up] in a line. They wanted them perfect, holding the snap string. After that happened, that night, Bedcheck Charlie came over. I mean, what a target that camp was! Straight up one side, and come back down the other; it's just models for them. Did anybody ever explain Bedcheck Charlie to you?

The Germans, what they did is they usually sent over a small plane, like a two-engine job, and they had the motors a little bit out of sync, so when they came over, you knew it was Bedcheck right away because you heard it, recognized they were out of sync. You knew he was here. That's to throw the fear of God into you right away, and they would drop a 25-pound bomb or something just to keep you from sleeping, just to get you edgy. They never really did much damage that I saw. Once I was in a house and they took a piece of the roof off. Scared the hell out of you, but it hurt the house, it didn't hurt anybody in it. So, that was Bedcheck Charlie. Of course, after Bedcheck started coming over, they put the tents back where they were in the first place, then they moved us up to a quiet front to learn—you go to college to learn how to become a doctor, but you don't really know how to become a doctor until you go into a hospital and learn how to become a doctor. Well, the same thing happens in the Army. You've heard that before. So, we went in for our baptism of fire. It was supposed to be a quiet front. They spread us out so thin… for a short time, it was okay, until the Germans got frisky. The Battle of the Bulge started on December 16, and then they started getting frisky down at our end too. Then we started to lose people. The guys learned what war is about.

I&R Men

My job at that point was taking care of the officers. I was in charge of the mess for the officers and the staff. How I got that job, I don't remember, but Captain McLaughlin gave it to me. Colonel Longo, we later got along very well, but in the beginning, he had an asbestos mouth. The coffee could be boiling, and he'd say, 'The coffee isn't hot.' I would feed the officers, and they were aggravated. They were prima donnas, and there was a big ego trip at that time. I went to the mess sergeant, and I picked up the food and cans, and I brought it to the room where the officers are going to eat. They had their own plates and stuff like that. I would give them what the GIs were eating. So, I would say to Sergeant Sedowski, 'What are the guys eating today?'

'Well, they can only have one piece of bread, because we're short on bread, or they could only have this, they could only have that. This is what they're going to get.'

I said, 'Fine,' and I would bring enough so each of the officers would get the same thing.

And then the first time the colonel said to me, 'Got any more bread?' I said, 'No, the men are only having one piece today. You know what the book said. The officers eat what the men eat.' Actually, the officers are supposed to eat after the men eat, but I didn't go that far. But this is what I started to do. I started to become unpopular, but not unpopular enough, and one day I said to the captain, 'Captain, you have to get me out of here. I can't stand these guys anymore.'

So he said, 'You come with me,' and that's when I got to be with Flatt and the captain. We became the Three Musketeers. Theoretically I was still the bugler, but I was kind of hanging out with the captain. So, his driver's name was Flatt, F-L-A-T-T it was. Captain said to me one day, 'You know anything about a .50 caliber machine gun?'

I said, 'I can take it apart and put it together blindfolded,' which was a lie. I'm sure he knew it.

He said, 'Get in the jeep,' because he had a .50 mounted on his jeep. He said to Flatt, 'Get in,' and we went out into the woods. He was pointing at trees and I was [shooting], chopping them down. He said, 'That's good.'

So, the three of us were always where we weren't supposed to be. His dodge was, 'I'm looking for another CP.' But when you meet the I&R [Intelligence and Reconnaissance] platoon out in no-man's land, you know you're too far out.

*

We never knew what we were in because they kept bouncing us from the Third Army to the Seventh Army, from the Seventh Army to the Third Army, and did you ever hear of the other Battle of the Bulge, Operation Northwind, which came on the heels of the first Battle of the Bulge? This was another thing that you don't hear about much. Just in the last couple of years you start to hear about it, and they're starting to write about it. It was a hush-hush, not popular thing, mainly because some officers way up there made some mistakes;

we lost more people than we should have. Anyway, this was considered as bad as the first Battle of the Bulge. The 101st by that time had come down. We were more or less on the bottom of the bulge. Everybody thinks of Bastogne. They don't realize that the bulge, the front, was over 80 miles, the bulge front. We were on the southern tip of it, which was also close to Alsace-Lorraine. During this Operation Northwind, Hitler's baby, even the 101st took a bath. We were attached to the 101st at that time. We never knew from day to day what we were in. It got to the point we didn't even ask because it didn't make any difference. Wherever we went, they were shooting at us anyway.

We were maintaining a line. Of course, we kept moving and the line kept changing, naturally. Sometimes, it went back, and sometimes it didn't, and we were taking the bad stuff. A lot of guys were getting hit because we just didn't [have the manpower]. The problem there was that they started bringing everything up in the main body up towards [the relief of] Bastogne, and they were taking people from us down below. We were spread out pretty thin, and we couldn't fill in because they were still taking people away from us. So, it got to be a little bit hairy because we were always understaffed, and we didn't have the support we should have had.

[Our biggest concern was] Tiger tanks. Did you ever see a German Tiger tank? Well, at one point, a little later on, the I&R platoon ran into an ambush. We're still trying to figure out who gave the order that caused this, because you don't send an intelligence and reconnaissance platoon out on a night reconnaissance. That's like committing murder. They sent the I&R platoon out on the night reconnaissance, traveling down the road in jeeps. You can't see a foot off the sides of the road, but everybody off the sides of the road can see you like daylight, especially when the moon is out. There was a lot of reflection because there was a lot of snow, so you're a sore thumb going down the middle of the road, so you're going to get killed. But you can't see anything. So, how can you have a night reconnaissance when you can't see anything? That's the name of that game.

Well, the next day, I volunteered for the I&R platoon. The captain said to me, 'Do you know that's a dangerous operation? You can get killed in that operation.'

I said, 'I'm playing the odds, Captain.'

He said, 'What do you mean by that?'

I said, 'Well, right now, as it stands, it's three to one. With them it's 28 to one. I'm going with them, if it's okay with you.'

He said, 'Okay.' He said, 'Pack your bag. Go over to join them right now. But if you change your mind, I'll take you back.'

So, I said, 'Okay.' He was a hell of a guy. He really was one hell of a guy, and we got in a lot of trouble.

On The Road

[The primary mission of an I&R platoon] is to find the enemy and report back. Take prisoners, interrogate. You have no choice but to engage. Generally, when you find them, they find you. Sometimes, they find you before you find them because your neck is out. There's hardly ever a day when you're not engaged, sometimes more than once. If we're that close, sometimes we just engage them because you really can hardly get away from them without it. Most of the time, they see you first. But you know, you're coming around the bend. We came around the bend in the road. There was a bank over here. We came around the bend, and then boom, we almost ran into a bunch of Germans with a horse and a wagon. There were like 40 or 50 of them. We split up into squads, two squads, 12 men in each squad. We almost ran into them. Of course, they got more scared than we did. So, we just started popping.

That day, I'll never forget that day. I might be a wise guy. Came across a carbine, and I said, 'Gee, why carry the heavy end one when I could carry this little carbine?' We had the little skirmish, and it was close. This German was in the ditch, and I came down on him, and he was coming up with his rifle. I [pulled the trigger of the carbine, it didn't work] and my buddy in back of me took care of the German, and I threw that carbine so far. You could tell me it was a good weapon, but it didn't work for me, so I just got rid of it.

We were always in jeeps. It was seven jeeps, four men in a jeep, 28 men. We were assigned our own medic, because there was an aid station back at headquarters company anyway, so they gave us a medic. We had two squads, and we split most of the time. We took parallel roads. The medic, the lieutenant, the driver, and the platoon sergeant were in the seventh jeep. He had the big 694 radio, so he could call the artillery if a Cub came over or something, have a little conversation if we needed help. [Standard issue] for an I&R platoon was two radios, one for the platoon leader and one for the rest of the platoon. We ended up with one in every jeep. We stole everything we saw. [*Laughs*] You've got two squads. One radio between the two of them, that's not possible even. How do you keep in touch with anybody? Some dingbat with a glass eye wrote the book.

[We improvised a lot]; there was a .50 caliber machine gun on the lieutenant's jeep. We were supposed to have one .30 caliber machine gun. We had a .30 caliber machine gun, every jeep. We had a couple of bazookas that we acquired. We had grenades. We had a couple of 60-millimeter mortars, and we had grease guns and more BARs than we were supposed to have. We were fired on. On the way to Dachau, we were fired on coming out of the woods. There was a little knoll to the side.

This almost sounds comical, I know. We laugh about it all the time. There's a little village right in front of us. We dragged all our crap up on the hill. Those Germans in that village probably thought they hit the point of a division, because we unloaded on them. We hit them with bazookas and mortars and everything you could think of. Made a lot of noise. We were great bluffers.

Lieutenant Short used the three-man assault at the time; he had an order, I don't know why. The two point scouts, myself and Larry Hancock, and Howard Hughes, who was a great BAR man, went in and we cleared the first few houses, and then we waved the rest of the guys in. We took close to 200 prisoners! We broke up their weapons, told them to put their hands on their heads and walk back up the road. The reason we were in a big rush to get to Dachau was that we were being pushed like crazy. What are you going to do with these guys? So, that's what we did, and then we took off, but we needed that stuff. A bluff works, it really does. We were great poker players.

Lieutenant Short was a great guy. His father was General Short. This guy, he's a bag of bones, nervous as a cat, came up from private right up into lieutenant, all in the field. I guess he was in Africa, he was in Italy—I know he was in Italy. It was nerve-wracking with him. I mean, he would get up [during a firefight]. I said to him one day, 'What do you think you are, George Washington crossing the Delaware?' He'd stand up. Things are going on.

'You guys go over there! Watch that over there!'

I said, 'Get down.' He was a pip. He was an absolute pip, but he watched out for us.

This captain came out with us one day. He wanted to see me. He was new. He was put in charge of us too. He messed up cannon company, so they put him in charge of intelligence. Yeah, it's the truth, and he came out with us one day to see how we operated. We got into a little skirmish. He had this Italian Mauser, I guess it was, this 'blunderbuss,' and he flopped down next to me, right over here, and he let go of that thing, and I thought my head was coming off. When we got finished, I stood up and I went right into his face and I started... I called him everything you could think of. I was really mad. My whole head was ringing. I had a problem from that time on, and he... 'Your fanny is court-martialed. When we get back, you're dead.' Lieutenant Short walked over to him, and he said, 'You're not going to do a thing. I saw what you did!' I'm cleaning this up a little for you. He said, 'You better not come out with this again, not if you want to go home,' and that was the end of that. That officer never looked at me again.

This is probably the best bunch of guys I ever worked with in my life. I mean, Larry and I, we worked point together a lot, most of the time. As a matter of fact, they took us out of point one day, and we got nervous because the guys up front hadn't worked much. So, every time they saw a bush, they stopped. We weren't getting anywhere. So, the lieutenant finally came back and said, 'Would you guys mind going back up to point?' Because you know I'd be happy to do it.' We trusted ourselves. We didn't trust anybody else. We worked point most of the time. It wasn't that bad.

*

Larry and I almost didn't ever talk when we were out. I mean, we'd be on opposite sides on the road. We never walked the shoulders. That's where the mines are. We'd look at each other, throw a signal, and I knew what he was going to do, and he knew what I was going to do. We worked together so much. We'd go in. You're running across a lot of little villages. You don't do this in a big city, but you're running through one village after the other. They're all farm villages and so forth. So we cleared the first few houses, and then wave the rest of the guys in. It isn't like we had a lot of men to work with. We did a lot of things like that; we threw the book away. For example, for the I&R platoon, I think in the book it said when you're coming down the road and you stop for any reason, this jeep backs on like this, this jeep goes like this, the next jeep goes like that [*gestures with hands indicating vehicles turning, reversing, lining up parallel*]. Theoretically, that's good. You can go in any direction if something happens, right? Well that's good if you're still alive, because all the mines are on the shoulders of the road, so you back up onto the mines, and you blow up. We never hit a mine. We never hit a mine. You look at any film of troops moving down the road. They're walking on the shoulders on the road, so that the tanks and the jeeps and the armored guards can go through. They're the ones that are stepping on the mines and blowing up. So we ignored the book. We did what was expedient; we just really never thought about it. We knew what we were going to do. We just stayed away from shoulders of the road, period. Said there was nothing to worry about, as far as we were concerned. As far as the middle of the road is concerned, most of the time, if somebody is putting something in the road, you can see where the road had been disturbed. Well, you go around those things. These become second nature, so we never had a problem. But if we came upon tank tracks, and if we saw tracks in the snow, well, we just turned around and went the other way. What are you going to do with a Tiger tank? The armament is that thick [*moves fingers several inches apart*]. Everything we had would bounce off of it. So, there's no point in it. If you happen to be in the Fort Knox area, which is outside of St. Louis, right next to Fort Knox is Patton's Armor Museum, and it's the most marvelous thing you ever saw in your life. There were a bunch of us together, it was a Rainbow reunion, so we were all together. Here's this Tiger tank, and you know it scared us. You get scared just looking at it. They had cut away one side and put plexiglass over it. They had three full-sized dummies sitting around a table playing cards in the tank. You saw the steel on this thing, and it's still a scary thing. Of course, now we have bigger than that, but that was just a scary piece of work. [And the German] burp gun, nothing could shoot faster than that. Did you ever hear one? It's just unbelievable. That's another thing. It seemed like almost every German had a machine gun. It's just that later on, as our stuff started to come over, we had so much stuff. Even though they were destroying it, we replaced it so fast, where they couldn't replace theirs. The Tiger tank actually I think had a problem moving their turns. Did you know that? But it really didn't make any difference if it was a little slower because things were bouncing off of it anyway.

The I&R man's adventures were just beginning. The men soon found themselves at the gates of Dachau, and the next day, burst into Hitler's Munich home.

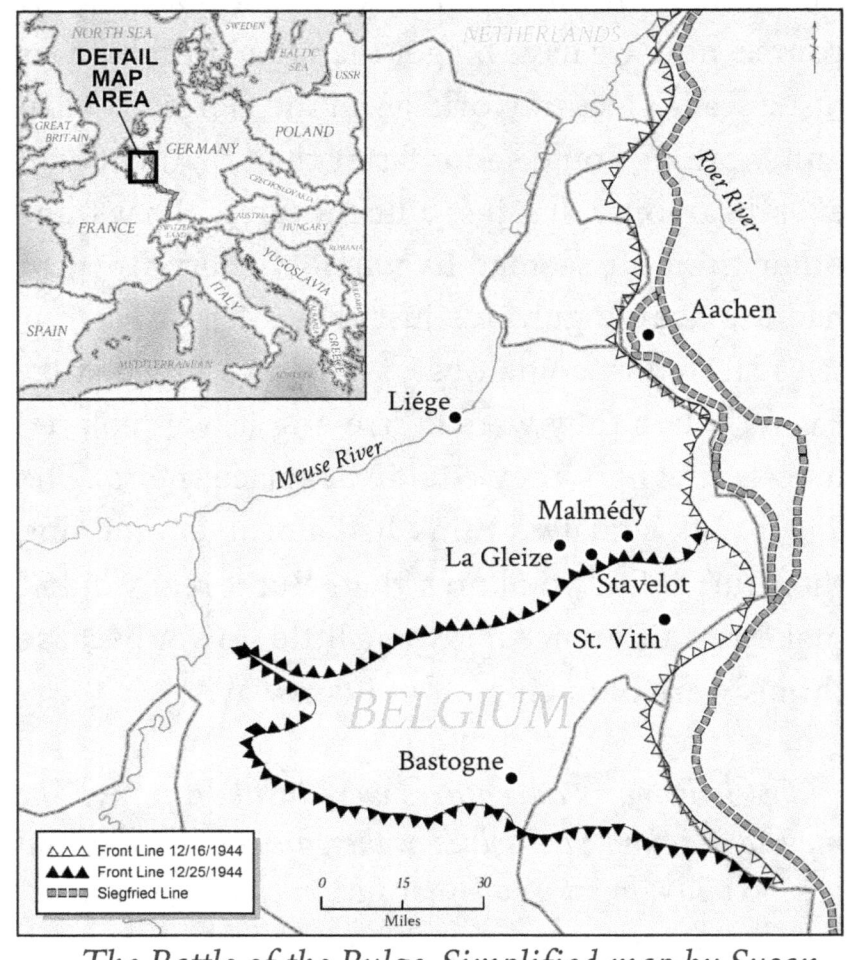

The Battle of the Bulge. Simplified map by Susan Winchell.

PART TWO

SETBACKS

'I woke up early in the morning, and I heard a lot of commotion. I looked over from the haymow, and God, there was a line of stretchers, stretcher bearers, and all at the barn. In the passageway, the guy looked just like my company commander on one of the stretchers there! So I hurried down the ladder on the side; by that time they had him in a van.

[A few hours before], he had said, 'Foley's back, let him take your place for tonight.' He said, 'You're all set, report to the medics.' Foley was going to take my place, cover for me.

So when I saw that company commander in a stretcher, in the ambulance, I said, 'Captain, what happened?' He started crying, he was hurt pretty bad, he said, 'Foley got killed.'

[My friend] that took my place got killed. And then the captain said, 'Your [new] company commander—be good to him, like you were to me.' He said, 'I don't know when I'll see you again.' We had a little talk there, and then they took him away.'

—Paratrooper, Battle of the Bulge

**Timothy Horgan in uniform, World War II.
Source. Tim Horgan.**

CHAPTER SIX

The Cavalryman I

Sitting comfortably in his office at his home in Glens Falls, New York, 'Hometown, USA,' Tim Horgan affects a relaxed and friendly demeanor when speaking with a high school senior [sixteen years later, now an Air Force doctor] for our school project. Like his young interviewer, Mr. Horgan had just turned eighteen during his senior year. He was drafted two weeks after graduating high school in 1943, and was trained to be part of a tank destroyer outfit and then sent to Europe, where he wound up eventually assigned to the 2nd Cavalry Reconnaissance with Patton's Third Army. In his 19-month tour of duty, Mr. Horgan participated in the Battle of the Bulge, where he was awarded the Purple Heart after one of his friends tripped one of their own boobytraps, forgetting it had been set up.

'That's how I got my Purple Heart—I was watching a guy on fire right in front of me, trying to pull off his clothes. A hell of a sight, that poor guy, well, he's just gone. He burned right up in front of me, went right down; I was trying to pull off gasoline-soaked clothes from my buddy who just went up in flames. It was a hell of a sight, and just in two or three minutes, it was all over with, boy.... but I got my hands burnt up.'

Near the end of the war, after crossing the Rhine, Mr. Horgan was part of the liberation of the Flossenburg concentration camp and the famous rescue of the highly prized Lipizzaner dancing stallions. After traveling back to Europe in 1994 around the 50th anniversary of D-Day, like many of our veterans, nearly 50 years after the end of the war, Tim began to share his World War II stories.

Timothy J. Horgan

I was born in 1925 in Brooklyn, New York. I went to St. Francis Prep. That was when they were in Brooklyn at the time, now they are out in Queens. And they are greatly increased, up to 4,000 students. When I went there, they only had 400. On December 7, 1941, I was not quite seventeen. And I went to the movies, every Sunday afternoon, I'd go to a movie. We stopped at a candy store and found out everybody was crying in there, so we asked why. We found out it was the bombing of Pearl Harbor. Well, I was young and didn't quite realize exactly what was going on, not until I could absorb it more.

I turned eighteen on January 18, 1943. I had to go up to register with the draft board and they said, 'Fine. What are you doing?'

I said, 'I'm going to school.'

'When are you going to graduate?'

I said, 'June.'

They said, 'Fine, we will see you then.' And sure enough, the second week of June I get a postcard in the mail; come over to the Grand Central Palace in New York for my physical. So I went through my physical there. When you have finished your physical, then they say 'there are tables over there and go pick your table': Army, Navy, Coast Guard, whatever. [*Gestures to imply tables in a row*] So I picked the Army. And then I got sworn in on July 14, three weeks after I graduated high school, and they gave me two weeks to clear up all my business. August 4, I had to go back to the draft board. That morning they took me on a subway, the Long Island Railroad, out to Long Island to Camp Upton, which was the indoctrination camp out there at the time. I stayed there a week or so and then I got on a train again for two days and wound up down in Waco, Texas, Fort Hood. We got down there in 130-degree heat. Well, all of us New York boys had to go ahead and get acclimated to the weather. So we didn't do anything for about four or five days so we could get our bodies adjusted. That was tank destroyer training I went through; that lasted until the day after Christmas, when they gave me a ten-day furlough to go to Fort Meade in Maryland. So I come home, and I was home for New Year's, then I had to go back to Maryland. We stayed there a couple of weeks and then we got out of training again, went on up to Massachusetts to Camp Miles Standish, which was a debarkation camp, which means you assemble all of your troops together from the camp right outside of Boston, go down to the harbor, get on the boats, and go in the convoys over to Europe.

Replacement

I had just turned nineteen and I landed in Liverpool, England. It took us fifteen days to get over, which is a different story. In Liverpool we got out and went over up in the hills of Wales for a couple of weeks of training. Now this was in February or March of '44, and we knew the invasion was going to come, but we didn't know when. In May I was still a replacement. See, back in '43, the whole graduating class of young fellas was destined to be replacements, because once you get into combat, well, you got to keep feeding the troops in. So anyway, they started setting up replacement depots, which were to take the troops that are landing in the Liverpool salient, put them on a train and bring them down to our camp set up temporarily outside of the town of Taunton; this is southern England. And we would process all of the GIs over 36 hours and we would let all of the goodies they would bring stay. A lot of guys would come over with dress shirts with all tailored or whatever, but [we'd say], 'Buddy, throw it in the pile in the corner.' And we told them, 'Two of this, and one of this, and three of these or four of these, over there...' Get them out in 36 hours, get them on the train, and ship them over. And this was right after D-Day, June 6. Luckily, I was there. My buddies whom I went overseas with, they hit [Normandy] on D-Day D+3. But if I didn't take this job, temporary job, I would have been with them. But I stayed there all summer long because we didn't have the facilities in France yet, through June, July, August, the end of September.

Then they opened up Le Havre in France, so that the ships went right over to Le Havre to unload the soldiers coming over; so then I got into the replacement pool and then I got assigned to the 2nd Cavalry Reconnaissance, with Patton's Third Army. There was a history, big history of the 2nd Cavalry Reconnaissance, they go back 150 years; my Colonel Reed was a graduate of West Point, 1922. His first assignment was Fort Riley in Kansas, which was a cavalry [camp]. So he started in the cavalry with General George S. Patton; he too was a West Pointer, and he too was a cavalryman from way back; in fact he was in the Olympics—well, that's part of another story. Both were cavalrymen in a very aggressive organization. And you learned a lot between Colonel Reed and Patton. Patton didn't take any guff at all and Patton, he was a military general—not a politician—a military general. He'd get his assignment and go, he wouldn't take any malarkey, he would just go. I never met him, but I saw him, moving into some town, I don't know, I can't [remember]—when you go into combat, you don't know what day of the week it is. You don't get any daily newspapers and you don't get the news on the radio. [*Chuckles*] So you just go from day to day to day. So in this one town, he came on through, in his jeep, his escort, and there are his pearl-handled guns; he was noted for his pearl-handled guns. And also an Eisenhower-cut jacket, and his riding britches, because he's a cavalryman, riding britches and high riding boots, that was his thing. So I saw him once coming on through, it was in France and [maybe early] November. Again, you don't know what day of the week it is, or the month. But I got over there and it was about then that I was assigned to the cavalry—when the Third Army was running across France, and the only way you could stop General Patton was to stop his gasoline supply. [*Laughs*]

The Battle of the Bulge

We actually were in Germany when the Battle of the Bulge was beginning. The 2nd Cavalry was in Germany, down in Saarbrücken in the Alsace-Lorraine Saar region of Germany. We were on our way, going through Germany, but all of a sudden Hitler pulled this invasion up there in the north of Belgium and Luxembourg; that was the weakest part of our line up there at the time. When they came on December 16, I was down in Saarbrücken, and two or three days later, I think it was, when Patton got his orders to make a 180-degree turn, go due north, we went up into the Battle of the Bulge. I was in Luxembourg at the time, at the southern end of the bulge on the Moselle River; that was a good barrier for the front line. I stayed there, January or December; oh about the 20th or 21st or whatever day it was that we landed up there. And that was a feat in itself taking a whole army and moving it in two days right up north! But I stayed in Luxembourg for the Bulge, and by the way that winter was the coldest winter in fifty years, and I mean cold! All of us GIs, we didn't have winter clothes, and we tried to layer up: two pair of pants, two jackets on. I had three pairs of socks on, one on top of the other, and every day I'd get up and rotate them, 1-2-3, 2-3-1, so that the sock which was next to my skin and took all of the perspiration would then be moved to the outermost layer, and the other two socks were on the inside.

Patrol Duty

A lot of the GIs got trench foot. Our boots weren't waterproof and the snow and cold; that was a rough, rough winter. In fact, see, we weren't equipped for it; we didn't have our winter clothes. It was all light, light stuff, and in the Battle of the Bulge we had these white parkas like a sheet so that we'll go on patrols, and most of the patrols were at nighttime. So when you went on patrols at night you blend right in with the terrain; it's all snow on the ground, and I mean a couple of feet of snow. Finally, that came until about the middle of

January. The army was really relaxed in the equipping of the GIs over there. I really felt sorry for the infantrymen because they were in the foxholes all the time; they had no place to get warm. At least I could go ahead, get into a house, on the first floor, always on the first floor for security reasons—the back door was our escape route, but never the front.

We were right there on the Moselle River in a small little town called Ahn. It was in wine grove country, and the wine grove country has the mountains and the hills that come down to the river. So at daytime, you couldn't walk around because the Germans were on the east side of the river watching you; if you go walking around in the town, they will take potshots at you, and conversely if we saw them walking around, we would take potshots at them—I mean, you know, you had to break up the monotony somehow or other. [*Laughs*] That's how it was, so you had to be careful, and we had our patrols that'd go back and forth; at nighttime, walking up and down that road, to see if the Germans had come across the river and come in on their patrols—they'll come in and play havoc with us, so we would have to go ahead. We had to go out every night, always had guard duty into the wine groves. Your eyes and mind wander a little bit when you are out on guard duty. Two hours on, four hours off, two hours on, four hours off. So when you are out there for two hours, it is cold, but you just have to look and listen, see if you see any enemy patrols going up and down this road; I can remember in January, when it was clear, cold, blue sky, and now and then you would have clouds going by, you know, partly cloudy, but you would see those wine groves [seemingly] moving up and down. You know how a wine grove is, with the poles sticking up to keep the vines of the grapes? And every now and then, when it was so clear, and then a cloud would come across and it would change your opinion because you would look out again and your eyes would play tricks on you, and you would think that they were marching on you. [*Laughs*] Oh yes, and you are out there, and you just look and listen, you don't talk, a cold two hours. You come on in from guard duty, come back into the house again, and it was no warmer in the house because there was no central heating in those homes over there, it was all in the fireplaces. And you couldn't start a fire in the fireplace because the smoke would go through the chimney, the Germans would see the smoke coming up, throw a couple of mortars over on you. So what we actually did is, in the back of the house, we would go ahead and break through a pane of glass, you know there were nine panes of glass in their window, break out one of those, get the stove pipes, rearrange it to put it out that window on the first floor, so by the time the smoke got to the top of the roof, it had dissipated. But then that wasn't that warm either, so you had to be in sleeping bags and it was cold, really cold.

That was rough, Battle of the Bulge. You had guys losing feet with the trench foot, we weren't clothed. When you had to go on patrol, even the infantry, they would get shot and fall on the ground in a field. You couldn't go out and get them because then you would be subject to being shot, so you would have to wait until the nighttime to go out and get them. So you got out there at night and that's after five, six, eight, ten hours, and the guy's frozen. It was below zero; the guy's all frozen on you. But the Battle of the Bulge was a rough affair. That was a rough affair.

I had been promoted to corporal and that there is the jacket that I had when I was 160 pounds, a few pounds ago. [*Chuckles, rubs his stomach*] I can't get into that thing today. But I have it and I have my ribbons on it and my battle stars and whatnot. This patch over on this right shoulder there is the 2nd Cavalry patch, and on the other side is the outfit I came home with, which is the 90th Infantry. We were spearheading a lot for the 90th Infantry. See, what cavalry reconnaissance does is goes out on the drive, on the point, or come in between the two drives, between two divisions going through. We'd have to flush out in between; be sure that there were no enemy pockets in there that would come around and cut off the drive, so we are cut off. So we were either on the point or flushing out in between the drives in the towns and back countries, dirt roads, two-lane roads, make sure there were no enemies around. But we'd draw the fire first.

The Booby Trap

I was wounded during the Battle of the Bulge. And in this town we stayed in, we had to have security, so we set booby traps in certain areas. So when you come out of the house that you are staying in, you would go 20 steps this way, take a left, 15 steps, take a right or whatever because the booby traps were set with wires. So if anybody's walking around there, they'd trip a wire [whistles], and the booby trap would go off, so that is how we kept our security. This is right after what they declared to be the end of the Battle of the Bulge, the 25th of January, but that still lingered on into February. But at any rate, you never drank the water over there, because you didn't know if it was contaminated, you never had milk, forget it! Even in England you don't drink milk. So what you did is, you drank wine, not powerful wine, but just wine; everybody over there drinks wine. You always had a bottle of wine, you'd take a sip of wine a couple of times a day and that's like drinking water.

So one of my buddies there—see, around a platoon, there were thirty of us in a platoon, three teams of ten. He went ahead and he was looking to get a couple of bottles of wine, so he went down, a couple of houses down there, and into the basements. You always had a wine cellar in the basement over there. So he went in, and he picked up a couple of bottles of wine, but in the corner of the building we had a booby trap set up, a couple of sticks of dynamite with buckshot shells taped around it, sitting on a five-gallon can of gasoline. He came out, he ducked under the wire, but he had his gun on his shoulder, and the point of his gun was still up and he came right on through; he didn't duck down far enough, and he tripped the wire. When it exploded, the gasoline came all over his clothing.

We heard the explosion, I came out of the house, I was the second guy out to go down and see what happened to him, and here he is all up in flames! So my first instinct is to get rid of his clothes. I went at him, and I was literally trying to pull his clothes off, and I got quite a bit of his clothes off, but he was still on fire and after a minute or two he just fell right down in front of me, dead. And we take a look at him; he was already dead from the buckshot; you could see all of those little holes all over his body. But his skin and his upper chest here [*gestures to chest*], was just like a stuffed pig when you spick the pig on an open fire, and the smell of skin is something you don't want to smell.

My both hands were all burnt, enough that I had to go back to the medics, and they put balsam on me, and they bound me up with mittens—I called them the white mittens—but they were gauze; that's what I had for about a week. It wasn't enough to send me back to the hospital or keep me back out of the outfit—no, no, they put me back in the front line again! So I had mittens on there for about a week. I had no duty; the only duty they gave me was to get on the telephone in wherever we were set up for command, and I was working the telephones so I could go ahead and get a telephone up this way [*gestures holding a phone up to his face*], but nothing else.

That's how I got my Purple Heart—I was watching a guy on fire right in front of me, trying to pull off his clothes. A hell of a sight, that poor guy, well, he's just gone. He burned right up in front of me, went right down; I was trying to pull off gasoline-soaked clothes from my buddy who just went up in flames [*lets out sigh, pauses to compose himself*]. It was a hell of a sight, and just in two or three minutes, it was all over with, boy. I pulled off most of his clothes; the only thing I couldn't get off was his collar, his belt. I could get the other clothes off, and see, it was a double stitch, double layer of the clothes, but I got all this off [*gestures to chest region and leg region*], and pants off, and everything else…but I got my hands burnt up. So that's my Purple Heart story. And I understand they put me in for a Bronze Star, you know for bravery of doing that, and somebody came on back and said, 'Well, our quota for the month is up, so we can't issue another Bronze Star.' [*Laughs*] I said fine, whatever, whatever. Let it go. [*Laughs again*] But I suppose I was thankful nothing else happened [to me], and after a couple of weeks, I was back to normal again—well, I still had sensitivity in my hand, my skin, but I could still move around.

Mr. Horgan recovered from his physical injuries. The other scars would take years.

CHAPTER SEVEN

The Paratrooper II

Fresh from the failed Market Garden operation, Albert Tarbell continues his story with the 504th's unexpected insertion into the heavy fighting in the Battle of the Bulge.

Albert A. Tarbell

So, we're back to France, doing parachute patrol. This was right about the 17th of December, and we went off to Reims, France, where I was supposed to be doing the chute patrol; we had two non-coms from each company working with the MPs. We would get ahold of the paratroopers before they would be arrested by the MPs—they would fight the MPs instead of giving up to them, whereas we could talk to them, and they'd listen to us, because the paratroopers, they were just like that; they didn't want nobody bossing them around. But they would listen to us, especially a non-com paratrooper, talking to another paratrooper.

On the night of, I think it was the [16th of December], we were bringing these guys in, and all these guys were singing and raising hell and all drunk; [we were] taking them back to camp. Well, we didn't know what was going on; when we got back to camp that morning, we're already at warning. I was going by the CP, and I've gone up to my room and I heard this one guy say, 'Well, jeez, Sergeant, I've never fired an M-1!'

He said, 'That's all right, son. You'll learn. You can learn fast. Where we're going, you'll learn fast!'

When I got back to the barracks room there, my bags were all packed—my sergeant packed all my gear and everything. I said, 'We're going out on range to fire today?'

He said, 'Yeah. We're going on the range, all right. We're going back on the front line! The Germans broke through!' The Germans went over, right into the 'bulge.'

The rest of the night, we helped the orderly room distribute clothes, equipment, and I got some of the [new] guys who were just coming in from England, replacements, assigned.

Moving Out

About 8 o'clock in the morning, the trucks started coming in. Open-top trucks, Air Force trucks, semi-tractor trailer trucks. We loaded on there and took off. We didn't know where the hell we were going. We drove all that day. We got to the end of the day there; we got up towards Bastogne. Then from Bastogne, they re-routed us. They said there's another outfit coming in to go there, the 105th's going to go there. So we went on, going towards Roeselare, Belgium, but nobody knew what was going on; we didn't know what was going on!

We saw one guy coming out through the woods, and we asked him what's going on around there. He just threw his helmet on the ground and kept on going—he would not talk to us! So that was quite an [eyeopener], seeing [that]... The Germans had broken through and there was a lot of heavy fighting, from St. Vith and all through those areas there.

The 504th was about to angle with the notorious Waffen-SS Kampfgruppe Peiper, led by Joachim Peiper. With their seventy-ton Tiger II tanks and a penchant for war crimes in the east and now in the west, they were determined to take the crossroads and bridges that would get them to Liège. Just hours before, Kampfgruppe Peiper had murdered 84 unarmed GIs who had surrendered.[12]

'They Turned the Flak Guns on Us'

Well, I believe the name of the first area where we stayed was in Rahier, and we were there, I think, a day. Meanwhile, Colonel Peiper's panzer outfit was trying to cross a bridge near there, and they sent the 1st Battalion in there, and they had a fierce fight there, and they stopped them. G

---

[12] Joachim Peiper (1915-1976), notorious commander in 1st SS Panzer Division Leibstandarte SS Adolf Hitler, responsible for tolerating, condoning, and ordering the abuse and murder of civilians and GIs who had surrendered, particularly the Malmedy Massacre, where 84 GIs were murdered by his men on Dec. 17. At his war crimes trial after the war, it was alleged that his unit, Waffen-SS Kampfgruppe Peiper, was responsible for killing a total of 350 unarmed American soldiers and about 100 Belgian civilians over a one-month period, as well as other atrocities when they were dispatched to the eastern front. Source: USHMM, Holocaust Encyclopedia. *The Malmedy Massacre.* encyclopedia.ushmm.org/content/en/article/the-malmedy-massacre

Company, and our 3rd Battalion went in and helped them also, just across the valley from us; I think the name of the place was Monceau. And as we got up on the top of this hill there, the knoll, we looked out on the side to our right, you could see three [enemy] flak wagons out there. We didn't pay much attention to it; we thought they were disabled flak wagons, but Lieutenant Rivers said, 'Get those guys before they get back to those flak wagons!' They weren't [abandoned]; the Germans had left them and gone some place, and now they were running back there when they found out we were coming up this knoll.

Well, we started shooting at them and we couldn't reach them. And they turned the flak guns on us, and they hit the trees above us, and oh, man, they peppered our company! [*Shakes head*] We must have lost over half of our company; we lost all the new officers we had, but it was all shrapnel wounds. I think there's only one guy that got killed, and he took a direct hit—it was a captain from a service company. Another guy got hit in the leg, a direct hit. Other than that, they were mostly all shrapnel wounds and flak wounds from the flak gun.

We had quite a battle there, most of the day, and we did finally end up getting into Monceau, and we went into fighting all day, and oh, yes, I ended up helping carry the wounded back into the trucks. We had some trucks back there, and we took three truckloads of wounded. And those trucks couldn't get out, either; they were more or less bottled up in there.

We could move around on that knoll—we took over the knoll; we had all that knoll, and on the sides there. Anyways, we headed out, and towards dark, we fought on, and that evening everybody was so tired out.

I went over to check the trucks later. It was dark, and those guys were still there. And I especially remember one of my buddies, he had gotten hit in both legs and both arms, but they were flesh wounds, didn't break any bones. I remembered I wanted to check on him and see how he was. By that time, he couldn't move his arms and he couldn't move his legs, and he just stiffened all right up. But I guess they did finally move the trucks later on, but at dark they still hadn't moved, they couldn't get them back to the medics.

Anyway, we ended up in one building there after fighting, early in the evening. And we fell right asleep, and we always just slept wherever we could in the building. I woke up early in the morning and I went snooping around. I went in the other room, in the living room in this building, and there was this [dead] guy laid out on the table! God, I thought, we're in a funeral home! Here's a guy all laid out, funeral-like, so I told the guys, 'Let's get the hell out of here, we're in a funeral home!' And everybody got up and we got the heck out of there. You know, forty years later when I was back there, I asked one of the [locals], 'Where's the funeral parlor here? I want to show my wife where I slept that night and woke up and I found that guy laid out on the table.'

He said, 'We don't have no funeral parlors here, the nearest one is in Reims.' So then I told him about what happened, but he knew who that [dead] guy was. He said that so-and-so had died at that time of natural causes, and he was laid out in his home. This is where we were, see. So that kind of made me feel a bit better. But okay, I'm getting ahead of myself, forty years ahead.

'An 82nd anti-armor bazooka team covers a road near Cheneux on December 20, 1944.' Source: National Archives, public domain.

The Priest

The 6th SS Panzer Army's mission, which included Kampfgruppe Peiper, was to break through the American lines between Aachen and the Schnee Eifel and secure the bridges over the Meuse, working up to the city of Liège.

After our Monceau battle, we ended up in another CP, where our lines were very fluid; [we were constantly] sending out patrols. Nobody knew where everybody was, but we knew that we had to stop Colonel Peiper's group from making it, from getting through Cheneux, in that area. And at the CP that we were at, there was a priest there, and there was a hired man, and supposedly the farmer that owned it. I was kind of happy. 'God,' I said to the priest, 'I'm glad to see you! You're a priest! You'll be able to say Mass for us at Christmas while we're here!' This was a couple days before Christmastime, right?

He said, 'I can't do that. I can't do that.' You know what he said? 'I have to have an altar. I should be in a church to say Mass.' I thought, my God, my chaplain said Mass with a couple of beer barrels [for an altar], K rations [for the wafer host], on the top of a jeep, you name it, wherever he could, you know, whatever he could use for a [makeshift altar].

I told the commander and the first sergeant, 'I don't think those guys are what they are saying.' I said, 'I think they're darn German soldiers!' And just then over the radio they said, spread the word, pass the word along—they're dropping German paratroopers behind our lines! I don't know what became of those guys, but I had to notify the company to watch out for German paratroopers. And some forty years later, I met the priest at Cheneux. I said, 'Were there any priests here, how many priests were here [during that period]?'

He said, 'Two of us. Me and a younger priest were here, and we stayed in the cellar with the women and kids all during your fighting days here!' So those guys were not what they were. Forty years later, we found out that they were not.

But anyway, we moved out. Our lines were very fluid here, and they were moving around, and this and that. You really didn't know who to make [contact with]; we were trying to contact the American soldiers, the American divisions there, and trying to contact our own 3-2-5.[13] There were

---

[13] *our own 3-2-5-* Mr. Tarbell refers to the 325th Glider Infantry Regiment. "Originally, the 82nd Airborne was to defend Bastogne but the 101st Airborne drew that assignment and the 82nd was sent north to Werbomont. The 325th dug in around the crossroads at Baraque de Fraiture and held. During the intense fight in December 1944 the 325th decimated two German divisions." Source: The 325th Glider Infantry Regiment-Unit History. The 82nd Airborne, World War II. www.ww2-airborne.us/units/325/325.html

two divisions near there. And we made our way towards, I guess it would be toward Saint Vith, or in that general area, La Gleize, Werbomont, and through there. And on the 23rd, it was a sunny day, the first sunny day there was, the P-38s came out. They were raising Cain, and at this area where we had moved to, you could see way out, you could look down into the valley. You could see these German vehicles moving. I didn't know which way they were going, but there was a lot of troop movement, and the P-38s were bombing them and strafing them, and then you had a lot of air activity that day.

Christmas Is Here

And then we ended up in some area there, oh my God, after all day walking, it seemed like. And we just got settled in, and word came down that we had to move back out. And we had to go back all the way, it seemed like about ten, twelve miles. I took cross country in school, and you could hear the tracks of the tanks, or they were ours, or Germans, I don't know. And you could hear the trees being knocked down. Our engineers were knocking the trees as we were going through. They would knock the trees down, you know, blocking the roads. Every now and then I had a pair of pliers on me, PL29s, and I would get called to the front; we would come across a field fence. I'd cut the wires, cut the wire fence off so that we could come on through. We seemed like we walked most of that night, Christmas Eve. All that Christmas Eve we walked. We got into Bra, and then we set up a defensive position.

They said that it was a strategic withdrawal to consolidate our positions, more or less. That's what we were told, because they said that they had panzers, but our tanks were coming in from the south, and they were bottling in the Germans. And that was the way for them to get out, so [our line had] to come out, so that we can really hold them in.

We set up Christmas Day, it was so damn cold Christmas Day! And we didn't have no water for coffee or nothing; pumps were all frozen up. Well, we soon got set up, we had one hell of a gunfight there. The SS are right on our ass as we got there at Bra, and we were just there at the outside of town. We got hit pretty hard a few times. I think it was that same day, I took three prisoners into battalion, SS guys. That's why we knew they were SS hitting us. And I turned them over.

Just as I got to the CP, Colonel Cook was there and he said, 'Get them over here!' I took them over to him and he took his .45 out—they're prisoners but they were still pretty belligerent. He took his .45 out and he shoved it right in that first SS guy's mouth! All three of them landed right on their knees. I thought he was going to blow that guy's— 'I'm blowing your effing head off!' he said. Boy, they got down to their knees and all that bravado went right out of them fast. [*Chuckles*]

And I was glad that he didn't do that, because you hate to see anything like that, I don't care who it was. It took me off guard—here was my colonel, and he was going to kill these guys—but anyway, they were prisoners and we turned them over to the MPs. And that night, I think it's the same night, we heard some guy moaning and crying and moaning outside, he couldn't talk. And somebody said, 'Let him walk through, let him come in.' We let him in, and he comes into the CP, he had a grenade in his belt, and he had a hole you could put your thumb right through his forehead right in here, the side of his head where the bullet had gone through. [*Points to above left eye*] You could put your thumb right in that hole there.

He was incoherent. One of the lieutenants said, 'You better take him to the back and shoot him. He's going to die anyway.' And you could see the look on the guy's face, you could tell that he understood that, but he couldn't talk, that they had to kill him just to get him over his suffering. I said, 'Aww, better still, I'll take him back to the medics!' Me and another guy took him back to the aid station, and they said, 'We'll let him sit there. If he's alive in the morning, we'll send him to the hospital.'

I check back in the morning and then one of the lieutenants checked back too. I didn't know this until later; he checked back to see if that guy was alive. He was alive yet; he said, 'He's alive; he's on his way to the hospital, he's already gone.' So they shipped him back. But if he's still alive, he's had a headache ever since, I guess.

Airstrikes and artillery destroyed many German vehicles trying desperately to retreat. Kampfgruppe

Peiper was in shambles, units separated from one another and hindered by the terrain and the dark; having advanced to Stoumont by the 19th, Peiper now was cut off. On Christmas Eve, he abandoned his heavy armor and fled with his men, leaving behind his wounded and some American prisoners. Some historians place the victims of his murderous campaign at 362 prisoners of war and 111 civilians; he reported that out of a force of 3,000, only 717 of his men returned to the lines with him.[4]

*

'You're Going To Freeze to Death'

But anyway, we had a lot of fighting there. And winter fighting I think is about the worst you can do. You freeze. One time, we went on this area here and we stayed overnight; we marched during the day, and we got to this area, and we stayed overnight. We got in our sleeping bag, and I woke up early in the morning, I felt so good. I was so warm, so nice and warm sleeping. It had snowed during the night; we were sleeping underneath these pine trees and the snow had covered us just enough for insulation. Our boots had dried out and everything was all wet when we had gotten in there. We got up and they had a hot meal for us there! Whenever they could have turkey. We never got no Christmas turkey; I think it was days later before we got a warm meal—I think that was one of the first warm meals we had; even rations heated up in hot water was good, though. And coffee, hot coffee! After that, we got ready and then we started marching down the road. It was such a beautiful sight! It was bitter cold, but was such a beautiful sight to see. You're in this mountainous area, there's snow on the trees and it was just like you could have been on vacation someplace. Except for when you got tired, you know, you had to take a break. Take ten and have a cigarette.

That's where your training comes in. Just when you think you can't take another step, you take a ten-minute break and in ten minutes' time, you're right back up there. Ready to go. That's where your hard training comes in later to pay off, that gives you good physical condition. And we were always in good physical condition.

We got to this area here and they said, 'Put all your gear down here.' There's a big hill right near the mountain lake. So we put all our gear there and just sit down. We're going up here to attack, and they'll bring our supplies, bring our equipment up to us.

So we got up this hill here, and between the adrenaline and the climbing of that hill, we were soaking wet when we got to the top. And when we got to the top, we didn't know where we were. Half the time you didn't know who the heck was the enemy, the cold or the Germans. We started to get cold, and we had a few skirmishes there, and a few guys got wounded. But we didn't have no warm clothes or nothing. Nobody brought up our equipment from down the foot of the hill!

We had one blanket in our company, so we spread that out and we had six guys under there, trying to keep warm. Wounded guys, we covered them up with that. There was a tree right nearby. I grabbed that tree and I started walking around it, and I told some of the other guys, too, I said, 'Don't you go to sleep!'

I said, 'It's going to be awful cold tonight. If you go to sleep, you're going to freeze. You're going to freeze your feet. You're going to freeze your hands. You might even freeze to death.'

I said, 'If you feel like it's getting warm and cozy, get the heck out of there and start walking around.'

I started walking and holding on to that tree. And I would doze off and hold on to it; the next thing you know, there's about three other guys all doing the same thing I was doing. You can do that, walk and sleep. I just hung right on to that tree, and in the morning, those guys, some of whom had went to sleep, they were walking on their knees. They had frozen their feet and their hands—it was that cold; how cold it was! It was very cold.

*

We had penetrated behind the German lines. We didn't know we had walked so far back and over that mountain there! The colonel walked by, he was laughing, and he said, 'I had this guy follow me.' He was now a prisoner, a German soldier who had surrendered to him. The colonel was relieving himself when this guy surrendered to him! Guess we're all behind the line then, they didn't realize. I guess it was some artillery outfit that had gotten behind him.

We ended up, that afternoon, looking out down the valley and there was a German motorcade. We put all the fire we could in our artillery, everything into it. We did get one of the last vehicles; some of them were Rundstedt's headquarters people in that van.[14] There was a colonel in there; they were killed. And later on that afternoon there were some horse-drawn caissons moving out in the field way beyond. We could see them, and we called in artillery on them. And God, they just tried to pepper them there. That's the first time I'd seen horse-drawn caissons—there were sleighs, on sleighs and horses. They used a lot of horses in World War II. But from the distance that they were, we couldn't do nothing, all we could do was watch.

Anyway, we ended up moving again and attacking and this and that and oh, God, it was just hard to tell where you were; us being lowly GIs, down at the bottom of the pole, we didn't know what really was going on. All we knew was, well, there's another air raid, we got hit again. Another battle. And you never had no places for names, you only had coordinates—our orders, they were only in coordinates. You weren't given no name, like, 'Well

---

[14]*Rundstedt's headquarters people-* Gerd von Rundstedt (1875-1953), German field marshal during World War II.

you're going to go to Manlius today,' or 'You're going to go into East Syracuse.' All you were given was certain coordinates where you're going to go, and this and that, so that's where we went, [maybe why it's hard to remember exactly now]. We ended up in a lot of bitter fighting.

'Be Good to Your New Commander'

A short while after that, I think it was around about the 7th of January, I was supposed to go back to report to the medics—they said, 'Go back to the medics and have your foot inspected.' For trench foot, for frozen foot, to make sure I was okay, make sure I could get some sleep.

So I went back there, and I saw Doc Ketchen, and Doctor Shapiro, but first we had a nice bath, and got all clean, dry clothes—had a nice hot meal, coffee, and then we went to see the doctors. They checked us over.

Doc Ketchen said, 'Well, about time you got back here, Tarbell! About time you come and visit us.' We were laughing, kidding around. He gave us some 'blue heavens,' they called it, pills. They said, 'Drink your coffee, get a hot cup of coffee, take this and grab some blankets.' They issued us some blankets, said, 'Go to the haymow.' The aid station was in the [barn]. The barns, in Europe, the way they were built was one area is like a house, then you had like an area way, and then the barn, it's attached to it. We were in the upper barn, up in the haymow.

Four of us from the company were there, and just as we took that blue heaven and coffee, we went in the haymow with our blankets—there was an artillery outfit nearby us, we didn't know that, and they started blasting away! I was saying to myself, 'How in the heck am I ever going to get any sleep, with them guys blasting away?' That was the last thing that I remember—I zonked right out!

I woke up early in the morning, and I heard a lot of commotion. I looked over from the haymow, and God, there was a line of stretchers, stretcher bearers, and all at the barn. In the passageway, they had stretchers and stuff like that, so I looked over, the guy looked just like my company commander on one of the stretchers there! So I hurried down the ladder on the side; by that time they had him in a van. See, now I get ahead of myself again.

I was telling you about going to Paris on furlough; my buddy, Phil Foley, had come in from the 505th Parachute Infantry and he joined our outfit. He was with company headquarters and carried the radio and stuff like that, but he [had] had three court martials! And he was a holder of the Silver Star, and he also had a Purple Heart, and he was always after his third medal. So when he re-joined us around the 6th of [January], he came back and he brought me a nice present, a pipe to smoke; I liked to smoke pipes when I could. We had his Christmas packages, and we ate cookies together. He was telling me about his trip, this and that. That's when the company commander said, 'Foley's back, let him take your place for tonight.' He said, 'You're all set, go to the medics, report to the medics.' That's when I went to the medics. Foley was going to take my place, cover for me.

So when I saw that company commander in a stretcher, in the ambulance, I said, 'Captain, what happened?' He said—he started crying, he was hurt pretty bad, he had been hit through the back to the rectum, stuff like that—he said, 'Foley got killed.'

[My friend] that took my place got killed. And then the captain said, 'Your [new] company commander—be good to him, like you were to me.' He said, 'I don't know when I'll see you again.' We had a little talk there, and then they took him away.

Annihilated

We were waiting for our ride back to re-join our outfit, and I noticed there was a stretcher there, a person lying there, all covered up, and he had hobnail boots on. I figured him to be a German. I just went over there, and I uncovered him, to see who it was. It was the colonel; it was a United States colonel. It was Colonel Jurak from 555th Parachute Infantry; he had been killed that day, the same time that my company commander got hit, and Foley got killed. He had been killed that day. Jurak was a commander of the 555 and they were, in fact, annihilated in the Bulge, and they broke up the regiment, or the battalion, or whatever they were.

The 82nd Airborne got cleaned up and billeted. On February 2, they would jump off through the dragon's teeth on the Siegfried Line.

Private Leroy Johnson, 32nd Cavalry Recon Squadron, 1st US Army of Lakewood, NY, operates a traffic control telephone for the pontoon bridge from Remagen to Erpel, Germany, March 17, 1945. Source: National Archives.

PART THREE

CROSSING OVER

"The Rhine was more than a river. It was a sacred waterway to the Germans, the source of most of their legends and myths. And at this stage in the war, crossing the Rhine was the last barrier between the advancing Allied armies and the conquest of Germany. If the Germans could hold their beloved river, they might be able to stand off the Allies."[5]

*

'I got back to the boat and Fred was nowhere around, he was nowhere to be found. We think to this day that the machine gun burst got him, and you know the force *of the shot pushed him right into the Rhine River, and the current was very strong. We never found him, never found his body.*

We made it to the river. I started to get back on the radio to call back our situation, and I started to talk, and somebody said, 'Shut that goddamn thing off!' because, you know, as we're going down the river, everything's quiet and you could hear all over for miles.

The CP is saying, 'How come you don't talk? Give us your status report, give a status report!'

—Paratrooper, Rhine River Night Patrol

Ludendorff Bridge over the Rhine between Erpel (foreground, east side) and Remagen (background, west side) after it was captured by US troops on March 7, 1945. Source: US Signal Corps, National Archives, public domain.

CHAPTER EIGHT

'The Way It Was'

Measuring in at over 750 miles long and averaging a quarter mile wide, Germany's formidable Rhine River was the most effective barrier against Western invasion for thousands of years. So can you imagine being the first American GI to cross the famed Ludendorff Bridge at Remagen, Germany, on March 7, 1945?

As the 8th Infantry Division and the 9th Armored Division approached the vicinity of the bridge on the west bank of the Rhine, scouts were shocked to observe what looked from a distance like an actual intact structure still spanning the

1,300 feet of river when so many other Rhine crossings before it had been destroyed. Postponing a 'Destroy-the-bridge-NOW' order from above, the German commander on the west side was still ferrying men and materiel over the structure when the Americans appeared. Sergeant Alexander A. Drabik of the 27th Armored Infantry Battalion, a 34-year-old son of Polish immigrants, was tasked with leading his men over to the east bank to establish a foothold before it could be blown by frantic German engineers desperately trying to complete their charges. He turned to his men and said, 'Okay, who's going with me? I'm going across!'

The men moved quickly, literally running the equivalent of three football fields single file under heavy machine gun fire.

'We ran down the middle of the bridge, shouting as we went. I didn't stop because I knew that if I kept moving, they couldn't hit me. My men were in squad column and not one of them was hit. We took cover in some bomb craters. Then we just sat and waited for others to come. That's the way it was.'

In the next twenty-four hours, 8,000 Allied troops had crossed. Many thousands more crossed before the debilitated span collapsed ten days later, taking twenty-eight Army engineers to their deaths.

Ike was said to have claimed that the capture of the bridge at Remagen shortened the war in Europe by six months.

When Sergeant Drabik made it to the other side, he was confronted by a teenage soldier with a rifle. The boy lowered the gun and surrendered at the sight of the rest of the squad and company pouring across.[6]

'It wasn't a historical moment for me; I was too busy running. I didn't think about the bridge blowing or anything. I just wanted to get to the other side.'

That's the way it was.

CHAPTER NINE

The Infantry Sergeant

Larry Bennett wears a suitcoat over his sweater and shirt, sitting for this interview in Newburgh on the Hudson, his hometown. At 79 years old, he gives the air of optimism; he is a confident, well-spoken man who has done some remarkable things with his life. As a sergeant in the 86th Blackhawk Infantry Division, he served in both the European and Pacific theaters in World War II. He was awarded the Bronze Star with First Oak Leaf Cluster for heroic action in Vohberg, Germany, in April 1945, when he carried a wounded officer to safety under enemy fire after his company's medic was mortally wounded while attempting to treat the officer. He didn't go to college but worked in the chemical industry all his life. A lifelong Democrat, he was elected in a primarily Republican district to four terms in the New York State Assembly, guiding several veterans-related bills through the legislature to fruition.

'We crossed the Rhine on a bridgehead that had already been established. The Remagen Bridge had collapsed, but they had built a pontoon bridge just north of that. We knew we were getting close [to combat]. That afternoon we had passed through this town, and we saw dead Germans there and something that really amazed me, German horses that had been killed. They were lying alongside the road because the Germans had used a lot of horse-drawn artillery throughout the war. And then that night, we were near a town where there were some snipers, and I'll never forget this [sight]: there were several GIs lying along the road, and they were covered with blankets, and all you could see were their combat boots, and the guy next to me said, 'Sergeant, that's going to be us before tomorrow morning.'

I said, 'It's not going to be me.' I tried to be optimistic [to the point of] where I think I was saying something I couldn't really be that sure of. I just figured, I'm not going to get cowered this early in the campaign.'

Lawrence E. Bennett

I was born in the town of Newburgh, New York, on September 15, 1923. I was only sixteen or seventeen, and it was on a Sunday afternoon and a group of us were playing touch football. I got home around five o'clock for dinner and that's when I first heard that Pearl Harbor had been attacked. I had an Irish grandmother who was very optimistic, and never wanted to give you bad news and her reaction was, in her Irish brogue, 'Sure, and you'll hear nothing about that tomorrow,' which did not prove to be true.

[Later], I took what was called the voluntary induction. I was working for the Glenn L. Martin aircraft company in Baltimore, Maryland, at that time, although I lived in the town of Newburgh, and I was eligible for a deferment—they used to give six-month deferment, but I wanted to get in the Navy. I wanted to get into service, and in December of 1942, they stopped enlistments because they claimed the Navy and the Marine Corps were getting a disproportionate number of people, so they had what they call a voluntary induction—if you volunteered to be inducted, they would see that you got the branch of service you wanted. It sounded pretty good to me.

My draft board was in Baltimore, and I went down about seven in the morning to start the induction process, and ended up about 11:30, and at that point I thought, well, my physical examination was for general service, so I need a branch. I said, 'I want to go in the Navy.' And the gentleman said, 'I'm sorry, the Navy took thirty-four [men] and they were out of here by 9:30 this morning, and the Marines took ten [men], and the rest of you will go with the Army.' That was my first example of 'be careful before you volunteer for anything.' [*Chuckles*]

In February 1943, I went to Fort Meade, Maryland, after I was inducted, and about two days after that I got on a troop train. Of course, everything was secret then, you didn't know where you were going, but I knew we were heading in the general direction of south. We had gone to Cincinnati, Ohio, and places I forget. I said, 'This is great, I'm going to go to Texas where they have a lot of Army Air Corps bases, and I'm going to get into the Army Air Corps. That didn't happen to be true.

They also had a lot of other camps there that were training infantry, so at about four o'clock in the morning, the train station pulled into this railhead and there was a very huge sign that said, 'Welcome to the 86th Blackhawk Infantry Division.' And I said maybe I'll get in the ordnance, because I worked as a machinist for Martin, but I lined up and they said, 'Company D, 341st Infantry over here.' That's how I started out. Our division took basic [replacement troop] training at Camp Howze, Texas.

In the fall of 1943, [we] went into the Louisiana Maneuvers area, which was the worst living conditions I had ever been under. It was winter, and don't let anyone tell you it doesn't get cold and damp in Louisiana. We finished our advanced infantry training, we were sent to Camp Livingston, Louisiana, following the Louisiana Maneuvers. We went onto short maneuvers again and were sent to the west coast to take amphibious training, so all the indications were that we would be sent to the Pacific Theater of Operations; however, the Battle of the Bulge occurred, and that changed those plans. Some of our equipment was already loaded on ships in San Francisco, but we were shipped to Camp Myles Standish, Massachusetts, and were sent to Europe and landed at Le Havre, France.

*

We were in a convoy, a very large convoy. I can't estimate the number of ships, but we were on a troop ship that carried 6,000 soldiers. And the division artillery commander was with us and his flag was flying before we left the port, and we figured maybe we would get a better escort than some of the rest. The voyage was fairly uneventful, except it was the wintertime in the North Atlantic, very rough in the winter, and when we [got] into the English Channel you could hear depth charges being dropped, because German U-boats were still very active at that time; in fact, they were sinking ships all the way up to the last day of the war. None of the ships in our convoy were hit.

We land at Le Havre [at] about midnight and the harbor area was almost completely destroyed. It had been destroyed by the Germans before they left, before they evacuated. We had to go down in landing nets, just as you would in an invasion. We got into small landing craft and went ashore and were put on these trucks, [which were] more like something you would carry cattle in, a trailer towed by a tractor, and there was some straw in it, and you lay in it until you got to a camp. We went to Camp Old Gold—they had a number of camps there named after cigarettes—and had a brief training period there before we went up to the front [lines], which was just west of the Rhine River at that time.

'They Had a Lot of Fight Left in Them'

We entered combat in early March of 1945 in the Cologne/Bonn area. [It] was actually a defensive position on the west bank of the Rhine, in the little likelihood that the Germans could come back across the Rhine, but they were sending extensive patrols, you know, to try and keep the American army off balance. We suffered some casualties there, but not heavy casualties. Then our next phase of combat we went across the Rhine River and into the general area of Siegen, Germany. At that time, they were attempting to seal off the

Ruhr Pocket and to make sure the Germans who were in the Ruhr Valley could not break out and possibly cut off the spearheads, which were further advanced into Germany at that time.

The first night when we were moving up, as we sat up on the Rhine, we were subjected to some artillery or mortar fire, but we had the river between the German army and us. Then we were moving up, and you could tell we were getting near a battle zone because you could hear artillery firing and see the firing in the distance. We crossed the Rhine on one of the bridges, a bridgehead that had already been established. The Remagen Bridge had collapsed, but they had built a pontoon bridge just north of that. As I said before, we knew we were getting close [to combat]. That afternoon we had passed through this town, and we saw dead Germans there and something that really amazed me, German horses that had been killed. They were lying alongside the road because the Germans had used a lot of horse-drawn artillery throughout the war to save on gasoline and so forth. And then that night, we were near a town where there were some snipers, and I'll never forget this [sight]: there were several GIs lying along the road, and they were covered with blankets, and all you could see were their combat boots, and the guy next to me said, 'Sergeant, that's going to be us before tomorrow morning.'

I said, 'It's not going to be me.' I tried to be optimistic [to the point of] where I think I was saying something I couldn't really be that sure of. I just figured, I'm not going to get cowered this early in the campaign.

Our objective was a town called Hagen, a large industrial town in the Ruhr Valley, and we moved up into an attack position. The next morning, we attacked that town and maybe about two days later, the Germans finally capitulated there. There were more anti-aircraft guns in the Ruhr Valley than anywhere in the world, because they used them to protect their industrial area, and they were using them as regular field artillery pieces, and they had a lot of ammunition. I'll never forget that one of our guys in the 86th [Infantry Division] later wrote a book about it. They later asked him, 'What do you remember about the Ruhr Valley?'

He said, '88s, 88s, and more 88s!' The Germans, even at that stage of the war, had a lot of fight left in them. [They] were still counter-attacking; you'd take a town and maybe lose it the next day. Finally, after about ten days in there, the German army surrendered. There were just thousands and thousands of German troops coming down the road with their vehicles, their field hospitals, surrendering en masse; I remember that very well.

The German Soldier

Even though we had met the German soldier and German army when they were on the decline, I would say they were good. They were well trained, their officers led them well. At the very end in Bavaria we noticed younger solders, maybe fifteen or sixteen years old, but in the Ruhr, German Army Group B was the largest army they had still intact. I did not particularly see a lot of young people, maybe nineteen or twenty, the age of some of us. As the war got near the end, as the Germans had done in Berlin, they put kids in. They were young. Having said that, some people fail to realize these kids, they had trained since ten years of age.

They knew how to handle weapons even though they were only fifteen or sixteen years of age. I remember saying to a German major who had surrendered, I said jokingly, 'You have kids in your army now.'

He said, 'Yeah, we have kids, but those that you call kids'—and he could speak English—'are better trained than many of your soldiers, because what we hear of your army, you take your people in and train them for 17 weeks in infantry training camps and then you send them to a division.' He said, 'These kids you're calling have been training since they were ten!' And they were particularly good with the panzerfaust, which was a German [anti-tank] bazooka. We met some of them in the Ruhr, they would be in the wooded area. They would attack a convoy and some of them would seem to disappear; that was a very lethal weapon. They could knock a tank out with that [or] a truck full of GIs. One of the regiments in our division was going to a town in the Ruhr Valley which they thought had been secured. Just before they got in there, they passed a wooded area, and they were attacked. About fifteen or twenty GIs were killed in this truck—the panzerfaust just hit it and blew it to smithereens.

I would say the [German] leadership was good. They knew how to take advantage of hilly terrain; they knew how to defend rivers. That continued right through the war. They were first-rate soldiers. The fact they were able to carry on a war against major allies like England, the United States, France, Russia, and survive proved they were good soldiers. I didn't agree with their ideologies, but they were good soldiers.

German Prisoners

General [Walter] Model was the German commander in charge of that and had a tremendous reputation as a defensive general. He had bled the Americans white in the Hürtgen Forest just previous to that [*shakes head*] and didn't give up very easily. General Ridgeway had sent him a note days before this asking that, on a humanitarian basis, that he surrender his forces now to save Germany from the further destruction of their infrastructure, their industrial buildings that were left and so forth, but he refused, saying that a General Field

Marshal does not surrender. So, in the last two or three days of the war, [that German army] started discharging their soldiers. He wasn't surrendering himself, but they would come down the road with a discharge pass, and they still had to be taken in as prisoners of war.

One of the worst sights I saw was right near the end. [The Germans] were surrendering at such a rate that [we] didn't have facilities for them. It was raining very hard, and I was cold, and to see them in these large enclosures, huddled next to each other trying to keep warm, and no sanitary facilities, and very hard to get food to them—even though they were the enemy, I thought of myself in that same situation. They were just helpless. There was nothing they could do, [though] they'd have their own Red Cross representatives trying to help them, they'd have some of their officers trying to organize them, but it was a very pathetic sight. It shows you what happens when you are not successful in a military operation, when somebody else has your fate in their hands.

[By that time, we were aware of the concentration camps]; we went into none of the large ones, but we saw some small concentration camps in the Ruhr. We also saw a field hospital where they had German and American wounded, and I would say at that point the Germans were doing the best they could for both their own wounded and the Americans who were being liberated. They were short of supplies, short of medicines, but some of the people we liberated were in pretty bad shape. We also saw a large number of slave labor camps where these people worked in these various factories in the Ruhr. [These people] were from Russia, from Poland, from anywhere, thousands and thousands of them—I guess it was that source of manpower that kept the German armament [factories] going, because they had drafted so many of their own people that they depended on this slave labor. Some of the factories were underground, and the [slave laborers] had come out of these shafts. It was pretty pathetic.

After the fighting in the Ruhr Valley, we were transferred to the Third Army, and we joined the Third Army just before they went into Nuremberg in about the last fifteen days of the war. When you're with Patton's army, you move pretty quickly. In that operation we were involved in four river crossings. The Altmühl, which is a fairly large German river, the Inn, and the other one that I remember most is the Danube, because by that stage of the war we had lost quite a few men. The medical aid man that was with our platoon was a very, very good friend of mine, and he lost his life about ten days before the war ended.

'A Hornet's Nest of SS'

The most street fighting we were involved in was in two towns, Ludenscheid [and] Hagen, which was a large industrial city. Street fighting in Vohberg, and the 342nd was heavily in Ingolstadt; that was house-to-house fighting there, mostly against SS troops. SS troops were very fanatical about defending, they just didn't give up easily. I don't recall seeing a large group of SS give up, where with the German army, the Wehrmacht would. The [Wehrmacht] would hide in basements, attics, and so forth, and the first chance they got, when things quieted down, you would see them come out, throw their weapons down or put a white flag in the window.

We had crossed the Danube River and there [was] a place called Vohberg, and we were told earlier that the German garrison may have pulled out, but it was a hornet's nest of SS troops who made up their mind that they were not going to surrender. In the initial assault, our battalion was hit pretty heavy, and we were very surprised—we just thought all we were going to see was white flags, but it was just the opposite! I was in the second story of a building with my machine gun squad, and the medical aid man was in that building, and we looked out on this field where the Germans were dug in, after we had cleared the village. At that point an officer of B Company, the rifle company we were supporting, walked right in front of the window—I can see it like it was happening today. He raised his arm like that [*gestures, in the air*], and a bullet went right through his sleeve, and he said, 'Look at that, a souvenir!' He said, 'I'm going to keep this shirt!' In two minutes, he was down.

The medical aid man left that covered position and went out to assist him. There were several wounded at the time and several people yelled,

'Medic, medic, medic, over here!' but there weren't enough medics to administer first aid to each one of them. So, our medic got about halfway between the house and where this officer lay, and he got hit, but he tried to get up. When the officer had gotten hit, he just lay there like he was dead, but the [medic] got [up and was] hit again. So, me and one other fellow left the building, went out and brought him back. When we got him back behind the building, a [new] medical aid man who had arrived by that time said, 'You guys wasted your breath, this man's already dead.'

We didn't know, but we also went back out and got the officer, and he survived. I remember this so clearly, because as we got him behind the building, and they administered blood plasma—and he was as white as a sheet—as he started taking that plasma, you could see his color start to change a little bit. He survived, [but] I never saw him again after that. He had gotten hit here [*points to the right side of torso*] and his thumb was almost shot off, and the last I saw of him was when they were taking him back down towards the river to evacuate him. The Germans had a lot of these wagons, particularly in the Ruhr, that they hauled wood and things on, and they had steel wheels and so they had him lying on this. I heard since he had survived the war.

I received the Bronze Star for that with the oak leaf cluster because my Bronze Star was not just for meritorious but was also for what they called 'heroic.' I don't want to try to appear to be a hero, but I was there, and I'm lucky I'm here. That same day I could've lost my life. Our battalion lost about 25 or 26 [men] killed and 40 wounded in practically one day, which is a large loss for that period of the war, when you think, 'Hey, these guys are done, we're going to see a white flag.' The Wehrmacht regular German army were more ready to surrender, these SS were not. I could never understand what was in their minds. They thought, 'We're going to turn this thing around?' You know, like a football game. 'We're behind, but we're going to win!' I could not understand their psychology, but I guess it was part of their indoctrination.

The General

I didn't get to see General Patton, but some of our people did. The 342nd Infantry Regiment of our division approached a city called Ingolstadt, which was a fairly large city in Bavaria around the Danube River. Again [there was] unexpected resistance, and Patton came up and asked the regimental commander how things were going, and he said, 'We're not making as much progress as we thought, and our casualties are fairly heavy. I don't know if we'll get to cross the river.'

And it's reported, I wasn't there, Patton said, 'Listen, I want you to cross the Danube River by 7 o'clock tomorrow morning. I don't give a damn if you have to swim across.' I guess all Army commanders are a little egotistical. He wanted the Third Army to be the first army across the Danube River. You know, all blood and guts. His guts and my blood.

War's End

When the war ended, we were in Austria. We could have stayed there, but after about ten days in

Austria, we moved back to Mannheim, Germany, and I guess it would be called the army of occupation. Very good duty, very light duty. Within a short period of time we were given orders, our division would return to the United States to prepare for service in the Pacific, which would have been, if the war continued, the invasion of Japan. So, we got back to the States and had furloughs, rest and recuperation, whatever that meant, and then we were sent to Oklahoma for a brief period of time and then shipped to the west coast at Camp Stoneman and proceeded to the Philippine Islands. So, we were in the Philippine Islands just as the war ended.

I was very happy [when we heard about the dropping of the bombs on Hiroshima and Nagasaki] because [coming back to the States] on the ship, we were briefed on what possibly could happen, and when they started to give the casualty estimates for our division, and any division that would have invaded Japan. I wouldn't be here talking to you today if that invasion had taken place, because based on what had happened at Okinawa, when the casualties were horrendous, it would have been Okinawa ten times that scale. The Japanese had five to seven thousand aircraft hidden in caves, they had, I think, still five million men in the whole army in Japan, and they had equipped civilians with spears. They were not going to surrender if the atomic bomb had not been dropped. That would have been a horrendous campaign that could have gone on until 1946. The casualties had been horrendous. Thanks to Harry Truman, who I've always admired, I'm here today, and many GIs that were scheduled to be in that operation will say that. I arrived in the Philippines at that time in August 1945, and I left late January 1946; I was discharged at Fort Dix.

After the war, I was in the National Guard for two years, the 170th Field Artillery of the 27th Infantry Division. I enlisted for a year, and I was extended for a year, but our division was not called up [for Korea]. Some Guard divisions were, but the 27th was not.

I did not [make use of the GI Bill]. I should have, but I did not. I came back and went to work for the Dupont Company in Newburgh, which was one of the largest employers we had. I worked with them for a good number of years, and they were purchased by another company called the Stauffer Chemical Company, so between the two companies, I had 31 years of service. While I was working there, I was elected as a member of the town board. Sort of a miracle in this Republican town to have a Democrat elected, but I was, and I went on to become supervisor and later on elected to the New York State Assembly and served there for 12 years. I served on the veterans committee, and I was very proud that I was able to pass the first bill to get long-term veterans care for New York State. It just seemed the language, [the way it had been written], nothing was happening. But since then, we've had several opened, [most recently] one in Queens, one in Batavia. That was one of the things I was pleased I could be in a position, as a GI, [as a veteran], to have some influence on legislation later on in Albany.

'The Spirit Is There'

I joined the American Legion, the Veterans of Foreign Wars, the Catholic War Veterans, and I'm a member of the Combat Infantrymen's Association as well. Now also, in 1985 our division formed an 86th Blackhawk Division Association; I joined that immediately. For six years I was the treasurer, and at that time we had over 2,000 members, so that six years was like a full-time job. There was something coming across my desk at home every day. I enjoyed it, and we had reunions every year. In the beginning, it was every three or four years a group of us got together. Then, starting in the early '80s, we started meeting every two years in Indianapolis. The last one we had was three years ago. Our numbers are really dwindling. We're talking about having another one, but it's hard. When we have our division reunions, some of the fellows do attend. We've had as many as eighteen; the last reunion in Cincinnati last September we had [just] seven. With the age and so forth, it's hard to get guys together. The spirit is there.

Our casualties were not as heavy as some other divisions, since we arrived later in the war, [but I remember two replacements in particular who came up with us]. One who came in came up at night, and he was obviously very nervous, as anyone would be. He said to me, 'I don't think I'm going to be alive by tomorrow morning.'

I said, 'You have to stop that talk. Just worry about getting through the next hour.' I remember he survived. Another member of my company, fellow by the name of Jim Kelly from Pittsfield, Massachusetts, he came over as a replacement and joined a division in the Ruhr Valley. He trained with a guy named Paul Holland. Paul Holland died on his very first day in combat. [Kelly and Holland] had struck up a real friendship on the troop ship coming over, and of course we're assigned to the same division, and Paul only lasted a day.

Reflections

Going in as a teenager, it made me suddenly a more serious person. One thing it made me value is, every day I live because I could have been in one of those military cemeteries overseas, or in a local cemetery here. I have a different attitude about life. Doing the best I can every day, and not looking too far into the future, or worrying about what happens. I think that experience of being in combat and possibly being killed does leave you with a different perspective on things. You seem to be able to put things in their place. I think GIs who have been exposed to that can do it better than many other people. Don't look too far down the road, don't worry about every little thing that happens. Just thinking how lucky I am, at seventy-nine years of age, to have gone through the Second World War as an infantryman, seen some combat, and be still alive and in good health to talk about it.

It's a blessing.

Larry Bennett lived until the age of 92. He passed away on March 9, 2016.

Mr. DiFiore at the time of the interview. NYSMM screen-shot.

CHAPTER TEN

The Giver

He sits in a hotel room with his interviewers, all decked out: red, white, and blue flag tie, a vest covered in ornamentation, military patches and regalia. He speaks quickly, almost as if he is in the present as he recounts his past as a 19-year-old replacement combat engineer. He does a good job of downplaying the pain of not being fully accepted into his new unit, even after weeks of combat, but he can't hide the fact that he is a sensitive man, formed in hard times, even to the extent of attempting to save an enemy soldier from a vengeful mob two days after the war was over—to the disdain of his own buddies and officers.

"My two friends and I were walking around, just looking around, and I heard a lot of noise—talking,

yelling, and screaming. I walked into the woods a little bit, there's about twenty people in there or so, grownups yelling and screaming. I then saw this young German kid about sixteen or seventeen years old. They had him stripped down to his jockey pants, just jockey shorts, and they had a rope around his neck. [Pauses] They were going to hang him.

So remember, the war had been over with now for a couple of days. Something told me, 'Don't let them do it!'

I went over there, and they were pushing me away. I said, 'You can't do that to him!'"

'Johnny D' DiFiore stepped up in the face of enormous social pressure to 'do the right thing'; this event exemplified his entire life. This interview was recorded in 2003 when he was seventy-eight.

'People who know me say that I'm happiest when I'm at the VA hospital; I am happiest helping our veterans—I just love going there and being with them. I have been doing it for well over thirty years because they need help. I'm a giver. I'm not a taker.'

Augustine John DiFiore

I was born in Yonkers, New York, on June 1, 1924. I was one of eight children, the fifth one. I came from a very poor family. We lived in a cold-water flat. At that time, with eight children, my father was working for the state in a WPA project, and his earnings were $25 a week. With that, we had to survive.

My two sisters dropped out of high school to go to work. They were the oldest, and I had an older brother. He dropped out of high school when he was about seventeen or eighteen years old, and he joined the army, the 1st Division, 16th Infantry, 1939. My other brother joined the Civilian Conservation Corps (CCC). He was 16 years old, and was sent out to work in the forest in Montana. When I graduated high school at eighteen years old, I tried to join the Coast Guard or the Air Force, but I was rejected because of my eyesight. So I found a job in a factory that made Army Signal Corps wire. It's two wires that are twisted and it's laid on the ground or trees or poles; the army then communicated on telephones. I worked there until they drafted me on March 11, 1943, when I was about eighteen and a half years old.

When I heard about Pearl Harbor, I was in my house. I remember it was a nice sunny day, and I heard it on the radio; it didn't weigh on me that much, because maybe I was ignorant of something about all this. But then as the days went by, I see everybody's getting excited. Most of the guys were joining the service. They were joining the Army, the Navy, the Marine Corps, young guys, they all wanted to go.

I had a very close friend and I said, 'Come on. Let's go. Let's join.' Then, we went down to Whitehall Street, New York City, to join the Coast Guard, the Air Force, and we got rejected by both of them. My friend was accepted, but I was rejected because of my eyes.

So he says, 'I'm not going in if you're not going.' So we waited until we got drafted. From Yonkers, we were shipped out to Long Island, Camp Upton. It's way out in Long Island. Over there, they gave us different tests, a lot of needles, and they gave us our uniform and an old 1917 Enfield rifle with a bayonet and everything. That's when I started to realize that I was in the army.

We were there a few days and then we boarded a locomotive train, that's what it was in those days. We traveled north and then after an hour to two hours of traveling, one of the officers, we can see from his lapel that he had an engineer insignia on it. They talked to us, and they told us that we were in the 204th Combat Engineer Battalion, and we were going up to Fort Devens, Massachusetts, for our basic training.

We did three months of basic training there. I was a squad leader. I really loved it. I was a kid, I was very strong. I could run. I was up in the front with a captain all the time, on the hikes and all that. I ate it all up, especially the food, because there wasn't much food in my house. We only got one dish of food, and that was it. Most of the time, we went to bed, we were hungry. So I really enjoyed what I was doing in the army, and I did well. I was squad sergeant for the three months, and then after, we were inspected and they said that the battalion needed another three months of training, so we stayed there for another three months.

When I finished the six months of basic training, my platoon officer, my lieutenant, came to me. He said, 'Johnny, we see by your records that you have a 120 or something IQ.' The army has a special name for it.

Harvard Man

He says, 'You want to go to officers candidate school, or do you want to go to ASTP?'

So I said, 'What is ASTP?'

He says, 'It's a college course, an engineering course, a two-and-a-half-year course. We'll send you to Harvard.'[15]

So I said, 'My God.' I heard of Harvard, but I was a poor guy, I couldn't afford to go to college. So I jumped on it, and said, 'I'll go.'

I went there and I met all these young fellas; a lot of guys were older than me and much smarter than me. So, we had a great time at Harvard; we

---

[15] 'The Army Specialized Training Program was a military training program instituted by the United States Army during World War II to meet wartime demands both for junior officers and soldiers with technical skills. Conducted at 227 American universities, it offered training in such fields as engineering, foreign languages, and medicine.' Source: *The Army Specialized Training Program. Shared Sacrifice: Scholars, Soldiers and World War II*. Ball State University. Wikipedia.

lived in a suite like three or four bedrooms, with two guys in a bedroom, and then we had our study room in the center. One of our roommates was a guy named Hal Holbrook, a kid. He was nineteen years old. Ever heard of him? The actor? He walked straight as a pole and he was like... It was like you couldn't touch him, but I got to be good friends with him. I think I was the only guy that was his friend.

He came from Ohio, his parents were divorced, and he had a grandmother that lived near Boston. We were always broke because we used to go out with the girls from Radcliffe, or Wellesley, or Sergeants Teachers College on Friday or Saturday night. We danced around a little bit like that. We couldn't go for much money; we didn't have much money. We'd only make $50 a month, and we had to pay the cleaning bill, there were cleaners there; the uniforms had to be clean and neat all the time.

We did good. He used to call up his grandmother and we used to meet her in Boston. She would take us out to dinner. I don't know, but she must have given him a few dollars. I remember one time we went to the Boston Symphony Hall, and I thought it was boring, but I guess we made it through. There were things like that.

*

The invasion of France was on the planning board. They needed replacements. So after nine months, they took me and a lot of guys out [of the ASTP program][16]. We went to the camp. We wound up in Camp Shanks, the embarkation camp in New Jersey. From there, you get all your equipment and everything like that. They put you on a train and take you down to Jersey City and get on the ferry, cross the river, and you get on the boat. The troopship was the *USS George Washington.* We left and we were in a 75-ship convoy. It took us fourteen days to get to Liverpool.

Now when we got to Liverpool, we took a train to Chester, it's a little north. We trained up there, marched around, and stuff like that. Then, we got shipped down to Winchester when they had the invasion, where all our power troopers were. After they moved out, we moved in.

---

[16] The ASTP program was terminated due to infantry manpower shortages coupled with the growing feeling by some top brass that stripping men away for college undermined regular troop morale.

Then from Winchester, they shipped us down to Southampton and we waited a day or two to get on the ship. It wasn't a big ship, it was an English infantry ship that could carry maybe a thousand or so men. It took us a couple of days to cross the channel, which was full of mines. The next day, August 1, they loaded us into the landing craft boat and led us into the water. We went to Omaha Beach; we tried to get off the beach as fast as possible, but we were loaded down with all the equipment, ammo and everything. We even had impregnated clothes on for gas, we had gas masks, everything. We finally made it to the top of the hill where the trucks were waiting for us.

I went over as a replacement to the 19th Replacement Depot in the hedgerow country. That's where we were organized. We had to dig long slit trenches, or fox holes, and we put our pup tents, with raincoats or whatever, on the bottom. We slept two or three guys together. We had our shelter at the top, but we slept in the hedgerows. There were only one or two cows there. A young French girl used to come in the morning, and she had a little horse and wagon, a two-wheeled cart, and she used to milk the cows, but most of the cows around were dead; when we got there, there were a lot of dead animals, a lot of debris.

We stayed there until I was assigned to the 166th Combat Engineer Battalion. The man that I replaced was a young kid, 19 years old. He had drowned coming back from a river crossing; my battalion made a lot of river crossings; they were always up in the front. There was a captain or the major, whoever was in charge, he always wanted to see who's up in the front. We were always up in the front.

'A Little Lost Puppy'

I told my kids [about my experience as a replacement soldier]. I was like, forget about it, like a little lost puppy. They didn't bother with me. They wouldn't extend their hand like a buddy. They were a very close clique; they had trained in the States down in Mississippi, Missouri. Half of the guys were from New England, half of the guys were from around Mississippi, and I guess they cliqued up and they don't know me, they didn't put too much faith in me.

I got all the dirty details. For instance, when it was guard duty time, I always got the 12:00 to 4:00 shift. There was another guy in my squad, they called him the 'Sad Sack.' I got a picture of him. They would put us two guys together. What was good about him was that he knew his weapons, his bazooka, and his machine gun, .30 caliber water-cooled. Everybody called me DiFiore or Brains; because they found out I went to Harvard, they used to call me Brains. They said, 'Okay, you and...' I forgot the other guy's name. 'You've got twelve to four.' Okay. I would just sit down and try to snooze a little bit; about maybe a quarter to twelve or something, the corporal and somebody else would take us out. We walked in the dark. [One time], we walked for I don't know how long until we came to these two guys that were lying on the grass with a machine gun. They said, 'Okay, we'll be back. We'll be back to see you in a couple of hours.'

At about 2:30 in the morning, I hear footsteps coming. We were on the grass, but they sounded like on a dirt road. So I thought it was the guys, right? So we kept walking and something. So, I yelled, 'Halt, who goes there?' Then all of a sudden, they started running. Meanwhile, I was lying on the ground with my rifle. After I yelled, 'Who goes there?' the third time and they kept running, I just let out three shots. I couldn't see anything and my friend there was at the machine gun. I said, 'Hold it, let's move out of here.' So I helped him with the machine gun, and we moved maybe about a hundred feet away. We waited and nobody came.

At about 4:30 in the morning, we hear the guys coming. I told the guys, 'Where the hell have you been? You didn't hear the shooting? Was that you guys?' They came a half-hour late, and I thought that's the way it was. You know, no concern [*shakes head*].

We went back, and the sergeant said, 'What happened, DiFiore?' I told him the story.

'The captain wants to see you in the morning, he wants to get the story.'

I told him, 'Usually we go on guard duty in the daytime, and we know where we are. I didn't know where anything was.'

He said, 'Well, go see.'

I walked out there now in the light, and we were on the grassy plain. About ten feet below us was like a wagon road, and to the left of that was the whole battalion! All the way, all our trucks and vehicles. I happened to be shooting almost straight but at a little angle. I didn't hit the trucks.

Captain said, 'Good thing you didn't hit the trucks, DiFiore.'

I said, 'Everybody heard me shoot, but nobody came out to see what was going on!'

'We Ain't Taking No Prisoners'

Now we had come to Frankfurt, that's the ninth largest city in Germany, and they surround the Main River. We parked our trucks and our platoon walked down this wide cobblestone boulevard to the bridge; it looked like the main bridge going into Frankfurt. It was a stone macadam pavement bridge, we had shovels and picks with us. They told us we're going down there to fill in the pavement because it was blown up. We got down there and it was a mess. You can never fill those right. It was getting dark, they really blew up the bridge, it was so bad. I was on the left side walking down. No sooner than we got on the bridge, I'd say about 8:30, a couple of mortars start falling on the bridge. So I hit the ground; I think about maybe three or four mortars hit.

I looked around and I saw nobody. I got up late and saw nobody. My rifle was there. I picked up my Garand rifle and started running back the way we came. I ran across the opening of the bridge until I came to the sidewalk. Meanwhile, the Germans must have somebody cornered; there was a big apartment house on the block on the corner, they must have had somebody there. The Germans started shooting 88 artillery, armor-piercing rounds, and as I was running on the sidewalk, these rounds were just ricocheting, skimming off the cobblestone streets and slamming into the buildings.

You can't believe it and I didn't count them. It must have been at least a dozen of them, but I just kept running. Something told me to keep running. I got halfway down the block, and I heard heavy footsteps behind me. I turned around, there were two German soldiers that had their hands up in the air right away! I saw that they didn't have their steel helmets on. Usually, when a German gives up, they take off their steel helmet and everything else. They were yelling, 'Bitte! Bitte!' 'Please! Please!'

I just turned around and something told me just keep running. So I ran for maybe a hundred and something feet. That was the corner of the big apartment house. I ran around the end and ran another hundred feet to the end of the building. There was a driveway, my platoon sergeant was there.

He said, 'DiFiore, where the hell have you been?' What can I say?

I said, 'Nobody told me to get out, you know, let's go.'

So he said, 'Okay. The guys, they're down in the basement. Go down the driveway and get down in the basement.' Then these two Germans come right up behind me.

He said, 'Where the hell did you get them?'

I said, 'They followed me!'

He said, 'We ain't taking no prisoners.'

With that, I said, 'F you.'

I ran down the driveway and the Germans, I guess they must have sensed that. The Germans were at least 40 to 45 years old; they weren't kids. They followed me and I ran down the steps into the basement and all the guys were there. It was a dark basement; there was maybe a couple of flashlights and some candles.

As soon as they saw the two German soldiers, they got around them and started to search them. I just walked away because they seem to like to take control, these were the kind of guys who you could never tell to stop or whatever. I just walked away, and my friend came to me and he says, 'What happened?' I said, 'What's the matter [with them]? Nobody told me to get out of there; I didn't know what the hell to do!'

We walked out of the basement, and we rounded a corner. As we round the corner, I saw a steel door. Nonchalantly, I just opened the door, looked, and it was a big room, at least 30 feet wide by about 40 to 50 feet long. It was all mattresses with people in there, mostly women and children or old people, because I heard a lot of whimpering and crying. Candles, here and there. So right away,

I closed the door. I didn't even enter it, I just closed the door and told my friend, 'Don't tell the guys.' I don't want to expand on that, because... [*pauses*].

We stood there for about another hour or so, then the sergeant said, 'Let's go.' We walked a couple of miles up the road, either way. Meanwhile, these armor-piercing 88s were landing, they were really something. I don't know how [we got out of there]; I still say it's a miracle. We went about a mile up the road and we slept in another house.

'We Were Supposed to Draw Fire'

The next day, they drove us back to the bridge again. It was a nice sunny day. They said, 'Okay. Go back to work.'

We didn't even get to the bridge when they started shelling us again. Right on the left corner was a three-story old brick building which was an old pharmacy, and on the side of it was like a concrete grease pit. I don't know if you have seen it around, like, a car would go over it and the mechanics would work underneath the ground, a little room underneath; so about half a dozen of us, we ran down there. The shelling lasted about an hour and 45 minutes. I timed it on my wristwatch. My mother gave me that when I graduated high school.

After it ended, we went outside and there was our squad truck and the kitchen truck all blown up. So we waited while the sergeant went to get a couple more trucks to take us out. When we got into the trucks, we went up the road a couple of miles, and then we saw what the whole story was. A couple of miles up the road, A Company was put to work the previous night and was putting up a Bailey bridge across the Main River. The sergeant said we—I was in B Company—were supposed to draw the fire while they put up the bridge! So we crossed that bridge into Frankfurt. We went into where the railroad station was, and they told us to unload again. We're going to fix the streets, but the cobblestones were piled up as high as the gutters. We were there for maybe an hour or so. He said, 'Okay, load up again. We're moving out.' That's the way it was with Patton—he didn't let you rest, and we moved out.

Mostly, we made river crossings, we took the infantry across the rivers. We had plywood boats, two engineers, one in the front and one in the back; you get about 10 or 12 infantrymen. They get in the boat and put their weapons down on the bottom of the boat. You give them a paddle and tell them to paddle. No picking up your weapons when you go across—you paddle across [to get to the other side as fast as you possibly can]. So what happened one time as we cross this river, there was a nice sandy beach, they got off and start running. The first thing you know, the beach was loaded with booby-traps, teller mines and bouncing betties; it bounces up about three or four feet and then explodes. Sometimes it's full of ball bearings, or nails, anything. A lot of infantry guys were wounded. We were now on the other side, we heard them yelling for the medics. My lieutenant, Fred K. Lawson, said, 'Come on. I need some volunteers.' I was in the 3rd Squad. The 1st Squad sergeant said, 'We'll go with you.' They took about three or four boats and went across. Now, the lieutenant, when he got on the beach, the poor guy hit a tripwire and it went off. He was killed right there. The squad sergeant and the corporal were wounded. Another guy was wounded. It was a pretty bad mess. They let the guys stay there until everything calmed down a little bit, before we all went over there to help out.

Seeing General Patton

Another time we helped put a heavy pontoon bridge across the Rhine River, that's when Patton came. He pulled down his zipper and he pissed in the river; we were all clapping. [*Laughs*]

I saw him again. One time, I was with another friend. We're running outside of this town and there was a tank staying with us. We had our bazooka; they give us a bazooka instead of a machine gun. Patton came by in a staff car. He said, 'How are you doing?'

I said, 'Okay.'

He said, 'What were you guys doing? A big Tiger tank came down here.'

So, my friend was the bazooka commando, all I did is put in the rocket. He said, 'I would shoot and then run like hell.'

Patton said, 'I would do the same thing,' and then he took off. You're supposed to salute, give your name and outfit.

We wound up in Czechoslovakia, just before Prague. That's how far we advanced and because Patton just wanted to keep going. He got word to pull out. We pulled out of Czechoslovakia, came down into Austria. We followed the Rhine River up into Regensburg. Then on the banks of the Danube River, in Regensburg, we put our pup tents. That's where we slept for so many weeks.

We finally move into German cavalry artillery buildings. They were nice two-story buildings with stables underneath. Stone and brick. We lived there when the war was over. Patton had his headquarters right across the street from it. One guy I knew was a surveyor in our company. We had to build an airfield for the Piper Cubs; it was a big farm area. We had to flatten out the area so the Piper Cubs could land. That was the only way of getting messages to and from different cities and different outfits, through a Piper Cub. That's what we did for Patton.

'They Were Going to Hang That Kid'

There was another story I wanted to tell you. This was in Czechoslovakia, two days after the war ended. We were in this little neighborhood, half a dozen houses; that's how small this whole neighborhood was, but there was a work camp. When they had these displaced persons, like Polish or whoever they were, they lived in the stockaded work camp, in the factories or fields. My two friends and I were walking around, just looking around, and I heard a lot of noise—talking, yelling, and screaming. I walked into the woods a little bit, there's about twenty people in there or so, grown-ups yelling and screaming. I then saw this young German kid about sixteen or seventeen years old. They had him stripped down to his jockey pants, shorts, just jockey shorts, and they had a rope around his neck. [*Pauses*] They were going to hang him. [*Pauses again; looks down*]

So remember, the war had been over with now for a couple of days. Something told me, 'Don't let them do it!' So, I went over there, and I told them, 'Nix, nix, nix,' and they were pushing me away. I said, 'You can't do that to him!'

I tried to explain to them that the war was over. They said, 'No.' They must have said something, and I couldn't understand them. So I called to my friends; they didn't want me to interfere. My friends came over and I said, 'Well, look, they are trying to hang the kid here.'

They said, 'Let them hang the Nazi bastard!'

You know, the war was over. The people were pushing me, the kid screamed, 'Help me!'

I said, 'Okay!' I grabbed the kid's arm and took the rope off his neck and dragged him with me... [*Pauses*]. He was crying. The kid was crying.

I took him to where my lieutenant and sergeant were. I said, 'Here, they were trying to hang the kid in the woods.'

They said, 'What the hell did you stop them for?'

I said, 'The war's over!' I wasn't a killer.

*

After the war, we were in Regensburg. When the war was coming nearer to an end, the Germans were giving up themselves, just hundreds of thousands of them. They were in their vehicles, in our vehicles, [on foot], maybe hundreds of thousands of prisoners. We were told to build a stockade, a prison camp for ten thousand prisoners there, because after the war, a German soldier couldn't walk the streets unless he had his discharge papers. I guess they had figured everything out.

Our job was to build this camp and we used a lot of German prisoner [labor]; there were German and Hungarian prisoners. My job, I had a truck, I usually drove about 30 miles outside of Regensburg; [there was] a big lumber camp there, and I used to bring the lumber orders, what kind of lumber they wanted, and give it to the manager of the lumber camp. I used to hang around, and the twenty to twenty-five German prisoners that I used to bring, they used to help cut the lumber down into whatever we needed, then loaded it up on the truck and then I would drive them all back to the stockade. That was my duty after the war, until the end of August.

From the end of August, I think it was a Sunday. Bob Hope came to Regensburg with his troupe and performed at the airfield there. He put on a big show, there were ten to fifteen thousand GIs there. The next day, Monday, we were shipped out. They had the trains, they had the boxcars, the 40 and 8s, the same box cars that [probably] would carry the Holocaust victims. There was hardly any straw on the floor, nothing. They put us in there, and for four days and three nights, it took us to Camp Lucky Strike, where we got on a boat and came to Boston.

'I'm A Giver'

I was 19 years old, and I tell you one thing, we had a lot of faith in General Patton. We thought very highly of Patton, especially when he went up to the Bulge, because they were hurting up there bad. We weren't afraid of nothing with him. I just cried [when I learned of his death]. I didn't think it was an accident. He was too good of a man. He believed that we should have gone to... he wanted to go to Russia. When we were in Germany, deep into Germany, the people used to come and tell us—the soldiers too, when we were taking prisoners— 'Let's go fight the Russians now!' I mean, what the heck do I know? I was only a kid. I was just trying to stay alive, and I followed orders. I did whatever my sergeant told me. I was very obedient and disciplined, I never strayed. These guys were really veterans, the guys that I was with. I just toed the line and I tried to do the best I could.

I used to write to [my former comrades-in-arms]. They were mostly from New England or Mississippi or Missouri. They sent me an invitation one time that they were having a 45th reunion up in Warwick, Rhode Island. At that time, I had a problem, an anxiety problem. I couldn't drive and I love to drive. So my kids said, 'Okay. We'll drive you up to Grand Central Station, put you on the Amtrak train. You take the train up there and then you take a cab to the hotel.' That's what I did, I went to the 45th anniversary, me and my wife. It was very, very nice, but even up there, nobody put their arms around me. Nothing like that, you know. They just shook hands, and they didn't even talk to me, maybe because I was a replacement and these guys, they started from the beginning. They had a lot of reunions which I didn't go to. I could see [they had] a thing. They kept to themselves, it was their own clique. That's okay, I know life is like that.

I'm very happy with my family and my church. That's my life, my family and church. [I think my military service] was the best thing that ever happened to me. Of course, I was alive! But the experience gave me so much confidence in myself and making me independent; I'm an independent guy and I don't go looking for help from anybody, but I do give. People who know me say that I'm happiest when I'm at the VA hospital; I am happiest helping our veterans—I just love going there and being with them. I have been doing it for well over thirty years because they need help. I'm a giver. I'm not a taker.

Augustine J. 'Johnny D' DiFiore passed away on March 31, 2016, a couple months shy of his 92nd birthday.

CHAPTER ELEVEN

The Forward Observer

Robert C. Baldridge was a forward observer and frontline artilleryman with the 9th Division. Born on November 9, 1924, in Omaha, Nebraska, he attended school in the east and was able to get into Yale and then joined up via the Enlisted Reserve Corps. In this 2004 interview, he recalled nearly constant combat, punctuated by moments like witnessing the collapse of the famous bridge at Remagen spanning the Rhine.

'Me and my crew at the time went up to a big hill and set the OP post up there, and stayed there for about ten days, firing into Germany, firing at targets that we could see. It was a wonderful OP post for visibility. Seven or eight days after we'd gone over, I saw that *bridge collapse all of a sudden, from the bombing that had weakened it, and kept weakening it further. By that time, we had a lot of pontoon bridges that troops could go over on, but there were Army engineers working on trying to shore up that bridge, and all of a sudden, that bridge collapsed, and about as I recall, [twenty]-eight engineers died and drowned as it collapsed, and I saw that happen from the top of this hill. They were maybe eight hundred, maybe a thousand yards at the most, away. I heard the noise and saw all of this dust coming up. That was the end of the bridge.'*

Robert C. Baldridge

I read [about the attack on Pearl Harbor at school], in the *New York Times*, and of course heard what was going on, on the radio. It just enthused all of us to get through, get out and get moving and get into the service. Actually, I was not a senior yet, I was upper-mid or junior year there. I was just seventeen and I was able to get into Yale for two or three terms and then enlisted in the Enlisted Reserve Corps.

Like many boys or young men, my father was a battery commander in the artillery in World War I and he was back in service in an administrative job as a major at the time in the Air Corps, so I wanted to go into the army because of his army service in World War I, and I wanted to go into the artillery because he was artillery all the way and had been in Artillery ROTC in World War I. I wanted to follow in his footsteps.

I was in a 155mm Howitzer battalion under then Lt. Col. William C. Westmoreland. He was absolutely superior, the best. Some people outside our 9th Division thought he was like a Boy Scout, but he wasn't any Boy Scout. We respected him because of his knowledge and his ability to command the battalion. You didn't call him 'Westy' except behind his back; he was most admired. It was ridiculous, in our opinion, whether you were an officer or a private, this baloney that he took from Mike Wallace as a result of the problem in Vietnam. I am sure if he had to do it all over again, he would have made some adjustments in there, but I'm telling you we honored and respected that man up to the limit.

He knew that I'd been to college and that set me somewhat apart from most of the guys in the division. It turned out that he had an eye on me. I didn't know it at the time, but I ended up getting a battlefield commission during combat towards the end of the war.

Mr. Baldridge and the 9th Division waded onto the Continent at Utah Beach on June 10, 1944, D+4. They then went up near Cherbourg and were near Aachen when the Battle of the Bulge began.

The Fire Direction Center

I had a lot of experience being a forward observer and all of a sudden I am put into the Fire Direction Center at battalion headquarters. That's where the mathematics are done and the commands over wires—the telephone wires and radios are sent to the guns for firing. I did that for about three months, then I got a promotion. I was a gunner corporal—a guy that ran a gun underneath a sergeant who was head of the gun section. Being the gunner corporal, I was second and I was the guy who looked through the panoramic telescope and made the adjustments to sight in on the aiming stakes and so forth. I did that for a number of months. That's what I was doing during the Battle of the Bulge in Belgium in the winter, which was cold.

You had to be careful not to touch the barrels of the guns, or your fingers would stick to them. The only way you could get them off was to tear the skin off your hands. We learned about that, but we were acclimatized. Nobody caught cold or anything like that. The worst part of it was not to let the snow—we were in three to four feet of snow all the time—not to let the snow get into your socks. We didn't get the shoe packs—the rubber boots—until later on; all the guys in the rear were getting them. We had to be careful—we were advised to do this and knew it—we just had extra socks that we would carry around in our hip pockets. We'd try to dry them overnight and keep the socks, keep your feet, as dry as possible so that you didn't get trench foot.

We had plenty of food; we never went hungry, but several times we were under severe limitations on shells, the shortage of ammunition for the howitzers. We were told how many rounds we could fire from the experts in the Fire Direction Center knowing from headquarters further on up how many rounds we could expend depending upon the targets and the problems at that time. The shortage of ammunition at times was as serious as the shortage of gasoline, which everybody knows about. But that finally got changed and we had plenty of ammunition by the time we hit the Rhine River.

The Guns

I was in combat the entire time until V-E Day, which was close to a year, with the exception of a rest period of just three to five days after the Normandy Peninsula was cut and solidified. Otherwise, we were on the line continually until the end. To give some rest, you'd get pulled back from the front line maybe a mile or a few miles, but you were still in combat ready [status] under the possibility and probability of being shelled by enemy fire plus the V-1s and the V-2s, and all of that. Then you'd go back into the front lines. Then another one of your regiments or another division would get some period of rest where you just weren't under direct fire attack constantly.

We suffered thousands of casualties; only two divisions suffered more casualties than the 9th. If you're in the battery and not a forward observer, the guns could shoot as far as sixteen or seventeen thousand yards—they would usually be going over the front line as opposed to trying to hit the front line. But, if we could hit the enemy, they could hit us, so we are talking about [a range of] from a few thousand yards to maybe ten thousand on the average. Now a forward observer would be up close in the range of yards or a few hundred yards; occasionally, you'd be on the point. Sometimes when I was a forward observer—depending on the geography and the position of the enemy—you might be out in front of the front line. The German 88 was a wonderful weapon, absolutely fabulous. The weapon was an anti-aircraft weapon and a direct firing artillery weapon, just by lowering the barrel. It could hit a plane up at twenty thousand feet! We were under fire of the 88s quite a few times, and if you heard them, you were all right because you didn't hear the one that got you.

Crossing the Rhine

A critical discovery and subsequent capture of the Ludendorff Bridge during the Battle of Remagen in early March 1945 by the US First Army helped to shorten the war. The bridge and supplemental pontoon bridges ferried Allied forces to the German town of Remagen on the west bank south of Cologne, one of the few bridges over the Rhine that remained intact, although the Germans tried to destroy it multiple times before it finally collapsed on March 17, 1945, taking twenty-eight Army engineers to their deaths in the swift current of the river.[7]

The next real target area was the Rhine River. Of course, there was a lot of feeling about getting a bridge safe without it having been blow up by the Germans across the Rhine. The 9th Armored Division accomplished that, and my division happened to be right close to them—we were the second division over the Rhine, with the 9th Armored being the first division over the Rhine. The 9th Armored Division's assignment was to stay on this side of the Rhine to contest and continue battling on the Germans that were in that area; there was a whole German army down there on our side of the Rhine.

I went over the very second day, something like March 8, after the Remagen Bridge was actually captured.[17] We were the first division after the 9th Armored to get over. Me and my crew at the time went up to a big hill and set the OP post up there and stayed there for about ten days, firing into Germany, firing at targets that we could see. It was a wonderful OP post for visibility. Seven or eight days after we'd gone over, I saw that bridge collapse all of a sudden, from the bombing that had weakened it, and kept weakening it further. By that time, we had a lot of pontoon bridges that troops could go over on, but there were Army engineers working on trying to shore up that bridge, and all of a sudden, that bridge collapsed, and about as I recall, [twenty]-eight engineers died and drowned as it collapsed, and I saw that happen from the top of this hill. They were maybe eight hundred, maybe a thousand yards at the most,

---

[17] Remagen Bridge-sometimes termed 'the Bridge at Remagen,' the Ludendorff Bridge was constructed during World War I for war use on the Western Front by Russian prisoner slave labor. American GIs commonly referred to it as the Remagen Bridge.

away. I heard the noise and saw all of this dust coming up. That was the end of the bridge. But we didn't need the bridge anymore and, in fact, weren't using the bridge because everybody knew it was unsafe at the time.

The New Jet Planes

We lost three of our casualties who were nearby at that time from the strafing that the German planes had been doing on that bridge since we had first taken it. That strafing included the new planes, the new jet planes that the Germans had.

When you saw those, 'oh boy,' [I thought], another super weapon like the 88 that they had; one of Hitler's secret weapons. We didn't know what the hell they were! We had earlier been subjected to the V-1s. The 'V' in the German language stood for the 'vengeance' weapon—the V-1s and the V-2s. So, those were the ramjet pulsing engines. The pure jets, of course, were not pulse jets, and you could see how fast they went. Our pilots at the time, they learned how to avoid them, and hopefully come down on them from the top. Our own pilots learned how to down these jet planes, if they were able to get up high enough above them to come down on top and figure out where they were headed for and before the jet pilot could really see them.

*

After Remagen, we headed due west into Germany and participated, along with many other divisions, in encircling the Ruhr River Valley, which was a big industrial area of Germany, encircling and then cutting it up. That's where the German commander Model, he didn't surrender, he killed himself because a German field marshal doesn't surrender; he wasn't going to surrender his army. This is quite a story, that we found out later. He knew that he was completely surrounded and that to stay fighting, just everybody would be killed. He wanted to surrender, but he couldn't, so he issued an order to his army dissolving the army and saying to everybody in the army, whether officer or private, that the army is dissolved so you can, in effect, go home, if you can escape. Then he went out with his jeep driver into the woods somewhere and shot himself and was buried right there. He was found about twenty years later and was properly removed and buried wherever his family was buried. That was Model. He saved a lot of German lives by dissolving his army, which had never been done before, but he didn't surrender. As a result, his family and he and the army weren't in disrepute.

Nordhausen

On March 30, 1945, the men of the 3rd Armored Division overran the notorious Dora-Mittelbau concentration camp complex near the town of Nordhausen, which gave it its common name. It was a subcamp of Buchenwald, established after V-2 missile sites were being heavily targeted by the Allies. It became independently run by the SS and grew to over three dozen subcamps including dark, unventilated tunnels mined out of solid rock, where prisoners suffered brutal conditions, neglect, and abuse. Sickened slaves died by the thousands, and near the end, were selected for 'extermination.' SS Major Wernher von Braun was the lead scientist for the project. [18][8]

---

[18] Wernher von Braun-(1912-1977) The 'father' of the United States space program, von Braun's Nazi past became more evident after his death in 1977 at the age of 65, and he remains a controversial figure. His contribution to American rocket science is unquestioned, leading to the development of intercontinental ballistic missiles but also allowing President Kennedy's wish of seeing a man on the moon by the end of the 1960s to come true. Still, his official NASA biography skates rather lightly over his Nazi

From there we went on through to a mountainous area that wasn't too far from the Elbe River. That's where we went through and visited that terrible Nordhausen concentration camp, where the V-2s were being made. Wernher von Braun was the genius of that camp—the technical genius. I know that Wernher von Braun and a hundred of his guys came over to help start our [rocket] program, [but] he knew what was going on in Nordhausen. He was down there all the time! True, he wasn't in command of the SS guys who ran Nordhausen, he wasn't giving any orders to work these poor guys to death, which is what they did. But he knew about and, I guess, he couldn't or felt he couldn't do anything about it, and so he didn't. So, I don't want to hear anything about Wernher von Braun [not] knowing and seeing what he, in effect, allowed to continue on. I have

---

ties: "The V-2 assembly plant near the Mittelbau-Dora concentration camp used slave labor, as did a number of other production sites. Von Braun was a member of the Nazi Party, and an SS officer yet was also arrested by the Gestapo in 1944 for careless remarks he made about the war and the rocket. His responsibility for the crimes connected to rocket production is controversial." Source: *Biography of Wernher Von Braun*. National Aeronautics and Space Administration, August 3, 2017. www.nasa.gov/centers/marshall/history/vonbraun/bio.html

been down to our three centers where they make the stuff, and where they shoot it off, and where the command center is. I've got books on Wernher von Braun's history, and I always felt that America closed its eyes to what von Braun had been doing, merely to get a hundred experts over to save a few months' time in building our space program and allowed him and everybody else to become American heroes.

General Eisenhower, when he saw some camps in the Nordhausen area, he describes it in his book, and he had Patton with him. They got sick in their stomachs, and he sent out an order to all combat divisions: when they captured in any of these areas like the Nordhausen area—Nordhausen was the name of the city there—to parade every single person, German civilians, through the camps. Every person, including children over something like ten years old. If you were a child under ten years old, you didn't have to go, but ten-year-old children and up, everybody was paraded through those camps. They all said, 'Well, we didn't know'—the standard expression. 'We didn't know what was going on!' We saw that!

Nordhausen was a huge camp, and there were many other camps, of course. Here are these huge camps that were run by the SS troops, and they needed civilians, technicians, civilians to come in to lay wire, do technical work, and do things like that and those civilians would go back. What do you mean they didn't know what was going on? What a bunch of... we felt pretty strongly, I felt pretty strongly about that. 'We didn't know'—that was a hell of an answer! They got the answer to that as a result of the trials.

'No Hero To Me'

All I know is that I don't think von Braun should have been glorified and sent back to America with a hundred guys right away to help our space program get developed a few months earlier than it would have been. We had plenty of guys like Goddard, the Space Center. We knew a lot about it. Not as much as he did, and the Germans did, but how long would it have taken? I say a couple of months to have developed a V-2 type of program. So, I don't know that he should have been jailed or anything like that, but in answer to that question,

I think he should have been tried in some way and let off—tried in some way with his sentence a small sentence or let off instead of bringing him back to make him a hero. He's no hero to me.

The Russians

We were right on the Elbe River. All of the divisions were on it.

We [were halted, and] we got bored, we wanted to go on. Actually, we didn't want to go on, we'd been through a lot. We knew that we and the other divisions could have gone on and taken Berlin ahead of the Russians, timewise, but Bradley told Eisenhower it would be at the cost of one hundred thousand lives, that's in Bradley's book. By that time, we were just sitting there waiting for the Russians; we knew that we couldn't go over the Elbe. Everybody knew this, that the Russians would be at the Elbe soon, and we weren't to go over the Elbe. So, we didn't care. It just got boring. The 9th Infantry Division was right alongside just to the left, just to the north of the division that first met the Russians, which was the 69th Division. All of our divisions were just along the Elbe in a stream. Actually, our officers met the Russians the day after the 69th first met them. I think it was at that place called Torgau. Me and my battalion were probably maybe three miles north of Torgau when we contacted the Russians for the first time.

The Barter System

Then, amazing as it was to us, but obviously it had all been worked out and planned before, the day after V-E Day, which was May 8 or May 9, we packed up and moved back to the autobahn and went right down to the Munich area where my division, the 9th, was assigned to occupy in a big circular area around Munich. That was a nice assignment. I was in that area for six months until I left to go back home on points. Now, the orders from Army headquarters to everybody was no fraternization, absolutely no fraternization. That order turned out to be impossible. Consequently, it only lasted maybe two or three weeks. Then you could do whatever fraternization you wanted to because the Germans, they were so glad that we, and not the Russians, were occupying them, they couldn't have been more friendly.

Munich, as I mentioned, we were stationed at a little town called Pfaffenhofen, which is a suburb of Munich maybe ten miles away, fifteen miles away. Most of Munich had just been flattened, not by fighting but by bombs over the years. There was nothing there and in many other towns. Dresden's the famous one. Cologne, any big city like that, had been flattened by bombs for years and there was nothing working. There were no post offices. No shops open. No banks. Nothing was operating. The people that lived out in the farms, they were [the basis of the economy]—money and our pay and German marks didn't mean anything. You couldn't go into a store and buy anything. Currency of any kind was useless. It was a barter system that allowed the Germans to survive. You should have seen the kids that would line up at the end of meals, would line up to get whatever you had that they could eat. Somehow or other, food got into the city dwellers.

We had these little packs of cigarettes that came in the C-ration cans. They were all over the place, there would maybe be ten or twelve [in a pack]. The currency used for bartering, three or four cigarettes, the money was cigarettes—worth more than gold! I don't know. I never smoked, so I gave my cigarettes away. That got straightened out, of course, in due time, but you were talking due time, in six or eight weeks.

'I Can't Get Home!'

General Marshall set that [point system] plan up. As I recall, my point score was, I think, ninety. You could go home first at something like eighty-five for an enlisted man, or for the officers, maybe the score was ninety-five. Here I was ninety, I had more points and often thought why did I accept that battlefield commission? I should have said no! Here because I accepted it, I got more dangerous time as a forward observer, but yet here I was still sitting, I could have been home by now! So, then my point score came up where I was eligible to go home, and I didn't have to take so much baloney anymore because I was on the eligibility list to go home, but I couldn't get home because there was no transportation! The ships were all used. All the ships to take you back were returning with divisions—whole divisions!—that were scheduled to go to the Pacific, and any other ship was on its way to the Pacific to carry our troops from the west coast to the Pacific. There wasn't any shipping, so you just had to stay there.

I remember my father, who by that time was home—he'd spent two years in the Balkans, and he finally wrote me a letter telling me to stop complaining. I am eligible to go home, and I can't get home—'Stop complaining, that's all you write about.'

I wrote him a letter back and said, 'Dad, it's okay for you to write me to stop complaining about not being able to get home, but you're home!' So, he laid off any more such letters and I finally got home in January, after spending three Christmases overseas. I should have been home the previous September.

*

Using the GI Bill, it took two and a half years to finish up at Yale. I don't think it cost anything. I joined the 9th Division Association early and have been to six or seven reunions. They have a reunion every year and I've been to maybe six of them, after the fifty years. I am a member and former director of what's called the National Order of Battlefield Commissions. We have reunions every year. It's a smaller group, and all I can say is that I am on the young side, all of the members of my division having been through North Africa and Sicily, as I mentioned. They were all, on the average, six years older. They're dying off pretty fast now. Same thing with the National Order of Battlefield Commissions. I think I was the second youngest guy that I knew of to have been awarded a battlefield commission.

I am seventy-nine now, but all of these guys, all my friends and everything else, are eighty-six and eighty-eight.

It's sad.

Mr. Baldridge died a year after this interview took place, on February 19, 2005.

CHAPTER TWELVE

The Rocket Man

He speaks with an accent, an obviously well-educated man with an affable manner and a twinkle in his eye. Born in Vienna on the eve of World War I, twenty-five-year-old Rudolf Drenick immigrated to the United States just as World War II began. He wanted to fight the Germans so badly, he was upset when his superiors saw what they perceived as a higher value for the war effort in putting his intellect to work on a top-secret job—sorting through captured German scientific papers that laid out the birth of the rocketry age.

I had a grudge against Germany, and I was itching to get into the act! I had been active in the anti-Nazi movement in Austria for several years before the

Germans moved in, very much at the urgings of my father, and maybe this is part of the story. He was paralyzed from the waist down and he knew that we would never leave the country without him. So in the fall of 1938, he committed suicide, and that clinched the situation for us.

I was drafted. I was told that I couldn't enlist, not being a citizen. Oh, I really wanted to be in the infantry! But then the president of Villanova College had all kinds of strings he could pull in Washington, and I was yanked out of the infantry, to the dismay of my buddies, and to me, too, because I never got [to do what I wanted, which was] practice firing on the machine gun.'

Rudolf F. Drenick

I was born in Vienna, Austria, on August 20, 1914. I came to the United States in April 1939, just before World War II started. I came here with my brother, who was a year and a half younger than I. And we were welcomed by my uncle and his wife, who had come earlier.

I had gotten my PhD in theoretical physics on March 5 at the University of Vienna. I left Vienna on March 8 and crossed the border in Yugoslavia on March 13, so it was a quick action.

I had to learn English pretty fast. I think the attitude among the people who came here in '39 was different from the immigrants now. We tried to learn English as quickly and as well as possible.

First job I had was as a camp counselor for the summer of that year, '39, and in the fall of '39, I got a job as an instructor at Villanova College. Just before the summer, somebody advised me to send my resume to Catholic colleges in this country. And I got three types of replies. One was we have no openings, the other one was we'll pray for you, and one was well if we have nothing by September, come and see us, and that was Villanova College. [*Laughs*]

[When Pearl Harbor happened], I was at Villanova College, listening to a symphony broadcast in my radio when there was an interruption that said there has been an attack on Pearl Harbor. Except for being very excited, I don't remember any other reaction. But if anybody had asked me, I don't think I would have expected Germany to be the one to declare war on us rather than the other way around.

I was drafted. I was told that I couldn't enlist, not being a citizen. So I taught Navy V-12 programs at Villanova College, the special program in which we instructed sailors in the US Navy in mathematics, physics, and navigation. And that was my job, including navigation, which was a little bit odd for me, coming from the center of Europe, never having seen the ocean until I was already 20 or some years old.

'I Had a Grudge'

I was drafted into the U.S. Army. At first, I went to the infantry, which is what I really wanted, you know. I had a grudge against Germany, and I was itching to get into the act! I had been active in the anti-Nazi movement in Austria for several years before the Germans moved in, very much at the urgings of my father, and maybe this is part of the story. He was paralyzed from the waist down and he knew that we would never leave the country without him. On the other hand, he also knew he couldn't leave with his disability. So in the fall of

1938, he committed suicide, and that clinched the situation for us.

But then the president of Villanova College, who had all kinds of strings he could pull in Washington, pulled some of them, and I was yanked out of the infantry, to the dismay of my buddies, and to me, too, because I never got [to do what I wanted, which was] practice firing on the machine gun. Oh, I really wanted to be in the infantry!

I was first put in an outfit called a technical attachment to the War Department and was stationed in Fort Myer just outside the Pentagon. And there, I was used to translate and evaluate captured German documents, technical documents. And from there I was moved to the Ordnance Department, the first citizen member of the technical detachment, and there I got into the evaluation of the documents captured at the German proving grounds for the V-2 rockets. And I was with that, finally as a member of the Ordnance Department, until I was discharged in '46.

When I was drafted, I was drafted as a private. As I remember it, they did an IQ test on everybody, and I must have done really well on it, because I remember being interviewed with a sort of awe by the interviewer. I don't know how well I did, but at any rate I still was a private. [*Laughs*] [I could not be an officer], because I was not a citizen, and I was quite happy being a private, [even with a Ph.D. degree]. And I think to some extent in my early 'private' career they showed me that there was not going to be any honor scheme for Ph.D.s; I got KP of the worst kind. [*Laughs*]

The Secret Documents

[A lot of the documents were] from Peenemunde.[19] The way it happened is three enlisted men, all of whom were technical people with the knowledge of German, were all of a sudden shipped from Washington to Aberdeen Proving Grounds. And on the next morning, a major appeared with a staff car at our barracks and picked the three of us up. Now I don't know whether you have any notion of what it's like, to be a private and be picked up in a staff car and taken away, but I was. And the three of us were taken down to the

---

[19] *Peenemunde-* Peenemunde, on the Baltic Coast, had nearly 5,000 personnel halfway through the war. It utilized slave labor to construct and test the V-1 and V-2 rocket missiles.

firing line where there was a huge unused garage. There was a soldier there with a side arm guarding the entrance and the major unlocked the garage and we were taken in.

Operation Paperclip

By war's end, operations had moved to Nordhausen, where slave labor was utilized to the extreme to produce the Vengeance weapons. With the liberation of the Dora-Mittelbau slave labor tunnel factory complex, documents and as many as a hundred intact forty-foot-tall V-2 rockets were put under secure control, crated up, and shipped to the United States, along with some of the scientists and technicians involved under the top-secret Operation Paperclip.[9]

There was what looked like an acre of huge crates, the documents from the Peenemunde Proving Grounds, and they were marked 're-checked fuses.' Because as we learned later on, the Ordnance Department didn't want the Air Force to know that they found them in the mine in Germany and quickly shipped them to the Aberdeen Proving Grounds, and that's where we met up with them.

[Our job was to basically translate and then analyze] them. The major said, 'Here, evaluate.' So we got a crowbar, opened up the boxes, and started going through them. One of the problems was they were coded, full of code names, and we had no idea what they meant. So what we did is, we wrote the code names on the floor of the garage in chalk, and then piled the documents on them and gradually we began to gather what they meant. And then we also found a sheet in which one of the people at the Peenemunde complained about the misuse of the code names and there he gave away part of the secret. So gradually things began to fill in their place, but progress was very poor. We finally realized that we needed help.

Some help came from the Peenemunde scientists themselves. Five of them arrived at the Aberdeen Proving Grounds. The war was still not over. Germany had collapsed, but the war with Japan was still in full force. So here landed these five German scientists, and the people in the Aberdeen Proving Grounds obviously didn't know quite what to do with the enemy aliens at the time, so they put them in the bunch of barracks way out on the spit sticking out into the frozen Chesapeake Bay, and there were about three or four GIs, me included, who had to shepherd them around. We had to stoke the stoves in the barracks and take them to their meals in the limo, and of course, to the garage where the documents were.

They were very cooperative. At first, there was a, how should I say, distance between them and us, and sort of a wry anger to it, but working with them, we gradually warmed up. One of the Germans had lost his whole family in an Allied air raid, and he became friendly with a General Electric man who had been delegated to work with us who was Jewish, and who had lost his parents to the Holocaust. These two men became especially friendly.

[When we realized what these documents were telling us], we were fascinated. Fascinated. In fact, they changed the course of my life, and that's really what I think. I became interested in the application of mathematics to technology for the rest of my life.

*

I just missed meeting von Braun. One of the five Germans with whom I did work was his deputy, but I forget his name, sorry to say. [These German scientists helped with the code], but still it was a labor without end, but then somebody had the idea of inquiring among German prisoners of war as to whether anybody would be willing to help with the work, and about 150 or 200 did volunteer. They were set up in a special compound in Fort Eustis in Virginia. I remember going down there with an American major and we interviewed them. Most of them spoke English, some of them better than I. All of them quite interesting people and anxious to help the Allied cause. Their compound, which was a low security compound, was next to a high security compound. The German PWs from that came charging across the barbed wires, threats of what they would do to our volunteers when they got back to Germany. Our volunteers were quite worried. As it turned out, they were unnecessarily worried; when [the German PWs] got back they had worries other than revenge—their worries were how to live with what they did [during the war].

[The German prisoners] evaluated the documents, which were shipped down there by the ton and worked on by the Germans, who were as fascinated with the stuff as we were. A few of the documents pertained to Germany's nuclear program. Since I was a physicist, I was especially interested in them, even though I was not well-informed—in fact knew nothing about the American program—but my impression was that the German [nuclear] program was a low priority program.

[They were not close to developing an atomic bomb], I don't think so; the facility was in Norway. It was a heavy water facility, and it was a much smaller enterprise than it turned out later than the American enterprise. The American [one was] really drawn up in a very far-sighted and imaginative way.

The End of the War

I was delighted [when I heard about the dropping of the atomic bombs on Japan]. I mean, I was like most Americans, I really hated the Japanese and I felt they had it coming. I know there was some talk we heard that some of the German people thought that we would, when the war ended, join forces with the Germans and go against the Russians. I think that's probably right. My favorite story about the post-war Germans doesn't bear on this terribly, but I'll tell it anyway. One of the Germans among those who helped us with whom I got friendly was an ex-judge who spoke seven languages or something like that. And he wrote me a few times after he got back to Germany. And one of his letters said, 'Mr. Drenick, please tell me the truth. The Americans are making us eat peanut butter. The rumor is that they are stuck with warehouses full of peanut butter, they don't know what to do with them, and they now make us eat it. And we Germans feel it was bad enough to lose the war, but to have to eat peanut butter afterwards, that was going too far.' [*Laughs*]

During my stay early on in Washington at the Pentagon, I was at the south post of Fort Myer, which was a really grubby set of barracks, but they brought in a number of extremely interesting people. A Russian sea captain was one of them, and I remember two American [former] prisoners of war in Germany who had escaped from the

German prison by axing to death the guards, and they escaped that way. I was glad I was on their side at that point. Another fellow who turned up came from New Guinea, and his reason for being there was he was infected with molds, and they were completely new to the medical profession here. They brought him back [to study] for that reason.

[I was discharged in] September '46, [but I had contact with many of the men I served with] for quite some time. Because of the work with the German material, I was hired by General Electric and their guided missiles program. And another fellow who had worked with me in the army had gone to General Electric about the same time, so for a couple of years we were quite close. I left GE about two and a half years after I got there and went to RCA, and then I lost track of this one buddy with whom I was in contact. The others I don't remember being in touch with very much.

[Working with these documents changed my life], yes it did, yes it did. I was a theoretical physicist; I had met Einstein because of my thesis. I think he took pity on me, truth be told. [*Laughs*] I was in a seminar with another Nobelist, [Linus]

Pauling, because of the work I was doing. But after I went into the Army, I dropped physics until now, really. Now I am toying around with it again.

Professor Emeritus Drenick passed away on September 24, 2010.

CHAPTER THIRTEEN

The Paratrooper III

Welcome to 1945. The 3rd Battalion of the 504th Parachute Infantry Division had just come off the line after weeks of non-stop brutal cold and combat. Albert had nearly frozen to death and had just lost a friend who was instructed to take his place on the line, so that he might pay a visit to the medical aid station to have his feet looked at. In the shelling that followed, his friend was killed in his place, and he lost his company commander. The men were exhausted and were granted a temporary reprieve.

Albert A. Tarbell

At Rest

We [left the aid station] and there was some more fighting, and oh, God, always the cold weather, you know. You just get settled in one place, and you've got to move again! And then word came down we were being relieved. We're going to go for some R&R, some rest camp. And they sent us back to Reims, and we were there, I think it was a week or two weeks, and God that was so nice there! It was so nice. We stayed with an old couple, and they had two daughters. There was one that had just gotten out of a German jail, or whatever it was; it was run by the Germans anyway. She had been feeding Allied airmen in the woods, sneaking food out there, and somebody squealed on her. Anyway, they had her in jail for a while.

This other woman, her husband was doing forced labor in Germany, and they had a little three-year-old girl. Oh, they were so happy to receive us. Everybody was just open arms, you know. And the first night we got there, she gave us the top floor, their master bedroom. Down blankets, pillows, even the mattresses, you know, feathers, all goose down they have there in Europe. Just as we were falling asleep that first night, I could feel somebody poking around at the foot of my bed, raising the blanket up. It was the old lady. She had hot irons, wrapped in blankets, and she put one under my foot, and one under Brit's foot, to keep us warm. Oh, I said, I couldn't believe this; God, this is living!

And just as they went downstairs—they stayed in the cellar—the buzz bomb went over. You could hear the 'Rrr, rrr, rrr.' Everybody's saying, 'Keep going, keep going, keep going!' Because if [the sound] stops, you know it's going to come zooming right down. They were going into Reims, about 15 miles away, you could feel it when they hit, you could feel that jar. But that was heaven. They were so nice to us.

Later, the older girl said, 'Can you get me an extra sleeping bag?'

I said, 'Yeah. Okay.' I got it from the supply sergeant, he was a friend of mine. I gave it to her and then that was it. Word came down we were moving out, and we moved to outside of Saint Vith, and we went on an attack. That would be on the 28th of January, and it was snowing. We left early in the morning.

*

Our 3rd Battalion was leading in our area. J Company led first and we, H Company, would jump ahead, J Company would fall back, we kept [leapfrogging] like that. I Company would be next. The snow kept getting heavier and heavier and deeper and deeper. We were walking parallel, I looked down and I said, 'Look, we got company!' There was a bunch of Germans walking just below us. They were going the same way we were, and I don't think they ever saw us. We didn't see them [at first], either. So I said, 'Lieutenant Megellas,' I said, 'We got a lot of company here.' And boy he turned right around, just like a tomcat. Boy, it's just like we had rats cornered. They didn't want to fight, they surrendered. But he spaced our men right on them, we just closed right in on them, turned them over to the MPs. They picked them up, we left them there as prisoners.

We kept on going all that day. That's a long haul. I don't know how far we went. It was just knee-deep in snow, sometimes waist-deep. You didn't know where the heck you were, or how good it was, or whether there were [enemy] troops looking at you or waiting to ambush you. And then we heard them. When we stopped, Colonel Tucker got on my radio for a while there and he was talking to one of the other battalions. And a lot of the other officers had been saying, 'Oh, that colonel never knows what he's up to.' I verified it because he used my phone, my SCR300. The reason I remember it so well was that he had such poor procedure to talk on the radio. You would think he would have good radio procedure, you know, to talk and all. He just talked any old way he wanted, as long as he got his messages through.

At 4:30 p.m., as darkness began to blanket the knee-deep snow, it was decided that the battalion should stop for the night. Colonel Tucker had tried to get their bedrolls and packs, which had to be left hastily behind, brought up, but it wasn't going to happen. As a patrol returned and reported that the Germans seemed to be preparing a counterattack, Lt. Colonel Cook came up with the idea to attack first, with the hope of capturing the town for warm billets for the night.[10]

We learned that there were some [enemy] troops on the way to come attack us. One of the other guys said, 'I'll take the radio now.' We changed up. He took the radio, and I grabbed my tommy gun; I would be trying to patrol if I'm not with the captain or if I could get away from the captain, I would join a patrol. It was just something to do, you know, instead of just standing by idly.

The Mark V

I went on a patrol, and we took two [tank destroyers] with us, following us. We hit these guys head-on, it must've been a company of them, over 200, maybe about 300, [outside of Herresbach, Belgium.] Their tank didn't show up right away. We killed every one of them, it's hard to believe.

We went and got into Herresbach. Their tank came around the corner and he would have really done the business on us. But Megellas threw a hand grenade on the tracks and disabled it. He took a fragmentation grenade and he jumped up on the top, and he threw one down the hatch and disabled this Mark V tank all by himself, two grenades! That had never been done in World War II, which is one man with two Gammon grenades disabling a Mark V.

Now, they had around pretty close to two hundred guys killed. We never got one casualty in our company. They were going to put Megellas in for the Congressional Medal of Honor for knocking out the tank single-handedly, because he saved our company. That tank would have just really done a number on us because at that time, one of the TDs had gotten into the ditch and he was not in the position to fight them.

When we went into Herresbach, I was standing there at this burning building across the road and there was a tank right there, this knocked-out tank. I see this guy coming behind in the dark with his hands up. I said, 'Hey,' I said, 'we got a guy coming with his hands up.'

One of the guys said, 'Let's shoot him.'

I said, 'No, no.' I said, 'Let him come in. He wants to surrender. Let him come on in, there may be more out there.'

He came in, and he has his hands up in the air. And I could see the [Luger at his belt] right there. I said, 'Oh, there's my prize right there. I'm not shooting him.' He came right up, and just then this young whippersnapper, George Height, went right up, grabbed that Luger from his waist, and he surrendered. There was about seven others who then came out of the darkness to surrender. Now, you see, they waited. Had we shot that guy, they would have probably shot at us. They surrendered instead.

Height, he stayed in the army. He retired as a colonel, you know. And to this day I still rip him about that. He still gives me presents and favors. He said, 'I'm still beholden to you for that Luger.' [*Chuckles*] But you know, that was just one of those things. He was new, always following us around, when he joined the outfit during the Bulge. Lieutenant Megellas, we're still working on that Congressional Medal of Honor for him. At that time, General Gavin said he would get the Silver Star, but he said, 'We can't put him in for the Medal of Honor because there were no casualties.' At that time, now, you would think that would work in reverse. The first award never mentioned about him knocking off the tank, and then we had the award updated. We're still working on it, it's worded different now, and hopefully he'll get [the MOH] before he dies. He's 85 now. He's had one heart operation.

*

Anyway, we got out of that, but there was a lot of heavy fighting that following day. We spent that night clearing a lot of buildings of Jerries; we got a lot of prisoners, put them all in a big barn, put guys around them. Right after that incident about the seven guys that came out of the dark to give up, I went up to the farmhouse where they had come from, and here were all these tables, all filled with food. They were just getting ready to eat when [we caused] all this commotion. There was fried potatoes, there was brown bread. Of course, nobody likes brown bread. There's bacon there, I think there was eggs there, too. Anyway, boy, I sat right down there, we started eating just as the company commander and the first sergeant walk in and said, 'Tarbell, you're a hell of a man. You're a hell of a guy. You got all this food, and you don't tell us.' [*Laughs*] They sat down, and we ate. We got through eating, and this first sergeant said, 'Well, I hope the food wasn't poisoned!' [*Chuckles*]

Anyway, there was quite a bit of battle that day, and the following day, we had a lot of fighting, too. We were held up at one time by a bunker, they held up our whole outfit, machine guns, you know. They were traversing fire, but finally they ran out of ammunition. I was standing right by the bunker when they started coming out, had their hands raised up. They all wanted to surrender at a distance, and God, they were all older men. They showed us their wedding rings, they were giving us their wedding rings, and showing us their children's pictures and wives' pictures, you know. They thought we were going to kill them all, but we didn't, we just took them all prisoners, put them with the rest down there.

'It's Not My Time Yet'

Then we had some fierce fighting the following day, real bad fighting. I was all excited at the CP there, a couple of soldiers brought up a sleigh with two wounded German soldiers, and two German prisoners were pulling it. They were turned over to us. First sergeant said, 'Tarbell, grab somebody and take them to the medics.' I couldn't find anybody. He found a guy, said, 'Give Sergeant Tarbell a hand here, take these guys to the medics.' Okay, he walked over. First sergeant said, 'You go to the church, that's where the medics are located.' We went to the medics, and just as we got there a shell came in. It landed right in a snowbank. That's the last thing I remember because I was flying in the air. This other soldier that's helping me, guarding, he was between me and the church door. It blew us through the church door, and I come to.

I was lying on my back, and I could hear somebody say, 'Ugh,' like that.

This voice said, 'Well, he's gone, he's done.' I fell on my face. Somebody slapped me, said, 'Oh he's coming to, he'll be okay.'

I know they're talking about me, and I said, 'Oh my God, what the heck happened?' I checked to see if I have my limbs; I sat up and I looked at the guy who's next to me, obviously he's dead. He took the shot for me, you know. The concussion threw me right against him and through the door, we went through the door together. I was just thrown in the air, and he took all the pressure and it killed him. Do you know that I got up from there and I went right back to the first sergeant, I said, 'Who was that guy that just sat with me?'

He said, 'I don't know, I just grabbed him outside, because he was standing out there!' To this day, I still don't know who that guy was! There was no way I could find out because we were moving all the time, on the move. I think I had it narrowed down to one guy, I think was in G Company there, who died on that day, you know that one particular day.

Things like that, you know, happened. You wonder how the heck... to this day, I don't know what happened to my four prisoners, the two wounded journalists and the two guys, the two German prisoners who pulled the sleigh. For all I know, they might have got killed right there or they might have taken right off, I don't know. I never found out. That's what happened that one day there, it's just hard to figure out why the guy upstairs [decided] it's not my time yet.

The Siegfried Line

[In February], we ended up at Siegfried Line, and we had the bunkers to contend with.

One of the guys was very instrumental in getting [Germans in the bunkers to give up]. About the only way you could get those guys to surrender was if they ran out of ammunition, or if you could just coax them out of it. Fritz Toenjoest was one guy that was always instrumental in getting a lot of those guys out of there; one night, I think we had around ten or twelve bunkers surrounded, and he talked out the guys. He was German, born in St. Louis but of German descent, and he could speak German; I guess he told them there was no sense in fighting anymore. He was a good friend of mine, passed away a long time ago.

They say, 'Well, these German troops are inferior.' There is nobody inferior when you put him behind a loaded gun, I don't care who he is, there's no such thing as 'inferior troops.' That guy will shoot at you, and he will kill you. You go and you're still fighting him, you're still fighting a soldier.

We ended up fighting small skirmishes here and there, and we ended up near Aachen, Germany. In the latter part of February, we were supposed to make a river crossing there again, boy, nobody looked forward to that. We were practicing how to do that, and then we got [suddenly] relieved. That was unusual; we were going to make this mission and then they relieved us. We came by train back to France.

We went back to France, and we went to Lyon, France, this time. We started jumping in all of this and that. The new planes were coming out, we had to make a jump in this field here, and it was a beautiful jump. Everybody jumped, nobody got hurt except for the company commander, but the 508th, I think it was Headquarters Company, had a runaway plane, a runaway propeller, and it ran into a stick of guys and killed, I think, about six or seven guys. There were a bunch of dignitaries there watching that jump—I think Marlene Dietrich was there at that time.

The company commander broke his ankle, and everybody else came back saying, 'Wow, that guy refused to jump!' One of the guys wouldn't jump, he was endangering the whole plane, you know; he was going to face a court martial and ten years. Other than that, it was a very good jump. That evening, we were all back in Lyon in barracks. The captain was walking around with a homemade crutch. He said, 'Anybody want to jump tomorrow?'

I said, 'What are we going to jump for? We just got through jumping today.'

He said, 'The Army Air Force is here. They've got a new plane, and they want combat veterans to try it out, a C-46, it's got twin doors, one on each side. You can use both doors going out the same time, carry twice as many men.' First sergeant said, 'I'll volunteer to jump. Sergeant Shields will too.' He said, 'Give us a two-day pass [outside the zone], we'll take Fredericks with us.' He was the one who refused to jump, he was probably facing ten years.

'I'll think about it, but you can't go [outside the zone]. It's off limits.'

'We want to go there, nobody will bother us.'

'All right, but you stay out of trouble!' [*Chuckles*]

The next day, we jumped. I followed the jumpmaster, the lieutenant; Fredericks followed me,

Shields followed him. Beautiful jump, I could have landed standing up. I asked Fredericks, 'Why the hell didn't you jump?'

'Bah,' he said, 'I didn't feel like it yesterday!' [*Laughs*] He was one of those guys, you know, a little unpredictable. But he was a good soldier, in his own way.

Anyway, those are some of the things that happened there. I think we had Easter Sunday. We left right after that, I think around the fourth of April. We went back on the line, north of Cologne and the Rhine River, on the west side of the Rhine River. Of course, we didn't know what was happening at that time, but afterwards we found out that the 97th Infantry Division was coming down through the south, and that was always known as the Ruhr Pocket. Now, as they were working their way down south, our position was to hold the Germans from coming across the Rhine River, stay in that north pocket.

There were quite a few skirmishes there, and we had a funny thing happen there. We got word that there's a boatload of Germans coming over the

Rhine River under a flag of truce. There was a colonel, and a captain, and some enlisted men that crossed the river. They brought them over to our CP, the colonel to our CP, they sat down, we had their captain as an interpreter. He spoke beautiful English; he spoke better English than I did.

'We're here under flag, a truce, and we're protesting your forces shelling our hospital. We have a lot of wounded there!'

The company commander said, 'Well, that's not our department, but we got higher-ups coming.'

The guy from battalion showed up, and he said to the German colonel, 'Well, your fighting days are over!' They took him away, interrogated him at battalion or regiment, I don't know which, but they took him away from there.

Anyway, I ended up with the German captain interpreter. At that time, there was a *Yank* magazine on the table, with our General Gavin's picture on the front cover. I said, 'Read this, it's very interesting.'[20]

---

[20] *General Gavin-* James M. Gavin (1907-1990), third commander of the 82nd Airborne Division, was, at 37, the youngest major general to lead an American division in World War II. 'Jumpin' Jim' was known for taking part in combat jumps with his men, and the only general officer to do so four times.

And all this captain would say is, [*imitates pensiveness*] 'Very interesting. Very interesting.'

I said, 'Where did you learn such good English?'

'Oh,' he said, 'I used to be an editor of the English-speaking newspaper in Paris. 'That was my job,' he said, 'before the war.' I really loved talking to him.

So I noticed that when I first saw this colonel, the doctor, he had all kinds of decorations on him. Oh man. Oh man. And they said, 'Where are we going to put them for the night?'

I said, 'Well, you can sleep on my bunk.' I had my switchboard there and the radio there and my room was right next to it. I said, 'They can sleep in there.' I had my eye on that jacket; he's going to take his jacket off when he goes to sleep and hang it on that chair. He's going to end up without a jacket the next morning. Those decorations! [*Laughs*]

The Last Rhine Combat Patrol

That night we had to go to combat patrol, of all the times, we had to go on a combat patrol. They said, 'You're running combat patrol tonight with

Lieutenant Broadway.' Rufus Broadway, he was a new officer in the outfit. They said, 'They're going to put out the combat patrol and you're going to take your radio.'

I said, 'Okay.' So we went over the river in a boat, nice and quiet, nobody shot at us crossing the river—come to think of it, they must have thought that it was those Germans coming back, that boat, you know. When we got over there, even their foxholes were empty. We went onto the Bayer Aspirin plant; I think there was a Bayer plant right across from us.

There was a big viaduct there, we went on through, and then we got into a firefight further up, and they told us to hold tight right there; a little while later word came down, 'Head back for the boats.' But when we headed back for the boats, all those foxholes that were empty had soldiers in it this time; the Germans were in them and they were peppering us, you know shooting here and there. Just as I ran through the viaduct, the guy that was guarding me, his name was Fred Hoffman—on a patrol like that, all I could carry was the radio and my .45, no other weapon, so I'd have somebody guarding me, you know, in case I needed somebody to protect me—the fire came on through that viaduct; I just heard it and you could tell it was a machine gun burst. I got back to the boat and Fred was nowhere around, Hoffman was nowhere to be found. We think to this day that the machine gun burst got him, and you know the force of the shot pushed him right into the Rhine River, and the current was very strong. We never found him, never found his body.

We made it to the river. I started to get back on the radio to call back our situation, and I started to talk, and somebody said, 'Shut that goddamn thing off!' because, you know, as we're going down the river, everything's quiet and you could hear all over for miles.

'Stop that damn talking and keep quiet.'

The CP is saying, 'How come you don't talk? Give us your status report, give a status report!'

We had to sweat out getting shot by our own men when we finally got back to the other side, but we made it back all right.

I finally got back to my CP. I'm ringing wet from the Rhine River, the adrenaline. I lost my guard, he got killed, and there was the German colonel sleeping in my bunk, he's got his jacket on, he's got his arms folded right over it, like as if he was protecting everything he had on his chest. That was a hell of a night for me!

That was the last combat patrol of the Rhine River that we had. Two years ago, in Highlands, North Carolina, they brought that up. This Rufus Broadway is a retired doctor and he had us to his place in Highlands, North Carolina, and we had a nice get-together there. We had a beautiful get-together and we had a beautiful time.

Another thing that happened that I'll never forget, President Roosevelt died and we were in that holding position when he died. Everybody was so depressed. You know, what are you going to do? We didn't know who this Truman was, we never heard of him. How many of us are politicians? At 18, 19, 20 years old, you were right off the farm, or right off of high school and right into the Army, you're not into politics that much. We didn't know who the heck Truman was! That was one of the bad times, nothing you could do about it. We just stayed right in that area there, holding position.

Finally we got orders to move out, and we went by train from there to Hamburg, Germany. And from Hamburg we were trucked down to a small town on the Alt River, and we had a river crossing there, the pontoons were already in place. The 505th made the river crossing first, and when we got there, just as we got off the pontoon onto the dry land, we see this tank hit a mine on the road, and took this 40-ton tank and it just flipped it right over! That's how powerful the mine was. The Germans had planted sea mines and they had put detonators in there so that after maybe the 10th of each vehicle went over, it would set it off, so you didn't know when it was going to blow up, or where it was.

And so they said, 'Go over on the side, go over around it, and go alongside the road.' We had no sooner gone about 20 feet up ahead when a truck hit another mine and it blew the guys right out. I could see one guy, he looked like he must have been sitting in the back of the truck, it looked like if you threw a hat up in the air, you know, just flopping up in the air, and the truck went way up in the air! Boy that was [awful].

Now, we kind of had an idea that the war was going to end pretty soon, because we would hear Churchill's speeches on the radio every now and then, and he was pretty accurate. Usually what he told was the truth and it usually happened, so we knew the Russians were pushing hard on the Eastern front. Now, we really were [moving fast], and we started getting more prisoners giving up to us; groups, maybe platoon-sized.

We started getting jeeps up there to ride in. I said, 'God, this is the way to fight a war.' It was walking and running, and we were riding in jeeps across this open field; there was a whole line of us, we got to the end of this open field and there was a little bit of woods, and behind the woods there was three Tiger tanks sitting there! That's when I knew, I said, 'Hey, this war's winding down.' Those guys could have had a field day with us. They could have just wiped us right out.

So we went from one town to the other. One place there was a whole company, their platoon all lined up, ready to surrender to us. And then another time we kept on going, the truck traffic kept getting heavier, and heavier, and heavier. At one point, I don't know whether it was that same day, I think it was, or it might have been the day after, we got to this one point where it got so bad, we put outposts out to direct traffic. Zimmerman, myself, and George Height was with me again, it seems like everywhere I went he was with me, following me, so we directed traffic. 'Vehicles to your right, walk on foot to your left.' Those German guys were throwing their weapons away, and this and that, and oh man. And they even had a calvary ride through [to surrender], God, beautiful horses. But some of these solders were pathetic, you know, worn out, clothes worn and torn, beat up, you know, tired, battle worn.

Towards about dark, a staff car pulled up and out got, you know how you see in movies, German officers, got shiny boots on, got shiny long leather jackets on, the whole nine yards of it—that's the way these guys were dressed. One said, in perfect English, he said, 'Where is your general's command post? This is the commanding general here!'

From what I gathered after, it must've been the commanding general of that 21st German Army that surrendered to us. They wanted to surrender to us instead of to the Russians, to get out of the path of the Russians as they were coming in.

So I said, 'What do you want to see our general for?'

He said, 'This is the commanding general here, we're going back there with your general, and we're going to regroup and fight the Russians!'

I looked at Zimmerman [*turns head, makes incredulous expression*]. I looked at Height, and I said, 'Well, I'll tell you what you do, you just go right down this road here, to my right,' I said, 'there's some MPs down the road, they'll show you right where to go.' And I think that was the commanding general of the 21st German Army. They looked like they were in pretty good shape. We laughed, but they were serious. They probably were put in prison; our general wouldn't have had anything to do with them.

General Gavin commented on the incident, and what would follow, in his 1978 war memoir.

By midafternoon, I arrived at the charming German village of Ludwigslust in Mecklenburg. The streets were jammed with retreating German soldiers and their camp followers. Young and old, crippled and wounded, robust and ailing, men and women, but mostly men, were trying to get through the town to go to our rear.

Adding to the confusion were civilians and shopkeepers, piling whatever they owned in wagons and small handcarts, their faces stricken with fear for what would happen if the Russians were to capture them. Our troopers were attacking just beyond the town, and more were coming up. I was standing near the curb of a main street intersection, wearing a parachute jumpsuit faded from three years of war, carrying an M-1 rifle over my shoulder, looking like any other GI in the 82nd, except for the two stars on my collar and on my helmet.

An American GI came up to me and said that there was a German general looking for the American general who was in charge. I told him to send him over. He arrived, rather haughtily, I thought, and a bit threadbare, but otherwise impeccably attired in the field gray uniform of the Wehrmacht. It was set off by the red collar tabs and insignia of a general, and an Iron Cross dangled at his throat. When told that I was the American general, he looked at me with some disdain, saying that I couldn't be; I was too young and did not look like a general to him. It took only a moment to change his mind.

In the meantime, Von Tippelskirch came to my Command Post in the Palace, which, as it turned out, was a resplendent building, the like of which we had not seen at any time during the war. Von Tippelskirch offered to surrender his army group to us, making a specific point that he would surrender to me and that I was to tell the Russians to cease their attacks. Of course, I had no control over what the Russians would do, although I had already established contact with them, so I told him he would either surrender unconditionally or I would continue to attack until I joined the

Russians. The surrender document was typed while he and his staff stood about. When he signed it, he added in longhand, in very soldierly fashion, I thought, that it was to be effective upon entry into the American lines. The meeting had been cold and very proper.

By the time we reached Germany, there was much ill feeling on the part of the troopers toward the German military establishment. On that eventful day, a complete army group surrendered to the 82nd Airborne Division, more than 150,000 troops with all of their impedimenta. At dawn the next day I learned that the Mayor of Ludwigslust and his wife and daughter had committed suicide. I was shocked and puzzled. I could think of no reason for their suicide. From the day we crossed the German frontier, we had been anxious that our troopers behave properly and that they be in no way abusive to non-combatants. It was difficult to understand why, when the war came to an end, these three would commit suicide. It was two days later that we discovered the reason.

One could smell the Wöbbelin Concentration Camp before seeing it. And seeing it was more than a human being could stand. Even after three years of war it brought tears to my eyes. Living skeletons were scattered about, the dead distinguishable from the living only by the blue-black color of their skin compared to the somewhat greenish skin, taut over the bony frames of the living. There were hundreds of dead about the grounds and in the tarpaper shacks. In the corner of the stockade area was an abandoned quarry into which the daily stacks of cadavers were bulldozed. It was obvious they could not tell many of the dead from the living.[11]

On May 2, 1945, the 82nd Airborne Division and the 8th Infantry Division stumbled across the Wöbbelin concentration camp, a subcamp hastily established in 1945 to house prisoners being evacuated from other camps as the Red Army advanced in the east and the other Allies in the west. Living conditions were unfathomable; the GIs found nearly a thousand dead inside the gates.[12]

Mr. Tarbell and the 504th were some of the first soldiers on the scene.

The next day, near V-E Day, we started exploring around the city of Ludwigslust, and our company ran into a German concentration camp. It was not a concentration camp in the word, say, it was a starvation camp. It was called Wöbbelin, and my buddy, Shields, shot the lock off [on the gate]; we went in.

There were no ovens there—it was a starvation camp, where they brought the slave labors, a lot of political prisoners, and what have you. Germans, different nationalities, there were a lot of French Jews; I don't think there were any Russians in there, but there were Polish. Some Dutch people in there. They just starved their people there; we walked in there—it was, oh God, pathetic; you could just see... [*pauses*]; just bones, you know. You couldn't feed them. Somebody gave somebody something to eat, and they died. It killed them because they're not used to food.

I went into one building there, and you couldn't tell the living from the dead, because when they died, they had their eyes wide open. The starving guys are the same way, they look the same way. Couldn't tell them apart.

In the latrine, they had an open latrine there, guys were floating in there, so they must've gone to the bathroom and probably fell in there, and drowned in there, what have you. There'd be a pile of seven or eight deep, dead, and they hadn't got a chance to get rid of them, in mass graves or whatever.

It was just one of those things that the general would say, 'Hey, my God, I guess that's what we're fighting this war for.' It's an awful thing. Never forgot it.

We got back to the States, and you know I mentioned it and nobody believed me. They just said, 'Ahh, you're probably making it up,' you know. That's the way it used to be, you know. 'Oh, you're making it up,' probably. It wasn't until the Jewish people talked about the Holocaust that they said, 'Oh my God, they really had that?'

I said, 'They sure did!' Never left me! I always remember right to this day what I saw there. It's just unbelievable! You can't—their bodies, they weren't burnt. There weren't any ashes. There were bodies, they were alive maybe a day ago, maybe a few hours ago. They're starved to death! They died of starvation; you know how bad we feel when we miss one or two meals. Three meals, how bad we feel. These guys were worked and then starved.

The mayor there said that they [did their best], that the people there didn't know nothing about this. I understood in later years, that they were supposed to make sure that those people had food there, the mayor of that town, because it was in his district. They had plenty of food there, but the prisoners were never given none. [General Gavin] made all the people walk through there, through this place, and then right in the center square of the town of Ludwigslust, they buried a lot of these people right there. They would see, all the civilians, everybody, all of Ludwigslust, what happened there. They made all the people go through there.

The mayor killed his wife, his daughter, and then committed suicide. Killed his family, then himself.

You can't explain it, you know what I mean? Unless you've seen it, how bad it is. It's very, very bad. It was very bad. We felt bad. What are you going to do? All you can do is just go and get loaded. A lot of us did that. [*Raises eyebrows slightly, slowly nods head, knowingly*] We did that for years and years later, too, because nobody listened to you anyway if you told them, after the war was over, it was entirely a different thing, you know. They forget that very fast.

Then when Holocaust [awareness] came along, then the people realize that that actually happened, and that you were part of it.

On May 7, 1945, funeral services were authorized and conducted by the 82nd in the center of the town of Ludwigslust, in accordance with Eisenhower's directive that 'all atrocity victims be buried in a public place,' with appropriate grave markers and a stone monument to memorialize the dead. Captured German officers, town citizens, and hundreds of paratroopers were in attendance. The US Army chaplain's eulogy stated,

> The crimes committed here in the name of the German people and by their acquiescence

were minor compared to those to be found in concentration camps elsewhere in Germany. Here there were no gas chambers, no crematoria; these men of Holland, Russia, Poland, Czechoslovakia, and France were simply allowed to starve to death. Within four miles of your comfortable homes, 4,000 men were forced to live like animals, deprived even of the food you would give to your dogs. In three weeks 1,000 of these men were starved to death; 800 of them were buried in pits in the nearby woods. These 200 who lie before us in these graves were found piled four and five feet high in one building and lying with the sick and dying in other buildings.[13]

It would be years before the unimaginable extent of the Holocaust would be known, and to some measure, our knowledge of the greatest crime in the history of the world is still unfolding. The GIs were now sudden witnesses, without an audience who would believe them later on back home. There would be consequences, and trauma would be passed down.

CHAPTER FOURTEEN

The Cavalryman II

After recovering from trying to save his burning friend, young Tim Horgan made it across the Rhine, which he would revisit later in life. He also became involved in a famous rescue mission.

Timothy J. Horgan

Hitting the Rhine

Right after the Battle of the Bulge, we started going fast across Germany on the south side, because the First Army was up north, and we were in the middle, the Third Army, and the Seventh Army was on the south side of us. [The weather had cleared], the skies opened up [from being] all cloudy, snowy, and miserable, and then you had the P-47 planes come around strafing. What they would do is come down and take a look at the troops moving, come down and strafe them, the enemy troops, hopefully. [*Chuckles*] So to distinguish between us and the enemy, they issued us linoleum cloth, maybe about eight foot wide by three feet. And it had straps on the end, and we put those on our vehicles, and every day it was a different color. It was the color of the rainbow—there was a red one, there was an orange one, there was a blue one, there was a white one. We had to strap them on our vehicles so when the planes would come in and try to look for the enemy and strafe the enemy, they would spot us and then they wouldn't spray us; we had that for maybe about two months, because every day we were out in front doing the spearheading, reconnaissance—you know, go out and find out what's out there and draw the fire first, thank you. [*Laughs*] So, a little hairy, but remember I'm only 19 years old, so I can handle something like that, thank God.

Then we hit the Rhine, I crossed the Rhine in Frankfurt. When we entered Frankfurt, I can remember that was the first time I had a shower in three or four months. The outfit come on in and set up a great big tent that had showers all along it, so you go ahead and take your clothes off in the pile, get your shower, come out the other end and pick up clean clothes, look for your sizes and so on. [*Laughs*] But we crossed the Rhine in Frankfurt, and then we kept going through Germany and actually we were on our way to Prague in Czechoslovakia; I was about forty, fifty miles inside Czechoslovakia when the war ended.

The Concentration Camp

At the end of April, I was sent to the Czech border, and all of a sudden, this one day we are going through and come into this town, and come across this concentration camp, Flossenburg. I don't know if you are familiar with all of the concentration camps there, but that was one of the ones. We liberated it. That, my boys, is a sight you [don't] want to see, really. Did you ever see the movie *Schindler's List,* by Stephen Spielberg? He did a very good portrayal of it. Remember the *Band of Brothers* series? On one of those tapes in there is the concentration camps, and that's a true story. I don't know how anybody can say that that was false, it was all made up. I saw it! [*Points to his own eyes*] Well, we got in there and I'll elaborate on that.

I drove the M-8—it's like a scout car—and there were ten of us in the team. We had a lead jeep with three guys and a mounted 30 caliber machine gun, then the scout car, which was four of us—my commander, the gunner, radioman, and me as the driver—and then a third vehicle behind us was a mortar jeep. That's how we patrolled the roads, highway, back roads, two-lane roads, whatever. We got in the town and then we saw the concentration camp; the Germans from the camp were going out the other side of town from where we came in. But we got up there and [the prisoners] were so excited to see us, they wanted to get out, naturally, because they [knew they were now] liberated. But my sergeant was of Polish descent, and he grew up in the Detroit, Michigan, area, and he could talk conversational Polish. These people always had a couple of languages they could talk, and one of them was Polish. And he tells them, 'Okay, you are safe, you are liberated, but we can't let you out.' Because really if we had let them out, they would have run down the street, and after a hundred yards they would have fallen right on their faces, dead, because they were so weak and so excited.

So we kept them in there and I [took] my canteen of water and just give them, each one a little sip of that water, unscrewed that little cap you had on it, just give them a little sip of water. We broke our rations and gave them a little bit because they were so hungry, and they couldn't eat or drink that much. So they ate, and we told them the [MPs] were going to come the next day and let them out and take care of them. But it was my sergeant, he could talk the language, and he calmed them down a little bit. That was Flossenburg, the concentration camp, and right after that we got into Czechoslovakia on our way to Prague.

The Russians

All of a sudden, we get orders to stop—we can't advance anymore—which now I know from history, it was the Yalta Conference that Roosevelt, Churchill, and Stalin had divided up Europe. The Soviets were going to get Austria, Czechoslovakia, and then eastern Germany. The United States was going to get the southern part of western Germany, the British were going to be the north part of Germany, and Berlin was going to be split in three zones: the Russians, the British, and the Americans. Now you always know the Berlin Wall and all of that story, but that's the reason why we couldn't, that we had to stop. I was in the town of Klatovy in Czechoslovakia, and we couldn't go any further. So our colonel went ahead and got our F troop, which is a tank troop, and he put them on the outskirts of town, and he said, 'Don't let any Russian come in here.'

We couldn't advance, and it was only a day and a half, and we could have been in Prague; we would have liberated Prague. We couldn't go, so we had to wait until the Russians came to us. The next morning we look up and there are all these American flags. Now all of the European cities have a town square and there we are in that town square, and on all the buildings on the town square were American flags because we liberated the town. After a day or two, the Russians come into Prague and liberated Prague, we wake up the next morning we see all the American flags are down and all the [Soviet] flags are up, because the Russians liberated their capital.

After a couple more days the refugees didn't want to stay under Russian rule; they were migrating west to come over to Germany to come under United States rule, and they started bringing some stories with them, how the Russians treated them when they went into Prague. They trashed the place! The Russian soldier himself is a different breed; they didn't have any food, and they were really rough, tough. So they started coming across the border with these stories of what the Russians are doing; the next morning we wake up, the Russian flags are down, the American flags are back up because they liked how we treated them, and the stories changed [the locals'] minds. [*Laughs*] But then we had to pull back, we had been about forty miles into Czechoslovakia. That is where we stayed for the rest of the summer, on border patrol between Germany and Czechoslovakia; control the movement of refugees going back and forth. So that's where I wound up, in Czechoslovakia on May 8 when the war was over. You don't know what day of the week it is, you don't even hardly know what month it is. And all they do is we had to have, well, there was movement going on. The actual story, which I have now in my book, my history book when I go back, it was our sister squadron in the cavalry, and it only made up maybe about three to four hundred in each squadron. That makes up the group, so there was only about 800 of us and it was our sister squadron there under Captain Steward. He led this task force in there to, well, we... let me track it back.

Rescuing the Lipizzaners

[Shortly before the war ended], we captured a German general, and through his interrogation, he told us about a prisoner of war camp in Czechoslovakia in Hostau, Czechoslovakia. It was made up of American, British, French, and Polish prisoners of war. There were also a thousand horses in there, too, and about two hundred of them Lipizzaners. So as soon as he had mentioned the Lipizzaner breed, my colonel's ears popped up. He immediately called Patton, who said, out of spite, 'Get them, go!'

So Captain Stewart in our sister squadron led this task force of three to four hundred men, and he went into Hostau to go ahead and liberate the prisoner of war camp, and we did. Then we went ahead and got those horses out of there and we brought them into Schwarzburg, Germany, where there was a German horse breeding camp. The Germans knew the value of the Lipizzaners; the Russians, forget it! [Most would have just] cut the horses up for horsemeat. So we went ahead and got them into Schwarzburg; I was just giving support, I know that we got orders to clear this road, secure that town, so that there were no pockets of Germans around at all and be sure there were no land mines on the roads, there are no trees dropped across the road.

The biggest trick that the Germans had was stringing wire across a road, from one tree to the other tree, and if you remember your World War II pictures of the vehicles, you see that L-iron that they had in the front of the bumpers. Well, there was a reason for it, because most of the guys driving the jeeps would have their windshields folded down, so going down a road, you wouldn't see a wire, and all of a sudden, you'd catch it right there and be decapitated. [*Whistles and gestures at neck*] So that is why all of those vehicles had that L-iron with a little hook on the top, so if they did catch the wire, it would break the wire. So that was our job: be sure the roads are clear, that all the tunnels are cleared.

We did have one segment up there, our task force went in, where there was a little pocket of SS troops and they gave a little resistance, but thankfully we had more firepower than they did, so it didn't last too long, and they gave up. So that was our one little discovery, [their major concern being] these little pockets of Germans, that if you bring the convoy out, it would get ambushed. So that's my involvement of the Lipizzaner rescue, giving them support to be sure that they could get out of Czechoslovakia and into Germany. And then about the third week of May, the war had ended, and we had the horses up there, had a couple of veterinarians come in, and we transported them back into the Spanish Riding School in Vienna. We saved that breed.

I didn't realize it at the time. All I knew is we had a job to do, go out and clear this road, so that was my own involvement, but I didn't realize exactly what was going on until I could get into the history. But here in my [division history] book, in July of '45, when the war was over, we had the Russian Cossacks come in and put on a show for us. We are cavalry, and the Russian Cossacks are cavalry, and so there is a relationship between horse lovers. The pictures here aren't clear because they are too far away, but they were out there doing all of their tricks, horses go jumping to one side, the other side, and riding them and all that stuff, so I saw that in July, see, but I didn't realize what we were doing until after I could start reading some history. Then I put it all together.

All that rest of the summer, we were on border patrol between Germany and Czechoslovakia, regulating any movement of the refugees coming across the border; we were one week out on the border, there was a small little town in that area where we were billeting. So we'd go out a week, [come back] in a week, go out a week, and [then back] a week. Then in October, I finagled a five-day pass, but instead of going to Berchtesgaden in the Alps to go skiing—hell, I'm a Brooklyn boy, I don't know skiing—I elected to go to Paris. So I got on a train and went into Paris; I was in Paris for three days, and I had a cousin who was in Munich. So I said, 'Hey, I'll go from Paris to Munich.' I went on down to Munich and I looked him up and he was an officer, and he was in charge of the movie theatres in Munich for the GIs there, it was his job after the war was over. In Munich, you had town squares and there is an opera house in Munich that Hitler used to come on down to, the famous [Munich] Opera. So he would come into the opera a lot of times, and a lot of the time he would stay in this apartment right across the square from the opera house; it's this restaurant [at that time]. I asked a couple of GIs and they directed me on over to this restaurant. I asked the GI at the desk at the front, I said, 'Where's Lieutenant Malave?'

'Oh, he's down there.'

So I come in, it was a great big banquet hall type room, and it was at mealtime, dinner, so I went down there, and I surprised him. He was staying up—I think it was on the third floor or whatever—in this apartment. That was the apartment that Hitler used to rent out and stay! And it was only one bedroom and a living room and a galley kitchen. They set up a cot for me in the galley kitchen, and that's where I slept that night. My cousin had just got back from Ireland a week or two before that, and he brought back an Irish quart of whiskey. He intended to bring it home with him as a souvenir from Ireland; he told me about all the cousins over in Ireland—the word spread so fast he was there, he said, that they were coming over hills and dales, a ton of them he had never met, 50, 75 of our cousins came right out to greet him! So at any rate, he said to me, 'I can't keep this bottle, we're Irish.' We opened it up, and him and his two buddies who lived with him, the four of us, polished off the quart of Irish whiskey that night. [*Laughs*]

From Munich, I went back up to my outfit up at the Czech border. That was in October, and then about the middle of November I had the points. See at that time in order to come on home there was a point system; there was the high, medium, and low. If you had high points, which was all governed on the number of months that you are over in Europe, and number of months you were in combat or whatever, they made up the points. If you had high points, you come on back to the States in May, June, and get discharged. The low points, they took and transferred them back through the States and were going to send them down to Japan and the South Pacific to fight that war. The middle group was just in limbo waiting for these two groups to be processed to the States. So that is why it took me up until the end of November, when they assigned me to the 90th Infantry Division, on their way to come home. You have to go into a division group.

I left Marseilles, France, on December 8. I landed in New York the 26th of December, one day after Christmas! It took us so long because of this hurricane out in the Atlantic, and it's only a little Liberty ship, about 400 guys on it, and we had to skirt around the hurricane, so it took us four or five days longer to get around. So I come into New York harbor, the 26th of December. We were coming in—I was born down in Brooklyn, as I told you, also [lived] down in Rockaway—I don't know if you are familiar at all with the city, but that's right on the ocean. All the ships coming and going in New York harbor [would go by], you could look out because between there and Jersey is twenty miles, and the ships would come in from the Atlantic there—you could see the ships coming in from a far-off distance, maybe ten, twelve miles away. Here I came in on the ship, and could see where I was brought up down there, right on the beach of Rockaway. Came around the end, and there's Shore Road, Brooklyn, that's where I lived, that was only three blocks off the bay! And here I am and... [*sighs*]. But I'm home anyway. So we go and dock up in Jersey, go on down to Fort Dix to get processed and get discharged. By then it was all over with. It was the middle of August that the atomic bomb was being dropped, the two of them were being dropped then, and that saved a good million GI lives. Oh yes, that ended that war real fast. Real fast. So you know the war was over, so I had no fear there. I was thinking, now what am I going to do after service?

As I told you, I had gone to Saint Francis Prep, in Brooklyn at the time, so I went back to them and I asked them, you know I'd like to go to college, but I can't go in the city because I don't think I'd ever be able to make it living at home because I had to change my environment. So they said [to consider] Saint Bonaventure, our sister college up there, it's another Franciscan college, in western New York, or we have this other new one that just opened up a couple of years ago in '39, Siena outside of Albany.

So I had the GI Bill and went on up, applied for Siena, and I got into Siena in January of '47. I graduated in August of '50, three and a half years; I didn't want to spend too much time in college [because] when I was a junior, going to be my senior year, I got married on August 27 of '49; so when I was a senior I was married and graduated in August of '50. I came up here and I've lived here since. My wife had gone to nursing school at Saint Vincent's Hospital in New York City, so I met her down there, and she was up here when I was going to school. I would come up here on the weekends and, boy, they didn't have dorms in Siena at the time, just boarding in private homes, so I had a room in a private home. But on the weekends, I would come up to Glens Falls and stay over here in my wife's family home and things took off. We got married, had three boys [*Describes his family, with pride*]. Yeah, it keeps me going, glad to have them. [*Chuckles*]

Return to the Rhine

My second son and I went over to Europe in '94 to celebrate the 50th anniversary of World War II. We went to London, Paris, Luxembourg City, Munich, and Frankfurt on a ten-day whirl. That was quite an experience because I always wanted to go back over and see Germany; Germany is a beautiful country. In fact, I had one memory [from my time in Germany in World War II] which I had on my mind. Now when we hit the Rhine River, there was a road going along the west side of the river. A couple of buddies and I got up in this hotel, went up to the seventh floor, and they all had these little balconies outside of the windows. Now this is about the beginning of March, I guess. Now we go on up, we get out there and stand on the balcony, and here it is, a beautiful spring morning [in the middle of a war]. It was early—seven, eight o'clock—and you could just smell the spring air, and I looked up. Look to the right and there, down south of the Rhine River, or go to the left and look up to the north of the Rhine River, and I said, 'This is a beautiful country!' And I always wanted to go back and see it, and sure enough, I did.

Tim Horgan passed away on February 20, 2013, at the age of 88.

Nineteen-year-old Richard Marowitz hamming it up with Hitler's dress hat, 1945.
Source: Richard Marowitz.

CHAPTER FIFTEEN

The Recon Man II

Rich Marowitz, with a flair for humor and magic tricks, invokes a more serious tone discussing a transformative event shared by many GIs—the liberation of the concentration camp at Dachau. Set up in 1933 as one of the first concentration camps for perceived enemies of the Reich, it now burst at the gates with over 30,000 inmates and freight cars full of dead.

Richard M. Marowitz

The First Ones in Dachau

I'll tell you, we were the first ones in Dachau. Dachau was the only camp that had to be fought for. I don't know if you know that. The other, Buchenwald, and all these other camps, were walkovers. The Germans just left. The Germans didn't want to just leave Dachau, maybe because it was the oldest camp in Germany. It was in Germany. But they were giving us a pretty hard time, even dropped some 88s on us. We were pinned in the ditch. Of course, we got there a long time before anybody else did. So, we were waiting for the troops to come up to us. [Dachau was the objective], but of course, they never told us anything. They got us up in the morning, and they said, 'Here's your new map. There's Dachau. Go. You have to make contact with the tail end of the 20th Armored and be liaison between the 20th Armored and the infantry who are coming down.' Two-and-a-half-ton trucks were having a race, with the 3rd Division on the left, and the 45th Division on the right, and we [the 42nd] have to win.

Every five minutes, they called us on the radio and said, 'Where are you? What are your grid coordinates?' They said, 'What's taking you so long?'

So, we finally stopped, and lieutenant said, 'This is the way it is, guys. If we're going to be tactful about this thing, we're going to lose the race, and they're going to kill us. Our own officers are going to kill us.' He said, 'Or, we can just step on the gas and go like hell.'

So, we said, 'Let's step on the gas and go like hell.' The rest of it was like a bad movie. It really was. I mean, we went through one village and the Germans fired a panzerfaust over our head and blew us right out of the jeep. We dispatched them quickly and we got back in the jeep and took off again. These are the kinds of things that happened on the way to Dachau. That little town where we got the 200 prisoners, that's why we told them to walk back. We didn't have time for those guys. We had to get on the road.

Now, it's not uncommon to smell death. Different areas, you smell different things depending on what's going on; usually, it was farm animals that were killed, who had been strafed, they were bombed, or whatever, and they're bloated and they're rotting in the fields, and it stinks terrible. It just smells like hell. As we got closer to Dachau, we didn't discuss it. We were used to that. We all thought the same thing. We never talked about it, but later on afterwards, after the fact, we realized that we all thought the same thing—we figured we're coming to another bombed-out farm with a bunch of dead animals. That's what we thought! Nobody ever told us it was a concentration camp! There is a village of Dachau. So, on the map, we saw a village of Dachau. We were going to take the village. That's all we knew.

*

We cut one German convoy right in half. It was on a crossroad. We went through it, firing as we went, and they just went off the road. They didn't know what the... We weren't supposed to be there! So, what happened, they were fighting to get up to us because we raised so much sand on the way to Dachau that they had trouble getting to us. All of a sudden, we're pinned in this ditch, and an M4 tank comes out of Dachau. We jumped up out of the ditch, and the tank gun came down on us. It was a captured tank! Fortunately, one of our tank destroyers came up behind us and blew it away just in the nick of time. That day was the first time I kissed the tank destroyer, but that was a scary moment.

The Rainbow took Dachau. You can take my word for it, because we went in the main gate. The 45th came in the back end. They still think that they took Dachau. It has been proven, and it's been certified, that Rainbow did take Dachau. I can vouch for that. I saw a film on the History Channel, one of those channels, Discovery, and it was all 45th Division and how they went into Dachau from the back and the railroad side, and you get all the other jazz. Their officers all remarked, 'It was so quiet when we entered.' Well, sure, it was quiet when they went in because we got finished fighting before they got there.

So lieutenant colonel, the commander of the 2nd Battalion—great guy, tough as nails—he was sitting on the top of that tank destroyer, took a ride in on the tank destroyer. We're next to this farmhouse. He said, 'Did you clear the house?'

We said, 'No, sir.'

'Clear the house!' Well, snipers were all over the place. So, our job initially was to clear out the snipers, so we knocked off a number of snipers and took 25 prisoners out of the basement of that house who were more scared than we were, and we took three SS prisoners. One of them was really driving us crazy. He was in another house just up the street a little bit, and he was really giving us a hard time, so we finally did away with him, and when we got up into the house, he couldn't have been more than eleven or twelve years old, a squirt. Hitler Youth. They were just so brainwashed; we ran into a lot of those kids in their short pants.

On the siding, you saw pictures of it in the slides, outside of the camp, adjacent to the camp, there were actually forty boxcars of bodies and we found one man alive in that forty...there are some pictures of that one man, I don't know whether he survived or not. The prisoners were just walking skeletons, and they just dropped where they were and died. There were piles of bodies, of bodies that had been gassed and readied for the ovens. Some of them still lived because those boxcars were brought to Dachau to burn those bodies. It was a total mess. And the smell was not a farm; it was Dachau that we had smelled miles before we got there.

Well, as soon as I saw what the camp was... you really can't describe it. You really can't. It's not possible, it's not possible to describe it at all. But I'll never forget the 29th of April, 1945, I can tell you that. We didn't know anything about a concentration camp, and on the siding before you even get into the camp, there were forty boxcars of bodies.

[We also picked up] these two little Greek Jewish boys who were with us for a while, doing chores, washing, et cetera. Eventually, both got to Canada. Then one of them died, and the other I lost track of, and he ended up in Israel. At a Rainbow reunion in Seattle in 1995, one of my guys had gone over to Israel for a wedding and looked up Marcel. He had just retired himself; he had a wonderful family, did well in business, and Marcel treated them to dinner at his house. He then went into another room and came out with our

Rainbow map with all our names on it! So I said, 'Did you get a copy of it?' We had all lost our maps.

He said, 'No!'

I said, 'You may have done well in real estate, but you're too stupid to try to get a copy?'

So Sid said, 'I'll call him up.' So eventually, I got a copy of the map, which you can hardly read. It's a terrible copy, but I have it.

'I'm Throwing Her Down the Stairs!'

I'll also not forget the next day, the 30th of April, 1945, because twelve of us went into Munich before the rest took the town. A couple of our spies, or whatever the hell they were—I really don't know what they were—knew where Hitler's house was. We went to Hitler's house hoping, though we knew he wouldn't be there, but we were hoping... The town was ready to give up. Actually, in the afternoon, we just rolled in, we had no problem with it. These guys said, 'Don't worry about it. The town is not taken yet, but there's SS snipers in there.'

We went in there. We really didn't have much trouble, got to Hitler's house and banged on the door, and he had an English housekeeper who called us ruffians. 'Why is everybody so mad at Mr. Hitler, he's such a fine man.' My buddy Herb Herman said, 'I'm throwing her down the stairs!' He had a couple of other little words in there besides. [*Chuckles*]

I said, 'Forget it. Let's check out this joint and get the hell out of here.' You know, you're not comfortable when you're the only ones in town. So, we went through the place.

I ran into a bedroom. I didn't know whose bedroom it was, but it was gorgeous. Well, the whole place was nice. The furniture was all intact and the pictures were on the wall and the stuff was on the desks and everything was there. I went in and I opened up all the drawers, and they were empty, and the closet was empty, but I saw something dark in an upper shelf. I dragged over a chair and reached up and got it. It was the most gorgeous top hat I ever saw. I pulled it from the shelf and when I looked inside, in big, bold gold letters were the initials **A. H.** I could put two and two together.

It also stands for something else. [*Laughs*] I could picture his head in the hat, and I remember leaping from the chair where I stood, onto the hat, and jumped up and down upon it, repeatedly. I stomped it. It wasn't a collapsible hat, but it is now; as a matter of fact, I have it in the case, I thought you might be interested in seeing it.

Richard Marowitz and the inside of Adolf Hitler's hat.
Source: Richard Marowitz.

Now Herb tells me I walked out of his bedroom with the hat on my head and the comb under my nose and then walking around like Hitler, and the hat now has a life of its own. Shortly after, I heard Hitler committed suicide [that day]. Herb said that it was because he pictured a skinny Jewish kid from Brooklyn walking around with his hat on. [*Laughs*] It was a good day.

'These Things Come Naturally'

And then we were out of there. See, I&R is a peculiar situation. The war wasn't quite over. It was almost over, but it wasn't quite over. You get into a place and you take it, and right away, you got new orders. 'Go check out the road to...', and you're off again. They never even saved billets for us when we would get back. Well, first of all, they never knew if we were getting back, because we had a 75% turnover rate in our platoon. We would get back and report in, and they'd pick our brains and would ask a lot of questions, and then we would go out and liberate a house somewhere, kick some family out, and take over the house, and go to sleep, but we always left a man on guard with a radio.

[The replacements] have to depend on us more than we're going to depend on them. We want to be able to depend on them because we don't have a hell of a lot of guys. So, you bring them in and you do what you can with them right away. I'll never forget the day I went back to headquarters to pick up a replacement. I look at this guy. I have his name, Fritz Krinkler, and I look at this guy, and this guy is German. He still had a German accent. I'm bringing him. I said to him, 'Did you get tangled into the wrong outfit here?'

'No.'

So, I dumped him in a jeep, and I'm taking him back to the platoon. He said, 'Rich, I don't know what to do.'

'What's your problem?'

He said, 'Well, I'm from here.' His father got the family out just before Hitler slammed the door. He was able to get them out because he was German. He somehow got the family out just before it was not possible to get out anymore, and they got to the States. Fritz went to school for a few years, got drafted, came back over. He said, 'I have relatives here, Rich. I have relatives. I have friends. I have family here. I can't shoot at these people. How am I supposed to do it?'

'Don't even think about it.'

'Why not?'

I said, 'Because these things come naturally.' Of course, the next day, it came naturally because we ran into a situation. The Germans were hollering for us to give up. One of the guys, little Jackie

Walker, was stuck in the ditch by one of the jeeps, and he couldn't move. They had him zeroed in. We got into a little clump of woods, and Fritz followed me. I'm the one that picked him up. He knew me the best. So, he followed me up into the woods, and he said, 'Hey, I dropped my gun. I don't have a weapon.' So, I had a .45 that I was dying to give to somebody anyway, because that is the worst thing that was ever invented.

I said, 'Here, take this. Keep it.'

So, he's sticking the cigarettes out. I said, 'Don't smoke!'

He said, 'What's the matter?'

'The smell of smoke carries. There's a little breeze. You can see the smoke. Just sit with your back against that tree, and I'll sit with my back against this tree. You'll check me out and I'll check out.'

'Why? Where?'

'You hear them hollering up there, but that doesn't mean there aren't some people coming down around in the woods here. Just keep your eyes open and listen.'

'Okay.' He said, 'Well why are we here? We can get to the couple of jeeps that haven't come out of the woods yet. We can get out of here.'

'No, we can't.'

'What do you mean we can't?'

'Because we never leave anybody.' I said, 'Jackie is stuck in the ditch.'

'But we can get out.'

I said, 'Let me say it another way. If you were stuck in the ditch, would you want us to leave you?'

'Forget I said anything.'

He said, 'So what are we going to do?'

I said, 'Well, the getaway jeep took off.' The last jeep in line, we always called the getaway jeep. Something happens, that jeep takes off to get some help. So, about a half hour later, they came back with some of the Rainbow rangers, and then together we cleaned up the mess, and that was all over with, and we got Jackie. Nobody got hurt, and everything was fine. But Fritz, we went through another village that same day, and he was looking to kill Germans! He was a totally different man. I said, 'Fritz, you see how quick you learn? Nothing to it,' and he was a good guy. He was really good.

*

That's pretty much the end of the war. I mean, we're talking about April 30 was Munich. The war was over, what, May 6 or something? You just saw lines of Germans. The roads were just crowded with lines and thousands of Germans with their hands up on their heads, just giving up. The only action, or almost action, we saw was I think about two weeks after the war was over. They called the guys in our platoon out again. If there was a problem, get the I&R. They brought us into the CP, and they said, 'Well, there's German SS up in the mountains.' Now, we're in the Bavarian Alps. They either don't know the war was over, or they don't care if the war was over. There's some shacks up there, I'm told, [and we were to] break up their weapons, their radios, or whatever. So, you've got to climb about six peaks, which is another stupid thing. I mean, think about it. We've got to climb all these mountains. The idiot that's up there looking down is probably laughing like hell. We're going to be dead when we get up there, and that's going to be hours away. By that time, this guy is in another state. Insane. Anyway, officers have bad dreams I guess sometimes.

We found some shacks. We broke up some radios and stuff like that, but we didn't find anybody. Who's going to wait for us? You're going to sit up there and wait for us?

[I didn't have enough points to get out] until June '46, but I'm a pretty flexible kind of a guy. They pulled my record. Of course, most of them knew anyway what my experience prior to the Army was. So, they gave me a two-and-a-half-ton truck, and they told me to put together a van, some music, a group or something, and get some guys together and go around to the outlying companies that were spread all over the place to occupy and provide a little entertainment. So that's what we did, and little by little it expanded and expanded, and then we moved to Vienna, and then we took over a beautiful coffeehouse on the main drag with crystal chandeliers, and we had German waiters in tuxedos, and by that time we had a 12-piece orchestra. It was picked by General Mark Clark to broadcast in the States as a Christmas in Vienna. My brother was sending me special arrangements;

he was with Woody Herman at the time. We were having shows and all this other stuff. We had a hell of a time going there.

The first sergeant kept calling me. 'I got three stripes for you. I got two stripes and a diamond, a couple of rockers.' He used to give me all these things.

I said, 'I don't want that.'

He said, 'Well, you can take my job pretty soon. I'm going to go home if you would accept it.'

I said, 'I don't want your job either. I don't need it. I make more money than you do.'

He said, 'What are you talking about?'

I said, 'Well, we finish at the art club, then there's a truck outside from the Air Force, the airbase outside of town, and they load us up and they take us out to the airbase. We play all night for them. They feed us steak dinners and everything. They give us booze and broads and everything else and they pay us well.' When we moved to Linz, Austria, we were playing the showboat up and down the Danube. I said, 'You know, we're doing fine. I don't need your stripes.' So, I left still a PFC, but I made out very well.

*

[In 1946] I came home, and my father had just sold out his business. He manufactured ladies' coats. I went back to see my professor, my trumpet teacher, Charlie Colin, who was the best in New York, for some brush-ups. He was good. Dizzy Gillespie and all these pros used to drop in for a brush-up. Charlie straightened me out a little bit, and the big bands were breaking up at that time. The rumba bands got popular. You remember the Spanish craze? You're too young for that. So, I walked into Charlie's one day, and he said, 'Go up there to the studio. There's a new Spanish band auditioning trumpet players.' I went up there, and I could always read anything. If a fly walked across the page of a manuscript paper, I would read his footprints. So, it must have been forty trumpet players up there. I went and sat down. The guy said, 'Two more.' So, I went up and sat in the first chair, and he beat it off, and I played it, period, no mistakes. He called off another arrangement, and I played that. He said, 'Everybody else go home.'

I said, 'Wait a minute. Before you send those guys home, what's the deal?'

He said, 'Well, will you give me a few rehearsals?' Of course, I was the union, Local 802 New York.

I said, 'The union said you've got to get paid for rehearsals. I'll give you some rehearsals. But I only get Class A money. I don't accept anything less than Class A money.' At that time, it was 20 bucks an hour. Do you know what 20 bucks an hour was in 1946? Anyway, so that was a world off. I started to write.

He said, 'Okay, you got it.' So, I played. Everybody thought I was Spanish. I grew a thinner mustache than this. Little girls were talking. We were playing Spanish clubs in Spanish Harlem. These little girls were yakking, yakking, yakking. I turned around to the guy next to me who could hardly speak English, and I said, 'What'd she say?'

'She's after you, man.'

I said, 'I'm not after her, pal. I can't talk her language.' Anyway, it was fun for a while, and then my father decided to go back into business. So, I went with him, and we moved up to Albany, found a shop in Albany, and that was it. Since then, I ran two shops, and I sold out in '91, but I'm busy as ever.

*

In [World War II], I got away with murder. I really did—I [felt like] I was a civilian through the whole damned thing. The guys used to say, 'How do you get away with it? How do you get away?'

I would say, 'Get away with what?'

They said, 'You horse around with these officers. They ask you dumb questions and you give them dumb answers and they laugh at everything.'

I said, 'Yeah, what the hell?' They like to laugh, too. I was always a little bit off the wall myself.

I use this [Hitler top hat as a prop] when I go to the schools and talk to the kids. It gets their attention. Somebody said to me the other day, 'You're going to destroy the hat.'

I said, 'Look, I really don't care. It's a great teaching tool, and people will remember it. The kids will remember it because kids don't know anything about World War II.' If Hitler knew what I was doing with his hat... I'm getting the last laugh. PFC Marowitz gets the last laugh...

I never went back, and I don't intend to, I don't feel like I want to. But it is almost impossible to describe the feelings, so I'm not going to try. But when you looked around, some of these tough soldiers were throwing up and crying all over the place. It is not possible to really describe the number of feelings you get when you walk into something like [Dachau]. Because that's a scene that—well, first of all, nobody told us about the camp! We had no idea what a concentration camp did! We were going to Dachau, period. It was another village as far as we were concerned. That's kind of a shock to get all at one time. And yet, people in the village who were right next to the camps said they didn't know what was going on. People in Munich, which was actually only nine miles from Dachau, didn't know what was going on. Now if you want to believe that, the Brooklyn Bridge is still for sale.

Richard Marowitz passed away at the age of 88 on August 6, 2014. 'Hitler's Hat' currently resides where it belongs—the National Museum of American Jewish Military History in Washington, DC.

**Nineteen-year-old Charles Zappo, World War II.
Source: Charles Zappo.**

CHAPTER SIXTEEN

The Medic

I found this photograph as I conducted my research for this book.

Look at his face. A boy, really.

At nineteen, a baby-faced combat medic. And as a member of the 42nd Infantry 'Rainbow' Division, one of the first soldiers into the gates of hell, otherwise known as Dachau. What did those young eyes witness? What business did he have being in these circumstances? And what did it mean for the rest of his life?

Of course, we can ask this of any combat veteran, yet unless we were there with him, we will never truly know.

But this tiny, wallet-sized photo is haunting to me.

Charles J. Zappo

I was born in Buffalo, New York, on December 9, 1917. I only went up to the 8th grade, I had to quit school because my father got sick. I graduated from 8th grade and that's where it all started, I had so many jobs, it wasn't even funny [*Laughs*]. I'll give you just one basic job. I worked at the Curtiss-Wright plant making warplanes; in 1943, I worked there two years as an assembler before I left for the service. Before that I was in the CCC camp, if you ever remember one of those camps, I was out in the state of Washington for six months at a CCC camp. We helped the farmers, and my main job was soil conservation where you go along the rivers and planted little trees.[21]

I got one deferment for working at Curtiss-Wright because I was a sole worker in the family. Now, well before then I had volunteered for the Navy. I really volunteered because I knew I was going to get drafted anyway, and so I had passed the Navy test. Then, I was scheduled to go, say on a Monday, then on a Saturday, my mother, who

---

[21] *CCC camp*-Civilian Conservation Corps, a New Deal public work relief program (1933-1942) offering jobs for unemployed young men aged 18 to 25.

always opened up my mail [*chuckles*], she saw I got another deferment and I stayed. Then later on, I went to join the Navy again, but I failed the eye test. They gave you these circles with numbers in it, and you had to pick it out, but I was colorblind at that time with certain colors. [*Laughs*] I couldn't pass the test, so they put me in the infantry in August of '43; went to Camp Gruber, Oklahoma, I had basic training there, stayed at Camp Gruber probably ten months or so before we went overseas; before the army, I had gotten married. What happened is, after basic training my wife came over and stayed near the camp and I would go and visit her all the time on a fake pass. [*Laughs*] After basic training, they put us on a train and went to another camp; we left from New York City, I think it was Camp Dix, and we went and landed in Marseilles, France, right around my birthday in December 1944. In the meantime, my wife had a child I had never seen. I didn't know I had a child until I went into combat.

'A Horrible, Horrible Battle'

[I was sent over with the 42nd Infantry Division, the 'Rainbow' Division]. However, we went over there without any backing, we didn't have any artillery. Just the infantry fellas were over there, and we were waiting for the remainder of our division to come over. In the meantime, the Germans rolled through in the Battle of the Bulge. So they sent all of us green troops up there and on Christmas Eve, and there we lost quite a few people.

The first combat experience was really awful. [*Pauses in reflection*] When we went over there, it was the worst winter that Europe really had. And I just lay there when the Germans broke through, I remember that I was scared; I was in a foxhole and these German 88s were upon us, landing all around us, then our fellas were all around, the ground littered with our dead soldiers, they just lay there frozen. We lost probably fifty percent of our men; just green troops up there.

I didn't carry a weapon because I was considered a medical technician—I was a combat medic. And all we had was the big Red Cross stripe on our helmets and we had the armband with a cross on it. We weren't supposed to carry any weapons. We just carried medical supplies on us, we took care of a few wounded people there, but a lot of them were dead. I mean, after all, we administered first aid, and then of course the aid station was behind us, and they would cart out the aid station and then they went over to the medical battalion.

We really got hit pretty bad because the German tanks came right through. Gosh, the guys were all green troops, they hadn't seen any combat. We didn't have any artillery with us—they had just thrown us into battle. It was a horrible, horrible battle. That was the beginning. We were in Marseilles three weeks, and within three weeks we were thrown into battle! They didn't expect to see the Germans come through, but they had a huge offensive, really, and the Tiger tanks that came down through there... you'd be surprised. A couple of my friends, they were medics, they came out of that, they received the Silver Star for being medics. My experience was to be a combat veteran and you get a combat medical badge; I got the Bronze Star that came along with it. We had painkillers; our main pill was the sulfur pill. The sulfur pill then was just like penicillin, and you use that for, my God, they gave penicillin all over the place, but actually, we were there just to give first aid. Then, people in the back took over.

During Battle of the Bulge, I landed there at the front on my birthday, on Christmas Eve, and I was there probably about a couple months. And then when they stopped the attack, they sent us to an area there for a while.

Matter of fact, a lot of our replacements were from the Air Corps, because they took a lot of people from the Air Corps and put them in the infantry, and boy, you should have seen them. And we got a lot of replacements over there; I don't know, I think a division is around 15,000 men, and without the artillery and all those attachments, I figure I bet we probably lost six, seven hundred men there; it was a big loss—the fellas are just lying all over the frozen [ground] and it's so sad to see young fellas, you know, they just lay there. It was a bad, bad start. Believe me.

You talk about offensives. In March 1945, during our great offensive, we were the first troops to march into Germany, first to hit the Siegfried Line, and the first to cross the Danube. We crossed the Danube on little boats, and it was pretty dark, must have been early in the morning, probably three or four o'clock, and we were crossing when somebody lit up a cigarette and before you knew it, we were getting machine-gunned down there.

We captured cities like Wurzburg, about the size of Buffalo. We started from Alsace-Lorraine, we crossed the Rhine, we ended up in Munich. On the way to Munich, we came across a concentration camp. We captured Schweinfurt, the big ball-bearing city that the Air Corps really, really leveled. We had to fight from door to door in Wurzburg, Germany. I remember distinctly that we went into this store and found all of this champagne that the Germans brought over from France, you know? And the fellas didn't have any water or anything like that and they were emptying the bottles of champagne and were washing their feet with champagne. [*Laughs*] But an awful lot of fighting in Wurzburg; the ironic part about

Wurzburg is, I have a nephew that works the *Buffalo News* and they had all of these new printing presses put in. You know where they came from? Wurzburg! Over 40 million dollars' worth of presses, and they had Germans over there teaching them all to run it from the city that was completely leveled! [*Chuckles*]

Then we went on and captured Furth, that's near Schweinfurt, and Nuremberg. Nuremberg was another place that was on the way to Munich.

'A Horrible, Horrible Sight'

American soldiers view the bodies in one of the open railcars of the Dachau death train. Source: National Archives, public domain. United States Holocaust Memorial Museum.

And then we came across Dachau; actually we didn't go over there to 'liberate' Dachau. We were out there to capture Munich, but we came across Dachau. You probably know all about Dachau. Well, I went there, first thing we saw was [like] fifty freight cars filled with bodies before you enter the camp, men, women, and children.[22] The

---

[22] *fifty freight cars filled with bodies*- 'The train consisted of 30 rail cars with nearly 5,000 prisoners who had been evacuated from Buchenwald in the last

freight cars were surrounding the camp—the [bodies] were carted in from other concentration camps, and they were going to be cremated in the ovens at Dachau. They lay out there, and we saw the boxcars and all the bodies. They did find one guy alive; it was a horrible, horrible sight.

Of course, you got to remember that at that time we were going through a lot of deaths in the army. We were pretty hardened at that time, so we realized how bad it was. You knew it was bad. And as we were going through the camp, they had just us troopers and they were lined. Like my great-grandson says, 'Did you capture any of the Germans in the camp?' I says, 'No, Charlie.' They were shot. They were killed. A lot of them took over the striped uniforms that the prisoners were wearing, and they tried to escape, and the prisoners knew who they were, so they went out there and they clubbed them, and they shot them, and threw them in the moat, you know. So, as we walked through the camp, it was just a horrible sight. You saw the ovens and you saw the bodies piled up, piled up like sacks of flour. It was really the most horrible

---

days of the war.' You can see a short silent film of this at bit.ly/BOXCARS-DA-CHAU.

sight I have ever seen. And then they had about 33,000 prisoners here, I guess.

[*Reads from his narrative*] "The German lieutenants surrendered the prison camp to our General Linden, commander of our unit. However, German SS troopers, they were the elite troops, refused to surrender the camp, [so] inside the camp, I saw many dead SS troopers lying on the ground; they had made a futile attempt to defend the camp. Just prior to the liberation, they tried to kill as many prisoners as possible. I think they shot approximately 200 prisoners with machine guns. The bodies were stacked like cordwood; I saw bodies of women and children also. I saw the gas chambers where thousands of prisoners were led to believe they were showers, then they were gassed. We saw the bodies in the adjoining rooms. Bodies ready to be cremated, they were piled up all over the place like sacks of potatoes. And the stench in the camp was horrible. The prisoners had become like animals. As they moved the camp, many were dying even though they were being liberated. So Dachau was really a nightmare to all of the men in the division. Man after man was saying,

'Now I know why we are fighting. These Nazis are mad. People who operated the camps were insane.'"

[*Looks up from a narrative he was reading from*] Now in the nearby town, a few miles away over there from Dachau, I asked a few of the townspeople, 'Did you know what was going on in the camp?'

They said, 'No, we just hear the freight cars pulling in and out of the camp.' And nobody knew what was going on? Then I said, 'Well, couldn't you smell the fumes? Couldn't you smell the fumes coming out of the smokestacks?'

They didn't say anything.

[Now], as a medic, you see, we were there just in the camp as soldiers; I don't think we were there more than just a couple of days. We were marching on; we were marching on to Munich. What happens is, you have the medical battalion, and then they come in, and they're supposed to take care of all the men. Imagine taking care of 33,000 prisoners? They were all skin and bones, you know? And so, it was really a horrible, horrible sight. Just like I say, people in that town 'never even knew what was going on.' It's hard to believe they didn't know!

After that, what they did is, they went out and got all the people from the town, had them all come into the camp, and they had to bury all the dead prisoners. And carry them—you should have seen [that], they were carrying them on their backs, and dragging them, and putting them in trenches, and then they would bury them in the trenches. You can't imagine how terrible that [camp] was! So that's what happened, I mean, we weren't there [at that time]. We just liberated the camp, then we got to Munich, and we liberated [some people], there were about a quarter of a million slave laborers there. When they were liberated, they went wild; they went and looted the whole city and it was really unbelievable. [*Chuckles*] So, [it was more than] just the Dachau concentration camp.

Russians

We became an army of occupation and we ended up in Salzburg, Austria. [We had some contact with the Soviet troops]; I'll tell you a little story. There were Russians all over the place and we went to this great, great concert, the Russian troops were all sitting up in the front and they were all over the place. All of a sudden in the middle of the concert, you see all of these small balloons floating down into the concert. You know what those balloons were? [*Laughs*] And I thought that was a terrible thing, you know, you're in a concert.

When we were stationed in Salzburg, my buddy and I heard all of this singing down in the valley. So, we went down to the valley, and saw a trainload of Hungarians and they were trying to get into the American section. They wanted to get away from the Russians because the Russians had a bad reputation. And this whole train, they were elderly people and young people, and I talked to a few of them, and they said they had women and children on the train, they didn't have much food and needed some blankets. At that time, I was stationed in some mansion in Austria. It was a beautiful place. So I asked a few of the fellas to come up with me during the day and gave them something to take back with them. I gave them blankets and food and gave them a lot of clothing. They didn't want any part of the Russians at all, to be under Russian occupation. Everybody wanted to come over to the American side. And of course the Germans, I remember being in Austria and I got acquainted with a German and his wife, she was a pianist, and you see, when the Germans were in Austria, they got better treatment. They had had about a six-month stay in Austria, and they wanted to get another six months, so I helped them get another six months. I told them that we needed some signed papers, and they gave them another pass. He was thrilled to get the pass and stay there, but I miss the nice German people.

*

In January of 1946, [I finally had enough points according to] the point system [they had], so I got transferred to the 84th Infantry, because they were going home. And, while I was in Heidelberg, we heard that General Patton died; he was in Heidelberg, he got killed in that car accident.[23] It was an

---

[23] *we heard that General Patton died-* On December 9, 1945, the car Patton was riding in collided with an American army truck, resulting in a broken neck and spinal injuries. The others traveling with him in the car had only minor injuries. He died twelve days later on December 21, at the age of 60. One of his final remarks was, 'This is a hell of a way to die.'

ironic thing, this general like General Patton getting killed because he wasn't wearing his seatbelt.

So, we got on a ship in France, I think it was at Le Havre, and we sailed for home. It took us about seven days to get home. And when I got home, I saw my son, whom I had never seen. He was about fourteen months old and of course he starts screaming, you know, I don't know who the hell this guy is, and so we had a very bad start. [*Laughs*] You know, because here you are. You don't have a job; you really have no place to live. And then one day I was working in a piano factory, and it laid me off. And here I am with two children now, and living in a really bad, bad flat on the west side. And I decided to go back to school. I used the GI Bill. And I didn't have any high school. So they had what they call an accelerated veterans high school over in Elmwood Avenue. So, I went to working part-time and I went through and completed 4 years of high school in one year and got a diploma from our regular high school. And that was really a struggle. Then I enrolled in business college over here, Bryant & Stratton, two years. I majored in accounting, and I became an accountant; I worked at a bakery where I had to be a cost accountant and we used to ship baked goods to about a hundred stores. After that, I figured I'd start taking some civil service tests, because I could see I wasn't getting anywhere. I took a chance for the Internal Revenue Service, and I passed that exam. It's like an exam for New York State auditors exam tax department and I became a became a New York State corporation tax auditor all from that. I could work pretty damn hard.

Imagine going through all that, these kids can't get through four years of high school; of course, I only took the basic courses. But I go way back, you know, way back when I was just a kid I used to go out and shine shoes downtown, six, seven years old—could you imagine a kid going out there in the city? I had so many jobs it wasn't even funny!

*

At the end of the war, people were coming down from all the hills. I even had a lot of Germans surrendering, even to me, coming down with white flags. I was put in charge of this German POW camp in Germany as a medic, and I helped some of the Germans over there that were really sick. One guy had pneumonia, and I wonder if he still remembers me. And then I remember when I was in Camp Gruber we had a prisoner camp there, a German prisoner camp at Camp Gruber, and you know they went out there striking for more cigarettes. Then I had a brother that was a POW. He was captured in the Battle of the Bulge. Do you know what they were doing to these American prisoners? They were segregating them. If they were Jewish, they were put into the terrible camps. They thought my brother was Jewish, and they put him in one of these camps and they were digging tunnels.[24] I guess he lost 70 pounds or something like that. He went through a terrible time in that. What a contrast. And now, he died last year, but they're giving him reparations, to these POWs. As a matter of fact, I was over to the VA administration office over here in Buffalo. And I took a lot of this stuff [*points to notes on the table*] over there and they were all interested in this stuff. One of the POWs, he had things to do with the POW prisoners and their activities, I was

---

[24] *They thought my brother was Jewish*- the camp was likely Berga an der Elster, a subcamp of Buchenwald, detailed in Vol.6 of this series, *The Bulge and Beyond*.

telling one guy that Germany has given reparations to some of these prisoners, our prisoners, and he didn't know about it, because they put these fellas, our prisoners, into minor concentration camps. My brother, gosh, he almost died in that camp. But people don't realize what the fellas went through.

'You Don't Realize How It Is Going to Affect You'

Well, I tell you, I realize [now] how this affected my life, this thing I saw here at Dachau, I didn't realize it, but my wife says at night I'd be twitching all over the bed. You go through all of this, and you don't realize how it's going to affect you, throughout your life. That thing is affecting me, I don't know why, but as a matter of fact, this is the first time I haven't really broken down [trying to talk about it]. Maybe it's because [I had] my last breakdown with my grandson. But it stays with you—this post-traumatic stress that all these young fellas are coming home with, it's real. It's a serious thing. I go to the VA Hospital, they treat me real good. Matter of fact, I got my hearing aids there, and my glasses. Of course, if I live to the end of the year, I'm going to be 90 years old. And there's 1,200 of us World War II veterans dying every day! There aren't too many of us left around here. So I've been all over, and they want people to remember this stuff. I don't like doing this stuff anymore, but I do it because I feel I should do it, [because] people don't realize that it's just like this right here [*points to paper on table*], 'Lies about the Holocaust.'

If you were to see what went on in Germany…Hitler, he was a madman.

Charles Zappo passed away on June 19, 2015, at the age of 97.

The Brandenburg Gate amid the ruins of Berlin, June 1945. Source: Bundsarchiv.

CHAPTER SEVENTEEN

The Fall of Berlin

By March 25, 1945, resistance on the west bank of the Rhine River had all but collapsed, with German troops surrendering by the hour, now trapped by the encircling Allies. Another 325,000 would be trapped in the Ruhr Pocket in the next few weeks; by April 11, the Ninth US Army had reached the Elbe, just 50 miles from Berlin.

The previous month at Yalta, the Big Three had planned for the division of Germany into zones of occupation, with Berlin lying squarely within the Soviet sector. Evaluating the situation, Eisenhower concluded that an assault on Berlin from the west would be too costly, given that Berlin would revert to the Russians anyway. He decided to wait. The Red Army launched its final assault on Berlin on April 16. In the two weeks that followed, it suffered over 350,000 casualties, more than the United States in the entire European Theater of the war. The Battle of Berlin was the Red Army's costliest battle in World War II.[14] Delusional and unrepentant, Hitler dictated his last testament to his secretary, lashing out at the German people for failing him and his National Socialist visions, killing himself in the Führerbunker in Berlin on April 30. The victors would enter the ruined Reich capital, twelve years into its 'thousand-year reign.'

CHAPTER EIGHTEEN

The Paratrooper IV

Albert A. Tarbell

On To Berlin

We were soon thereafter on occupation duty. Guys on high points were being shipped back to the States, I think it was 85 points or something like that, they could come back to the States. The war was over in August, when they dropped the bomb. That stopped us from going, because we figured we were going to Japan or going to the Orient.

[The atomic bombs] couldn't have happened at a better time. We wanted to come home. We didn't want to go over there, you know. I don't think anybody liked the idea of jumping into Japan, I think that would have been wholesale slaughter. We would have lost a lot of men there, because they were going to protect their country. I think they would have protected it very well, very hard.

We started having few leaves and then started regrouping. They said we were going to go to Berlin, occupation duty. I went from Charlottenburg to Berlin by jeep; the colonel put me in charge of battalion beer and liquor supply after the war. That was a good duty.

I got orders to report to the medics. Good old medics. I went to the medics, Captain Ketchen and Captain Shapiro over there. They said, 'Tarbell, we got something here for you and your guys.'

I said, 'What is it?' Here was a flask, five gallons of 180 proof alcohol. They had checked; they said, 'Oh, we checked it, inspected it, it's good for consumption.' I was dishing out this alcohol, vermouth and grape juice, and the guys didn't come around for seconds. [*Laughs*]

I finally got detached service with Colonel Cook at his battalion. I still was carried in the company, but I worked at the battalion. When I went to Berlin, I couldn't get anybody to drink that vermouth [we 'liberated' weeks back], because we didn't have nothing to cut it with. One of the guys from officers' mess said, 'Hey, Tarbell, I got about six cases of gin.' He said, 'I'll trade you for that barrel of vermouth.'

I said, 'You got a deal.' I took the colonel's jeep and his driver, I had about six cases of gin. I took it to Berlin with us with other stuff we got, like schnapps from Essen, Germany.

That was quite a jeep ride, on the autobahn, in and out, in and out; wherever the bridges were blown you had a detour, then you had to get back on. We got to Helmstedt, and from there we went into the Russian zone; from here to Berlin, it's all Russian zones. You're going to see Russian guards every so often. They said, 'When they salute you, return the salute. You know they're liable to shoot you if you don't.' Or do something, you know, get pissed off anyway.

We're driving and driving, and I got so sick of saluting. God, it seemed like every couple of hundred yards or something there's a guard. We stopped at one place, we had a piss call, a relief call. God, there were a bunch of women working in a potato field or some kind of a field, doing something. They all come running over to us! You ought to have seen how quick those guards moved, boy, they just held them right back. The women were going to come over, you know, they knew we were Americans.

Anyway, we got into Berlin, and it was quite a city. Oh, that city was so beat up, God. The subways there, they had artillery there. They used to fire artillery [from] the subways and everything else. In a lot of places, the whole street was crumbled, and they had blocks and blocks of buildings that were all demolished. Do you know when we got there, we relieved another outfit that was already there? The people were already cleaning bricks and this and that. The other unit had set up work details, already rebuilding, they're trying to rebuild.

I understood that in order to get a heating or food permit, you had to work. Whoever we hired, they got a ration card to go to this soup kitchen and they were fed meals. We had two restaurants that I took over, one for the enlisted men, and the non-com club. I took care of the non-com club; my buddy Fritz took over the enlisted men's club. We had beer there, and I was getting liquor supply from the States. I'd bring that down to the sergeants, first sergeant, mess sergeant, took care of them guys first, you know, then all the others, everybody got something. We tried to break it up even.

It was a good living. We had football games at the Templehof—not the Templehof, but where they had the Olympics, the Unter den Linden ran right into it. Brandenburg Gate was nearby there. I went a couple of times to the Russian zone, but I didn't want to fraternize with the Russians at all— they were not people to fraternize with. We didn't get along, but oh, they bought watches from you. They'd buy a Mickey Mouse watch; they'd pay you three or four hundred dollars for it! They had never been paid in about six years; they were going to spend it all right there when they got paid. They bought things like that, you know, that they had never seen before. They were taking everything apart; they were taking plumbing apart and everything else, furniture—it was all being shipped back to Russia.

In one of the areas there, my company commander was in charge. A friend of mine got word one night that the Russians were coming in there and raiding this woman's home, taking all the furniture and everything else. This woman was complaining. The commander, he took Renner with him. He told Renner, 'Don't let that guy out.' He sent another lieutenant with him.

The lieutenant told the Russians, "Guys, that's not right. You're out of your area. This is in the American zone. You shouldn't be taking this stuff out of here. Don't move that truck.'

He told Renner, 'If that truck moves, shoot that driver.'

You know, we never figured that the Russians would go back to try to move it. The lieutenant went in, and he tried to pacify the woman. So what do the Russians do? The guy jumps back in the truck and told the driver to take off. Renner straightened out and shot the driver and killed him. He was the first American to kill a Russian soldier. They questioned him later, they asked the colonel, 'Couldn't he have just wounded him?'

The colonel said, 'I didn't train my soldiers to wound people. I trained them to shoot to kill.' My company commander went there, and [met with] his Russian counterpart, and they did a lot of finagling, and Renner got out of that. But that's the way the Russians were.

When we first went in on leave in Berlin, they said, 'You cannot go out on pass unless you have a .45 or a tommy gun. You have to be armed. If you don't have that, take a rifle, but you got to be armed.' I got on a tram, running near Hofstrasse. I looked at the people. My God, everybody was either a cripple or they were old people! I said, 'My God, what's my sidearm for? Not for these people.' I found out that night what it was for. The Russians would come over in our zone and they would raise hell. It was to protect us from them! Why, they were an awful bunch. They just went hog wild there, in Berlin, because I guess, after six years of [being invaded, German occupation], fighting the war. But their values and ours were different; we valued human beings and they didn't seem to care too much. At least, that's my impression of them. I didn't care for the average Russian soldier. Maybe we're just brought up different. I don't know.

View of the defendants in the dock at the International Military Tribunal trial of war criminals in Nuremberg, Bavaria, Germany. Source: National Archives, public domain. United States Holocaust Memorial Museum.

CHAPTER NINETEEN

Judgment at Nuremberg

Just before Thanksgiving in November 1945, Justice Robert Jackson opened the most spectacular set of trials in history. A man of unimpeachable credentials and integrity, Jackson was asked by President Truman to serve as chief prosecutor of the International Military Tribunal, as the court was formally known.

In the 1943 Moscow Declarations, the Soviet Union, Great Britain, and the United States published their joint statement that Nazi war criminals would be pursued 'to the uttermost ends of the earth ... so that justice may be done.' In late 1944, as it was becoming clear that the Allies would eventually prevail, high level discussions began to crystalize the process for the judicial accountability of the leadership of Nazi Germany responsible for the Holocaust and other crimes against humanity.

It was important to the Allied leadership that the trials be held on German soil. Jackson and others settled on Nuremberg as an appropriate choice, given that its Palace of Justice was intact, but symbolically, Nuremberg was the home of the early Nazi Party massive rallies, and the 1935 Nuremberg Race Laws, which set out to define 'Jewishness' and began specifically codifying acts to be considered criminal.

In the first and best-known trial (out of a total of thirteen, trying over 200 German defendants, lasting until 1949), twenty-one defendants stood trial. It lasted nearly a year, and one has to consider the gravity and general unprecedentedness of a war crimes trial; today, its significance for putting potential human rights violators on notice cannot be overestimated. Many of the GIs who were present at Nuremberg after the war understood on some level that they had a front row seat at a hugely historic moment, yet frankly, with the fighting over, it was a peripheral affair. Most were guys who had not collected enough points under the demobilization Adjusted Service Rating Score point system; they just wanted to get home.[25]

---

[25] *Adjusted Service Rating Score point system*-Witnessing the frustration incumbent with the Army's failed demobilization efforts at the end of World War I (where entire divisions were sent home at once, rather than individuals based on merit/time served) as General Pershing's Chief of Staff, General George C. Marshall ordered up a study for a more objective, timely methodology for getting the troops home in late 1943. It called for the following:
One point for each month of Army service
One point for each month in service abroad
Five points for each campaign
Five points for a medal for merit/valor
Five points for a Purple Heart
Twelve points for each dependent child (up to three)
Source: Bamford, Tyler. *The Points Were All That Mattered: The US Army's Demobilization After World War II*. National WWII Museum, August 27, 2020. www.nationalww2museum.org/war/articles/points-system-us-armys-demobilization

Alvin Cohen's Nuremberg International Military Tribunal ID card. Source: Alvin Cohen.

CHAPTER TWENTY

The Jewish Guard Keeper

Al Cohen was another one of the trio of New York's Capital District ETO Army veterans who visited my high school every year for a while, beginning in 2000. He was very active in many veterans' organizations, co-founding the Hudson Valley (NY) Chapter of the Veterans of the Battle of the Bulge, where he even served as president. In tandem with my slides and mini-introductory lectures, they would speak in turn of their experiences in the battle, crossing the Siegfried Line, and fighting into Germany. I would usually ask the soft-spoken Al to present last to the students, as he had a very special task, though it was lost to him as a nineteen-year-old, impatient to get home after the war's end.

'This was my ID card to get into the cell block as a guard at the [International Military Tribunal's] Palace of Justice in Nuremberg. We were supposed to turn them in when we left the war trials, but I hung onto mine just for the heck of it. At first, I was guarding one of the criminals. I don't recall who it was at that time, but on the right side the first cell was Goering, the second one I believe was Hess, and then Jodl, and so on Ribbentrop, and so on down the line. Von Schirach was head of the Hitler Youth, and he and Speer, they could speak very good English, and they would try and talk to us. We weren't supposed to, but we did. The first thing I say to any of them was, 'How do you like having a Jew guard?' Most of them, I think, understood English, but they wouldn't say a word. I've got a couple of their autographs, but nobody wants them. I try to get rid of them. Nobody wants them!'

This chapter is drawn from his testimony recorded in May 2000 and August 2001.

Alvin M. Cohen

I was born in Utica, New York, on October 1, 1925. [We lived there], I don't know, maybe for a couple of years, and then my father was transferred around. We ended up settling in Albany, where I went to the Albany public schools. Then I left school; I figured I was going in service, so I went to work at the American Locomotive in Schenectady. From there, I was drafted in '44. I got there in August, beginning of August, and it was very hot. September cooled off, and finally, when I left, it was December, and it was cold and damp. In fact, we're out in the field, and we've got a shipment of down sleeping bags out of the Schenectady depot.

We didn't like it down South. The people down there weren't too appreciative of servicemen. They like to take your money, but that was as far as it went.

[I had been in the New York State] National Guard, so I already had had some training. The Guard was now federalized, and some of the fellas from school were signing up because they got paid. I don't remember what it was, maybe seventy-five cents a drill. I figured, 'Oh, I'll go anyway, and I'll get some military training.' We had green, one-piece uniforms, leggings, and the old World War I helmet. We were drilling with shotguns. There were some rifles, shotguns, and Thompson sub-machine guns, etc., which I believe are still stored down in Peekskill. So, [basic training] was easier for me than some of the others. When we first started out, as an example, the sergeants were going to show us how to pack a full field pack, the old-style World War I. That's what we had here in Albany. He said, 'Does anybody know how to do it?'

I said, 'Yes,' and I raised my hand.

He said, 'Okay. Let's see if you can do it.' I did it, and then they gave me acting corporal. I got out of KP that way. After basic training, I came home. I had, I think, seven days' delay on the road. Travel time was about four days. I ended up with four days at home, and I had to report to Fort Meade, Maryland. They went over our clothes, gave us shots. After about a day and a half, they loaded us on the train, and we went over to Camp Kilmer, New Jersey, dropped our barracks bags in one of the empty buildings, and they marched us into a warehouse, gave us a brand new M1, new trench shovel, new web equipment. Out the other door, back to the barracks, we cleaned our weapons. They fed us. We got on a train over Jersey, crossed on a ferry boat, and up on the dock, it was a Queen Elizabeth tied up to the dock. That was the start of a four-day trip; there were about twenty-seven thousand troops packed in that thing. You couldn't move. We were lucky. We had about twelve of us in a compartment, and all our names started with C. Luckily, we all stuck together, right straight through until we were assigned to M Company, 359th Infantry, and it was the 90th Infantry Division.

Overseas

We landed in Gorx, Scotland, and they took us off. The ship was too big to tie up to the dock, so they took us off on a lighter, got us on a train, and we started down towards London. The transportation crew told us, 'If you get stuck, if you don't cross the Channel tonight'— this was on a Friday— 'we'll give you a pass to London.' Everybody's all excited they're going to get a pass to London. We got down; we ended up at Plymouth, and we got right on the ship. The next morning, we were all going to Le Havre; that was what I saw of London. [*Chuckles*]

Everything at Le Havre was pretty well beat up. They started marching us up the hill; I think they called it Camp Philip Morris, one of those names after a cigarette. As we're marching up, we see these little kids alongside the road, looking for candy and cigarettes. You couldn't get over it; they spoke French. It was hard to visualize that you're in a different country and they're speaking French but not speaking our language.

When we got up to battalion, they needed volunteers for heavy weapons. As I said, the fifteen of us or so that were in the compartment, we were all together. A couple of the fellas said, 'We're getting the mortar platoon.' That was 81-millimeter mortars; well back of the line. They started volunteering, and the rest of us knew each other, so we stuck together, so we all volunteered. We get up to the company, and they signed us to a platoon, heavy weapons. Well, we all volunteered for the heavy weapons platoon, but we ended up in this machine gun platoon. That was the best thing we did because out of the whole group of us, some of us went back to the hospital, but we all came back—out of the fifteen of us, only one fell and got hurt bad enough to come back to the States.

The Siegfried Line

I started out carrying ammunition. I had two cans of ammunition, picked up a leather strap someplace. It's strapped over my shoulders. I had one can on my chest, one on my back, inside my pack. They took the M1 away from me, and I got a carbine, and eventually, I became the second gunner. I carried the water jacket receiver. We'd be assigned to a rifle company, a squad of us. They were moving us around a lot to change different sectors. That was just before we went through the Siegfried Line. We got through there, and through the dragon's teeth, and there was a road, a bombed-out farmhouse. We had our squad in there, we had our machine guns set up outside. It was pretty much a holding position. We were lucky that we got through. We were moving around quite a bit. Our regiment was always stuck out in the woods someplace; we didn't get to see anything of the cities or towns. In fact, at the end of this month, I'll get back to a division reunion. I'll see some of the fellows that were in our squad.

The Siegfried Line were rows of dragon's teeth. It's like a pyramid that's cut off on top, without the point, rows of them. In between the rows, they'd have booby traps or mines to keep the tanks from going through. Where we went through, we were lucky the engineers had cleared the path; there were no mines when we got through there. We were up in some woods, and it was a log dugout, about six or seven feet tall, but it was sunk in the ground, just a little was showing. We opened up the door, and it's covered with sawdust, just like someone took a rake and raked it out. Right in the center was a German element, so nobody would even walk in there, but the lieutenant went in, put a rope around it, and then dragged it out. Luckily, it wasn't booby-trapped or anything. That's the problem we ran into. The Germans were pretty cute. They'd like to booby trap a toilet seat, places you'd least expect something.

'I'll Blow Your Goddamn Head Off'

In basic training in Arkansas, I had a run-in [involving antisemitism] with one fellow. Then once overseas, after we made the river crossing, we got a building to get in out of the cold to sleep in. The building was in pretty good shape, so it wasn't bad, though there wasn't any furniture in it. They brought up copies of *Stars and Stripes*. We were sitting on the floor, and I got through cleaning my carbine, so I clipped in. As I'm doing that, this one fellow who came in a short time before, as a replacement, he was off of some farm up in Northern New York, and he was looking at the paper, and he said, 'We're over here, getting our rear ends shot off, and the Jews are back in the States, making all the money.'

I finished putting a clip in the carbine; I put a round in the chamber. I put the safety on, I walked over and stood over him, and I said, 'What did you say, fella?'

He repeated it.

I said to him, 'I'm Jewish.'

He said, 'No, you're not.'

I said, 'Well, what am I?'

He said, 'You're Italian.'

I said, 'With a name like Cohen?'

He said, 'No, you're kidding!'

I dropped the muzzle of the carbine right down in his chest, and I said to him, 'If I ever hear you say anything about the Jews in front of me, or at the back of me, I'll blow your goddamn head off.'

The lieutenant sitting there never said a word. After that, he wanted to be my buddy when we wouldn't have anything to do. Other than that, I've had no problems. A lot of fellas had it a lot worse.

Our platoon leader was a tech sergeant, and he made battlefield commission, and he was terrific. None of the non-coms wanted stripes because as soon as you got stripes, you got hit. When he was with us, nothing could happen. In fact, at the reunions, I see my old company commander, our mess sergeant. Our battalion commander retired recently, maybe eight or nine years ago, as a major general. He stayed in; he had the 1st Division in

Vietnam for a while. Quite a few of them stayed in after the war.

We very seldom saw the other platoon; we never saw the mortar platoon. Even if we went back for a rest, they'd have one platoon in one building, another platoon maybe five miles down the road, in another building. Most of them were all bombed out. We never got to see them. In fact, at the first reunion I went to, there wasn't anyone there that I knew. They were all fellows out of our M Company, but they were either in the hospital, they were back someplace, and we never got to know each other; the only ones we really knew were the fellows in our own group. They tell us we're going back and getting off the line for three days. We get back to town, miles back, and they tell us, 'You're going to be here for three days.' The first thing you had to do, you had to clean crew-served weapons, then you cleaned your own weapons. If you had time, you try to get cleaned up. Usually, we didn't have time to do the latter. We'd be back for supposedly three days. Maybe four or five hours later, we're going back up, somebody's in trouble, so we'd come back and have to relieve someone. If we get in a town, the standing order was, if you're going to spend the night in the town, you had to take the civilians and lock them in the cellar. Sometimes, they give you a hard time about that. All you had to tell them was that the Russians are coming. They were very docile after that. They'd get down. We'd lock them in the cellar.

Pulling Guard Duty at Nuremberg

After the war was over, I didn't have enough points; most of the replacements didn't have enough points to come home. They shipped the low point men to the 1st Division at Nuremberg, pulling guard duty at the war trials. I start pulling guard at the war trials and the cell block.

This was my ID card to get into the cell block at the [International Military Tribunal's] Palace of Justice in Nuremberg. When I first got there, you didn't need a card to get in. Then, the FBI had a detachment there and they came out with this ID card. We were supposed to turn them in when we left the war trials, but I hung onto mine just for the heck of it. At first, I was guarding one of the criminals. I don't recall who it was at that time, but on the right side the first cell was Goering, the second one I believe was Hess, and then Jodl, and so on Ribbentrop, and so on down the line.

Alvin Cohen, second on left, watching sleeping prisoner at Nuremberg. Source: Life Magazine.

It was miserable. To stand in front of a door and look at Goering, or looking at Hess, we were looking at Speer, von Schirach, any of those twenty-two war criminals, they're just sleeping, and you're standing there [outside of the door, looking into the cell]. We have to watch them. I don't know, just, to me, it didn't sit right. Anyway, I suppose it was better than pulling guard out in the cold.

The doors were wooden, I can't say it was oak. The doors were about that thick. [*Gestures inches apart*] They cut squares in them. There's a metal grating, and light is hooked on it and shined into their cell. You had to make sure that they slept with their hands out, face exposed, and that they didn't try to commit suicide. This was right after one of them hung themselves. I did that for a while, and then I got so-called promoted to an escort guard. I used to take them up to see their lawyers in the courthouse. We pulled guard for two hours on, we stood in front of the cell during the day; they always had to be visible to you. They had a toilet there, a bed and a table with one chair. They used the toilet, and that was the only time they could be out of your vision, for how long it took.

'Fresh Air Fanatics'

There was one window in the back of the cell. In the spring and the summer it wasn't too bad, but in the winter, it was hot in the cell block where we were standing. It was freezing outside, the windows were wide open because all these German criminals were fresh air fanatics, and you had to stare at them continuously to make sure they didn't try and commit suicide. That cold air would flow in your face, and it was a rough job trying to stay awake. Two hours on, two hours off, and they had one room, which used to be a gymnasium, they had cots set up where we could lie down, rest, some of the fellas played cards or read. That same room was the room they cleaned out and then built the scaffolds to hang them.

[In this photograph], on the left side, I'm the third one, right there. It was in *Life Magazine* in January of '46. I didn't know anything about it; as it happened a friend of mine went to the dentist and sitting in the waiting room, she's reading through *Life Magazine* and found it.

They kept the most important ones on the first tier, that's the ground floor, like Julius Streicher, Jodl, Ribbentrop, I believe twenty or twenty-one of the most important ones. The second tier, there was a catwalk, and the flooring was like a piece of tin. Every time you would walk it would bounce up and down. They had four or five cells to watch. The less important criminals were kept there. The third tier held witnesses and some of the criminals.

One of the ones on the top floor was Ilse Koch. She was a notorious guard at one of the camps. She would take the skin off the prisoners when they were killed, if they had a tattoo or something, she would make lampshades out of them and all kinds of decorative ornaments. When you were on the third tier, which she was on, you had to watch them the same way by making sure they didn't kill themselves. She was a cute one; when she heard the guard coming, she would take all her clothes off and stand there naked. You had to look into the cells, so what happened—you had to look, she would write a letter to the commanding colonel or commanding officer of the prison. First thing you know, you were on the carpet for looking at her. After a while, I guess they got used to it, and that was the same with a few others.

At night, there is a grate with a light on the side of each cell. The light went over the cut-out of the door and that light shone into the cell continuously. I pulled that kind of guard for three or four months, and one day we got back to our barracks, and we fell out.

'How Do You Like Having a Jew Guard?'

Von Schirach was head of the Hitler Youth, and he and Speer, they could speak very good English, and they would try and talk to us. We weren't supposed to, but we did. They used to tell me that their parents used to bring them over to the Catskill Mountains [in New York state] in the summer. One thing I did when I pulled guard, the first thing I say to any of them was, 'How do you like having a Jew guard?' Most of them, I think, understood English, but they wouldn't say a word. At least they used to rotate us, they had a stone wall around a little courtyard between the prison and courthouse. It was like a garden, some grass and trees, for the use of the exercise of the prisoners, and they wanted somebody who had to be handcuffed to Hess when he was out in the yard with the other prisoners. I was elected for that. It wasn't too bad, but he had arms over twice as long as mine. At first, I was walking with one shoulder down, and then I got smart and made him hold his arm up. He didn't even speak to the other prisoners, but you could tell by the expression in their eyes. They acknowledged each other. I've got a couple of their autographs, but nobody wants them. I try to get rid of them. Nobody wants them!

*

One morning, the first sergeant read off the day's schedule and he wanted a volunteer; he needed a radioman, but nobody raised their hands—nobody ever volunteered for anything. Then the first sergeant grabbed me. He said, 'Do you know anything about a radio?'

I said, 'I know how to turn it on and off. That's about it.'

He said, 'Good, get cleaned up, get a jeep, get down to the [military] police station.' So I go down there, to the MP station, which was adjoining the courthouse where the war trials were, and I saw this lieutenant.

He said, 'What do you know about a radio?' I told him the same thing.

So he said, 'Good, you'll be the radioman here. From now on, you're on detached service. You have to go for twelve hours on, twenty-four off. If you want to, you can stay back with your company, but just be here to go on duty.' While policing Nuremberg, we had anywhere from twenty to thirty jeeps patrolling the town, day and night. So I became a radio operator for about four months.

The time that I had off, I could do whatever I want. I lived back with the fellas at the 1st Division. When it was time to go on duty to get on the radio, I would get picked up by one of the patrol jeeps on duty to take me to work. That was a good deal, but eventually it didn't work out because the division MPs weren't issuing enough citations for uniforms and being drunk and all that, so they brought in a special MP unit. That ended my job. I started pulling guard again in the cell block; I went back to guarding the prisoners for about a week, and after that I became, as they called them, an escort guard. I wore a white helmet and a white belt, and I would take the prisoners up to the summary court, where they had lawyers from Russia, France, and other countries, and they would interrogate some of these prisoners. It was amazing some of the stories you heard, one of them was how they provoked Poland into a situation. They sent over German troops dressed as civilians and they fired back across the border at German troops over there, and that's how they started the incident that started the war—it was things like that that were very interesting.

The Russian Delegation

Once in a while, we lived on the outskirts of Nuremberg, a town called Fürth. When I had time off, I'd go into Nuremberg, each company had their own beer joint. I'd go in with the PX sergeant, he ran it, and they had a bar set up in there. There were Russians in there, there were French, English, and everybody got along fine. No problem. Every Monday, you could look down at the Palace of Justice, and in the basement, there is a window. Every Monday morning, I'd see a two-and-a-half-ton truck back up with crates of bottles that looked like water. It was vodka. You can see that room was piled up high with cases of vodka. Next Monday morning, when they back up another truck, it was empty. That's how [fast the Russians at the trials] went through that stuff.

Finally in June, beginning of June of '46, they came around with a deal that if you wanted to sign up for six months to stay at the war trials, they'd fly you back to the States for thirty days, then you'd have to go back. The reason for that was that fellas that had decorations and combat badges were being shipped home and they wanted to put on a show for the other countries, so they wanted to keep their combat troops in to pull guard. But it didn't work, most of us went home.

*

I got out on July 3 of '46. A few years ago, my wife and I and twenty-five of the men from the division with their wives, we went back over to [follow our combat route and see Germany]. It brought back a lot of memories, especially when we went up to the place called Habscheid, where we went through the dragon's teeth. It brought back a lot of memories. Of course, I couldn't find the farmhouse that we slept in. That was long gone. And we toured the Flossenbürg concentration camp, which our regiment liberated, but at that time we were out in the woods someplace.

I was nineteen years old, the war was over, we were anxious to get home, [guard duty at the first Nuremberg trial] was just another job, really. But as we got older, those of us that were pulling guard there, it had a different meaning, it was part of history. Now when I look back, and I see all these programs about the war trials and everything, it's kind of like [a surreal experience]. [At the time], I couldn't wait to get home; I just didn't want any part of it.

Alvin Cohen was the recipient of the Bronze Star and many other awards and citations. He passed away on March 25, 2014, at the age of 88.

"Former Nazi Party ideologist Alfred Rosenberg in the witness box at the International Military Tribunal war crimes trial at Nuremberg.
Emilio DiPalma is the military policeman standing guard next to him." Source: National Archives, public domain.
United States Holocaust Memorial Museum

CHAPTER TWENTY-ONE

The Courtroom Sentinel

Leo DiPalma was the son of Italian immigrants who grew up in the western part of Massachusetts in the Great Depression. Like many young high schoolers at the time, he was shocked at the news of Pearl Harbor, and ready to serve when his number was called three years later at the age of eighteen. He gained combat experience as an infantryman with the 79th Division, crossing the Rhine in 1945 before being tasked with a new assignment in the 1st Division—standing guard, at the tender age of nineteen, over some of the most notorious war criminals of the 20th century.

'I pulled guard duty on the witness stand with von Schirach. He was head of the Hitler Youth. One day, there was quite a confrontation between him and Chief Justice Jackson. Of course, we could understand him. And he spoke decent English now, but most of his replies were in German. But through the interpreter, we could hear what was going on. They were arguing back and forth about the duties of the Hitler Youth. Well, they called a recess shortly after that, and he turned to me. I was on his left side. He turned to me, and he said, 'But the Hitler Youth is nothing more than your Boy Scouts.'

I said, 'Really?' He doesn't realize that I was a front-line soldier.

I said, 'I fought your Hitler Youth.' He never said a word [after that]. We found Hitler Youth that could take apart our BAR, our M1s, or any of our equipment. So they weren't Boy Scouts like he wanted to portray them.

I came back from the service, but I never thought about it. It's only been the past ten years I've had time to think about it. I'm kind of a low-key person, but I'll do anything to enlighten people that weren't even born at that time.'

Emilio Joseph 'Leo' DiPalma

I was born in Springfield, Massachusetts, June 3, 1926. I had a little job before I graduated. I was working nights at a defense plant, American Bosch. I, of course, graduated. Let's see, I graduated in February. I was a half class, you know. I worked there until September 15, 1944, when I went in the service. I was, let's see, eighteen and three months, I guess. [When Pearl Harbor occurred, I was still in high school]; actually, my dad had trouble with his car, and he was driving around with it, trying it out. I guess he'd had some work done. He stopped at my cousin's gas station. First thing my cousin said when he come out, he said, 'We're at war.' Of course, I didn't say anything. I wondered, with who? I got to thinking, I said, 'Geez, I probably won't go in, I'm really too young.' But turned out that I wasn't. The next day at lunch, we heard President Roosevelt say how we had gone to war, we had been attacked by Japan, gave all the details. Actually, as young as I was, it did make me angry, because it was an attack. It wasn't something that we had initiated or done wrong.

I was drafted September 15, that was '44. I went to Fort Devens, just to get squared away, I guess. Then they sent me to Camp Blanding, Florida. I had infantry training. Well, that, as usual, in a way, you're kind of glad you were going. At that age, you really aren't afraid of anything, you know. It used to be kind of a drag, every day was a drag. You would learn about this, you would learn about that. And the next day, you got the same thing. And you really wanted to go; you wanted to go in combat, you wanted to do your duty.

Well, from there, after basic training, I believe I had 14 weeks of basic training. Of course, in the meantime, or just at the end of our training, the Germans broke through, the Battle of the Bulge, and we were headed for Fort Ord, to go to the Pacific. They re-routed us, and I went to Europe instead.

Well, we went overseas on the *Ile de France*. I never saw so many soldiers on one ship in my life. They said there was like 12,000 of us on that ship; it doesn't seem possible, but it was a big ship. We were stacked five high. And of course, landed in Greenock, Scotland, immediately hopped on a train, and we went down to Southampton, England, and got onto a small English ship, and went to France.

Le Havre Replacements

We landed in Le Havre, and they gave us a meal, and we walked immediately to a railroad station. Then we were put on the infamous 40 & 8s, you know what those are? Each car was marked in French, 'forty men or eight horses.' I mean, you were like mosquitoes in there, I'll tell you. And we ran up into Belgium a short ways, a two-way repo depot, replacement depot.

And here we are, we had carried all kinds of equipment over. When we got to the replacement depot, we were outside of a big, big building, it looked like some sort of a castle. We were told to put all of our stuff in piles, neat piles. Your gas mask, and any clothes you're not going to bring, and stuff like that. All you're allowed to take was what you could stuff in your pockets. That just meant socks, maybe a pair of underwear, and handkerchiefs, that's about it. Believe it or not, they burned some of the stuff. I never could believe what they did. The gas masks, that really bothered me. Just being a kid, you'd heard about being gassed in World War I. And I thought, gee, isn't this, might they be a necessity? So we went up on the front lines without a gas mask; thank God we didn't need them.

I was a replacement to the 79th Division, 314th Infantry. I believe it was just one over-nighter, we stayed in a building there. The next day, we went up on the front lines and got put into squads that were missing men. I happened to be in Company B, 324th Infantry. You met the guys in your squad, and not too many older people. They were all pretty young at that time. I think probably the oldest one in the squad was maybe 28 years old, something like that, my staff sergeant. We did have a first sergeant; he was a former coal miner. He was close to forty! There was a man that I still think about an awful lot, serious, serious. He was a good guy. When he expected you to do something, he didn't just send you. He went with you. We had this captain, Mack, who was our company commander. Same thing. He was always up front with you. Very nice. Very good soldiers. Very good soldiers.

We didn't have that good of equipment. In fact, when we could, when we took prisoners, we took some of their clothes. Gloves, especially. Sometimes a sweater or a jacket. They always wore the long coats, too, if you remember seeing Germans. The worst thing with us was, that was winter, February, our shoes were terrible. Terrible situation. We had those, well, even with the GI shoes, are the six-inch boot, and there's the little flat sole on the top. The leather was turned inside out. You've probably seen those, the rough outside. And there was no insulation whatsoever. They did issue us some snowpacks. You know, the rubber bottoms. Well those were good, as long as you were walking fine. You sweat in them. But at night when you're in the foxhole, man, did they get cold. One of the worst things, like I mentioned before, the gloves weren't that good. I think you still see some of these here, around, they were khaki, not patent leather, but an imitation leather on the front. You couldn't even fire a weapon or do anything with them. So most of the time, you didn't have anything. Or if you grabbed a prisoner, they had fine, leather gloves, with a woolen liner on the inside. So where they were going, they didn't need them. So we used to take them from them.

'That's What You Call a Short Round'

I must tell you a little story about my very first night in combat. The squad I went to was in a house, this was right on the front lines. There were open fields there, and they tell me there was a river not too far up, maybe a half mile, or maybe less, I don't know. The very first night, our staff sergeant, squad leader, said, 'You'll pull guard with me.' There were two of us, went up. And this other fellow pulled with another guy.

So our duty, our guard that night, was just on the outside of the house. There was a road, a dirt road, and we stood there for a while. All of a sudden, an artillery shell went overhead. It went and landed, now I know, behind us. It's funny how you get up there and you're disoriented, you don't know where, which direction you're going in or anything. And then pretty quick, another shell came the other way. So I asked Morgan what the situation was. And he said, 'That one that went that way, that's ours, artillery behind us. And the other one coming in was from the German side.' He called it harassing fire. You only get an artillery shell every once in a while, you know. Well it got so that you could hear the gun go off, and you could hear it whistle overhead, and you could hear it land. And I was kind of paying attention to that.

Then all of a sudden, there was one behind us. I'm listening for it to go overhead, and it didn't. It whined and it landed, probably, I don't know, maybe 100 yards from us. You know? And I said, 'Who fired that?'

He said, 'That's what you call a short round.'

I said, 'Well, you've got to watch out for the Krauts and your own people while you're out there.' Yeah. Oh golly.

*

I actually went on the front lines in February, I think it was the third of February, if I'm not mistaken. You know, you're kind of gung-ho. I think most guys are gung-ho going up there. But it doesn't take long that you realize, this is not John

Wayne movies, you know. This is serious. You grow up an awful lot, while you're up there. I went up as a happy-go-lucky kid, and when I came out, I feel I was grown, you know what I mean? It's no fun. It's no fun. I do remember back in basic training, we used to go out on night patrols, compass patrols, find a certain spot, stuff like that. They had wire up for you, with bells on them. And you had to snip through it. Guys were all laughing and everything, it's a big joke, really, you know? I remember officers telling you, they used to chew us out.

'When you get over there', he called to them, 'Jerry doesn't fool around.' Meaning the Germans, you know. He was saying the right thing. It was truthful. I often wonder how some of the guys who weren't maybe as serious as I was, how they made out, wherever they went. So it's no joke. It's scary, when you're in combat; most of the guys, I found out, would do their job, and do the best they could.

Afterwards, hours later, and speaking only for myself, I used to, when things calmed down, I'd get the shakes. I've never felt like that before or after. It is a serious situation. If I had to do it over again, I would say, 'No.'

*

Let's see, so we went up through the Roer River. Well of course, the Germans were on the run. We were moving pretty fast, and the Germans were leaving; they knew your position. One of the worst things to me was when the artillery came in. They had some pretty good spotters somewhere. They'd come in and they would flood the area with artillery. There's hardly any running from artillery, so that's a scary situation. We had quite a few guys hit that way. At the same time, when we were chasing the Jerries running, they were sending up the Wehrmacht, which were the German professional soldiers. He was a good soldier. And the Hitler Youth, they remind me of the suicide bombers you have today. They didn't give a darn. They were crazy. They were. And you could fight them until you killed them all, really. And they very seldom would run. But some of them, 15 years old, 16 years old, even younger than that, probably.

Crossing the River

We got pulled back. We crossed; we came back to Holland. Exactly where we left from, I don't remember. But we came back into a small town in Holland, and we had a week of training there on the assault boats. This was in preparation for crossing the Rhine River. That was very interesting. They were like what today you'd call a, oh golly, what are they called? A jon boat, do you know what a jon boat is? It's just straight back and probably 15, 16 feet long. There was a bow, a squared-off bow in the front. They put two of them together, back-to-back, and they had what would you call them? The rings on the U-side, they'd back them together and you'd put a pin in there. So you had this boat that was double the length of one of them. The thing that surprised me was, you had an outboard motor on it, and there was a sailor. How he got over on the Rhine River, I don't know. But the Navy ran us across on these assault boats. Of course, the word was if the outboard didn't start, you start paddling. You know, it was a long way across that river. I think there was probably somewhere around 24 [of us in the boat] or something like that, you know. There again, we had thousands of guys going across. But some artillery did come in, and we had some casualties here and there, but not too bad.

On The Run

From there, we just went from little town to little town. Once in a while, you'd run across a company of men, or maybe even a battalion of Germans. But most of the time, it was just small groups. Like I said before, they were on the run.

We got almost surrounded, or cut off, one time. We jumped off at 4:00 in the morning. Again, I don't know what the name of this town was, but it was farm country. Well, there was a coal mine there, I remember that. And we stayed in a building at night, and early morning, probably 4:00 or so, we took off and went through the town, got off on the other side. It was foggier than heck. We climbed this hill; well this road kind of skirted the outside of that hill, on the outside edge, you know? We ran across a teller mine in the road. A teller mine is just a great big mine; it's an anti-tank mine. Someone saw it, and we had two TDs, tank destroyers, with us. They had stopped. The sun came through, and we got hit with everything the

Germans had, everything, really. The only thing that saved us was that we were on the side of this hill, and they were in the woods. If the sun had come out a little bit later, or we didn't stop for those teller mines, if they'd have cut us off from behind, we'd have been annihilated. But hey, everything turned out okay, and they got on the run again, and we went after them. We had a few guys hit that day.

Most of that [fighting in Germany] was the same thing. Little towns, little skirmishes here and there, nothing too serious. We went all the way across, we went through Duesenberg and Dinslaken and other towns I don't remember. Essen. We ended up actually almost into Czechoslovakia at the end. Because a lot of the Germans that were on the run, they changed their clothes and just melded in with the civilians right there. Once in a while, you'd find some guy walking around, and we [would see] that their uniform, blue, it's called a bluish-green, it'd be sticking down below their short pants. You picked them up as a prisoner.

The war ended, and we went to Czechoslovakia; we were very close to Czechoslovakia. Took our training, jungle training, for the assault on Japan. We moved down to southern Germany in the mountains. Again, I don't know exactly where we were. But we had 21 days of jungle training; it rained for 15 of them. And it was just unbelievable, really. The training we got was a lot different than what we had had for Europe. Apparently, that came from experience they had over there from island hopping. One day, we were in tents, and a newspaper came out, the *Stars and Stripes*. I remember reading a little article that said that the United States had developed a fuel, I believe it said fuel, the size of a tennis ball, that would run a ship two and a half times around the world. I wish I had saved the article now. I said, 'Wow, that's a pretty good piece of fuel!' It wasn't long after that, they dropped the atomic bomb, and that was the beginning of that. Whew! We didn't have to go over there, because we had been told that we were going directly from Europe to the Pacific somewhere, no home, furlough, or anything like that. That was kind of a celebration when they dropped the first bomb. Then the second bomb, I said, 'Well, thank God for that.'

The Slave Laborers

I never really saw anything deep in the concentration camps. I saw, well, lesser camps, where some people were there. I remember the, I call them the pajamas, that they wore. They were striped uniforms, and they were all begging for food, and starved, really. When you could, you gave them something. But there was no organized thing to get these people repatriated, you know.

We came back into around near Dortmund, Germany. And we had a battalion, Hungarian, I remember, Polish, and Russian prisoners all together. We had two camps that we were trying to separate and get these people going back to their respective countries. I found that the Russians, you couldn't get too close to them, even the men, really. The Polish people were just kind of a happy-go-lucky people. They had been through quite a bit.

Now, there were some soldiers, but most had been brought back as slaves to work in the factories and things. We fed them, and every once in a while, they'd send out truckloads. I don't remember exactly where they were going, but we weren't involved with that. I felt very bad for those people, because they all seemed like very, very nice people. I remember the Poles very much, because we kept them in, okay, trying to keep them from going out, because they would go out and raid for food and other things.

The Farm Raid

This one camp that I was at, where I was on guard on the back fence. On the back fence it was a flat area, and the fence was down at the bottom of a hill, probably 60, 70 feet down that way. We'd tried to keep the people in the place. One afternoon I was there, and there were a couple of prisoners, or what do you call them, refugees, slaves, or whatever. They came up to me and they said, 'Hi.' And they would say it in German, 'Komrade.' One was asking me all about my M1, he wanted to know what it was all about, and he wanted to know if it was automatic, and he used the word 'automatisch.' I guess that's automatic.

Then they left, and then they came back before my tour of duty was up. They made me understand that they wanted to get out at night. I really didn't care, really. One of them, apparently, had worked for somebody not too far from the camp there. They wanted to know what time I came back on duty. I came on that night at 12:00, 12:00 till 2:00. I told them, as best I could, 12:00, could you be back before 2:00? God knows what they were going to do. But I got out there on the back fence, and in the dark, someone called me. They came up and I said, 'Okay.' Well, they all understood okay. Well, there weren't two of them, there were about eight or ten of them. They went down that hill and took off. It was probably 20 minutes to a half hour later, I could hear some shooting not too far from us.

Now, that stopped, and it's getting close. And it's like a quarter of 2:00. And I said, 'My God, they're going to come back and probably get shot by one of our own guys.' Pretty quick, I hear from down at the bottom of the hill, 'komrade, komrade.' 'Yeah, okay, okay.' Well, they came running up that hill, and they had the biggest pig you ever saw in your life. They had gone down to raid this family's farmyard, and they killed a pig and brought him in. You know, we never saw that pig or the remains of it or anything. They took it and they cooked it and they ate it! Then another night, we were all asked to go to some sort of a show that they had. These were the Polish people. They put on a little [stage] show, with the hand shadows and stuff like that. Somebody had told somebody there that I used to play the accordion. Well, before you know it, they had me up there on the stage and I'm playing the beer barrel polka, and the place isn't enough for us. Like I say, they impressed me as being just a happy-go-lucky people, really.

'They've Been Drinking with the Russians'

After that, well, I got sent to Nuremberg. Shortly after we sent most of these people back to their respective [former homelands], where they were going. I had them all separated, anyway. I can tell you another little story, too, while I was still there. We stayed in an airfield not too far from there. One night, I pulled guard at this little hospital, and there were German doctors and nurses there. I remember an elderly man coming to me, he was asking me for something in Russian. Apparently, he wanted a pill because, well, I didn't know what he was talking about. But I came on duty later that night, and they were bringing guys in that were sick. Throwing up, dead. Apparently, they had gotten into a high-octane gasoline at this airfield, and they were drinking it. Yeah. The next morning, we got pulled out and in formation, and there's Captain Mack again, he said, 'Has anybody here been drinking with the Russians?' Nobody responded. 'Anybody been drinking with the Russians? Take two steps forward.' Nobody moved. He said, 'Has anybody seen Ziggen or Dempsey?' No, no one had seen them.

He said, 'Well, they've been drinking with the Russians. Ziggen is blind and Dempsey is dead. Now is there anybody here that's been drinking with the Russians?' It was then that about a dozen guys stepped forward. They were drinking high-octane gasoline! Can you believe that? Geez. Terrible, terrible. I mean, these were things that kind of make you grow up, you know? I wasn't even nineteen yet.

Nuremberg

Well anyway, from there, I went to... they started the point system for guys to go home. Many of the older fellas, gosh, they had a hundred and some odd points, they'd been up from Africa all the way up. And they went and they disbanded the 79th Division, and the younger fellas like me were sent to the 1st Division, which was located in and around Nuremberg.

I got the duty of working with the Army engineers. They were photostatting copies of captured documents. And I ran a Photostat machine. That was a good duty. I worked the night shift, and I stayed right in Nuremberg, right by the Palace of Justice. I wished I had saved some of the copies of the things that the Germans did. I can tell you a couple of them.

The Documents

There was, well, these commandants of these slave labor camps, they had to be ruthless individuals. There was one paper we copied that said how they would take people out for a walk out of the camp, and they'd have a couple dozen of them, make them dig a big hole. Half of them would get in the hole, and they'd bury them up alive—the other half of the guys would bury their own friends alive. Another [document detailed] that the commandant of the camp said that they weren't shooting enough prisoners. So they had these people marched out to work, wherever they were going, and marched back in. If they came in without their hat on, they got shot. So of course, all these people would be very careful with their hats, and they'd march in. So the guards bringing them in would run up to them and take the guy's hat off and throw it out of line. Well, if you stepped out of line, you got shot, and if you got back at the camp [without the hat], you got shot. That's terrible, isn't it? These are the things that [the Germans documented themselves]; they apparently took pictures of these, wrote these up, and saved them.

I don't know what they were going to do with them, but they were captured documents that they used in the trial.

Sergeant of the Guard

When that got done, when all the copies were made and the trial started, I went back with my company, and I pulled guard in the cell block. The cell block was sort of a center, like a star, and all these blocks went off this way [*gestures several radial corridors with hand*]. Well one of these blocks had the 21 bigwigs, Hermann Goering and Ribbentrop and Hess and all those guys. I pulled guard there for a little while. I was a staff sergeant at the time. I pulled guard on Albert Speer's cell, and Rudolf Hess. Then after that I was there for a short while. I became sergeant of the guard. I took my regular duties every other day for 24 hours. Luckily, I was asked to go up into the courtroom. I pulled guard with the courtroom guard at one of the visitor doors. After that, I was asked to go up onto the witness stand. That was very interesting, because from where we stood, we weren't too far from the interpreters. If they were speaking

German, and you could pick out [the English translations], you know, so you could know what's going on, that was very, very interesting. Very interesting. I actually had, at that time, the latter part of the 21 original prisoners, like von Schirach, and Raeder, and Donitz, and Sauckel, right around that area there. It wasn't long, and I got pulled off of there, and they made me sergeant of the guard. I was moving up real fast. I stayed there until July of '46.

'Goering and I, We Didn't get Along'

I had a lot of contact [with these prisoners]. Goering, he was the highest-ranking German soldier there. He expected to be treated like he was a high-ranking officer. The rest of them, believe it or not, they used to bow down to him, let him go first and stuff like that. He and I didn't get along when I took over sergeant of the guard.

One of my duties was, during a recess, when I opened the door, I stood at parade rest right in the docket where he was right in the corner. I'm sure you've seen pictures of it. He would turn to me, and he asked me for some water. 'Vasser, bitte.'

Okay. I go down to the Lyster bag, which was chlorinated, and I'd get him a little cup of water, and I'd bring it up to him. And he'd take a sip and he'd go, 'Bah, Americanich.' You know? He'd hand it back to me. Now there was no way of getting rid of the water; I used to have to walk down to the men's room on this side to get rid of the water and walk back up.

Mr. DiPalma later recalled that fed up with Goering's antics, he once met Goering's demands by replacing the contents of the cup with water from the toilet instead of the tap, which Goering found better than the chlorinated version. 'I guess I felt it was my little contribution to the war effort,' he added.

In the meantime, you know, I think he was just doing it on purpose, just getting rid of me. I think one of the things was that he didn't want to do any talking, didn't know if maybe I spoke German or stuff like that. I could understand a little bit. But what he didn't know is, we had some German-speaking GIs right there, and they picked up some stuff on him anyway.

Another time, at night when court was over, one of my duties as the sergeant of the guard was to run the elevator. The elevator was located behind a docket in one of the panels. The elevator carried six people: three prisoners, two guards, and myself, made it [one guard to one prisoner], going up or going down. Well at night, we had to get out of there and run and get our trucks to get back to our billet. Everybody would step back, and there's big confusion in the docket. [The Germans] let [Goering] go right through, you know. Well, one night, I grabbed ahold of Field Marshal Keitel, he was standing right there. I said, 'Come on, get in, get in.' And I dragged him in like that. He was indignant; he was going to let Goering get [in first]. I pulled somebody else in, and somebody else, and I left him, left Goering standing there, you know. I think that was one of the reasons why he would send me for water every day, he was getting back at me.

Another time everybody in the docket was stepping over one another, letting him get out first; they were going to lunch. He didn't want to cross the hallway where spectators were, he wanted to walk right across—he didn't want anybody to look at him. So this Captain Gilbert told us, 'Put him last.' Okay, so we put him last. Don't let him stand inside of the doorway. He would wait until everybody went by so he [would have to] walk straight across. Well, I pushed him out there one time, we carried a club, poked him in the back, you know. He turned around and he swung at me, and he hit me on the arm, so I gave him an awful belt in the kidneys. He never said a word to me [after that]. He didn't like me; I know he didn't like me. I had a couple confrontations with him, but other than Goering, the rest of them were all pretty good.

Albert Speer, many of them spoke English. I never heard Goering speak English. Albert Speer, he was Hitler's architect, if you remember correctly. I always felt sorry for him. He was the architect, but he kind of got, I think, using the right word here, sucked into being a Nazi, and he turned out to be a Nazi. Of course, this was all for glory, I guess, for himself. I think Hitler just used him. He was a very calm-speaking individual. Always spoke to the guards. He was quite an artist. He never did me, but some of the other guys that pulled guard on some of these cell blocks, on his cell, he used to draw pencil sketches of them, and they were good. Very, very good. Imagine something like that's worth a buck today. I don't have that.

Let's see, Streicher, he was a pain in the neck, complained all the time. Terrible, terrible. Going back just a little bit, when I pulled guard on the cell block, imagine standing there for an hour and watching the guy sleep through a little hole in the door, you know, it's awful monotonous. The guys used to talk to one another, and the other guys would get to laughing. Some of them [prisoners] didn't get much sleep at night. You kind of had to keep it down; when I was sergeant of the guard, sometimes you used to hear hollering down there, so I had to go down there and tell the guys to knock it off. Have you ever seen the old German pfennig? It's their penny. It's about as big as our half dollar. Well, one of the things they used to do at night, this wing had a terrazzo floor. These guys would roll these pennies down the terrazzo floor, and it sounded like a freight train coming down through there! [*Laughs*] I'm surprised that a lot of the

German prisoners could stay awake in the courtroom the next day.

Another night, I was in the guard office, and I had a cot there, I was laying there. I could hear some screaming. I said, 'Oh my God!' I went down there and the guard at Streicher's door, out of monotony, had taken a piece of paper and folded it, and he had ripped a little man out of it, so that when you opened it up, it was a man with just legs and arms like that and the head. And from off his uniform somewhere, he had tied a piece of string [tied to the neck of the effigy]. You had the light on just outside of the cell, and he's swinging the thing in front of the light, and it's [silhouetting] on the wall, a man hanging. [*Chuckles*] Jeez. I really don't blame him for trying to get through the hours, standing there.

Rudolf Hess, I think he was sane. He was trying to act like he had a mental problem. When they wanted [fresh air], in their cell, they only had one window and it was high up. The ceilings were probably ten or twelve foot high, and there was a window, like you had in the old style of schools, with the hook on them. And there was just the awning type, but they open [that way]. There was a window stick that we used to use, and the sergeant of the guard was the only one who was allowed to handle the window stick, so when Hess called for a window [to be opened], he'd do this generally in the middle of the night sometimes, he'd call for the window stick. One night I went down there, and I went into the cell, opened the window, took the window stick, and waited outside. He used to stand in front of the window and look out, and he'd mumble something. It wasn't German, I think he was just faking, really.

Let's see, von Schirach, I pulled guard on the witness stand with him. He was head of the Hitler Youth. One day, there was quite a confrontation between him and Chief Justice Jackson. Of course, we could understand him. And he spoke decent English now, but most of his replies were in German. But through the interpreter, we could hear what was going on. They were arguing back and forth about the duties of the Hitler Youth. Well, they called a recess shortly after that, and he turned to me. I was on his left side. He turned to me, and he said, 'But the Hitler Youth is nothing more than your Boy Scouts.'

I said, 'Really?' He doesn't realize that I was a frontline soldier.

I said, 'I fought your Hitler Youth.' He never said a word [after that]. We found Hitler Youth that could take apart our BAR, our M1s, or any of our equipment. So they weren't Boy Scouts like he wanted to portray them.

I kind of felt sorry, though, for Admiral Donitz. I guess he was the bigwig as far as the Navy was concerned. One of the things they had him on was shooting prisoners. I guess, when his U-boats sunk a ship, these guys would go around getting rid of the ones that survived. Well, we never did that. But I do remember when I was on the front lines, and we were moving fast, we take no prisoners. I never had occasion to do anything about that. But that could've happened up in our area, too. Why would they get him on that, unless it was because he put out the order, maybe? I mean, I think the old story goes, all's fair in love and war, right? You break the other guy's leg so you can go see your girlfriend, right?

The rest of them were all just no problems, really. No problems. Alfred Jodl, he was a signer of the surrender terms. He didn't talk to anybody. Him and Keitel, they weren't Nazis, but they originally were Wehrmacht soldiers, and they were good soldiers. But of course, they turned into Nazis afterwards, you know?

*

I came home in July, yeah, about three months before the trial ended. [I was not present when Goering committed suicide]; I think [he died] the beginning of October, as I recall. Everybody was trying to get their autographs. In fact, I have their autographs. All but Hess. Every time you'd ask Hess for his autograph, he spoke good English, because he spent quite a bit of time in England, he said, 'after the trials.' Well, you know what our favorite saying was? 'You won't be here after the trials.'

The Return to Nuremberg

I was discharged at Fort Meade, Maryland. Yep, that was a happy day. I got a chance to go back to Germany two years ago. I went with my number three daughter, she writes children's books, and writes a few other little things, whatever she feels like doing. The day we got into Nuremberg proper, I wanted to go down to see the courthouse, if I could get there. It was raining, we got a cab and went down there. I was amazed at Nuremberg to start off with. When I was there, about one third of it was just demolished. But they've done a wonderful job of putting it together, they repaired the buildings. You could see where the stonework was a little bit different and stuff like that, and they saved an awful lot of it. I was surprised at the U-Bahn, the subway that they have there now. It is beautiful. It goes out of the city to the airport, and it goes all over the place. So we got to ride that over there. But getting back to the day that we went down to the courthouse, walked around the complex there. I told my daughter, I said, 'There's the gate that I used to go in every morning.' So we get down there, and the gate was open.

The building where the courtroom was, when we were there, you couldn't go [directly] into that building. You had to go into the main part of the palace, and then go upstairs, and come across. The courthouse, I mean, the courtroom was up on the third floor. But that door was open on the first floor. And there were people there. So I walked up and I grabbed this young fella and I said, 'Do you speak English?'

He said, 'A little bit.'

I said, 'Can we get up into the courtroom?'

'Well no, the last tour just went up.'

I said, 'Tour?'

'Yes, today's the first day that they started tours.'

I said, 'Well, I was a guard here during the trials.' Well, he went over and talked to this elderly gentleman, and the guy comes running over, and didn't speak a word of English. You know, he said to me and my daughter, 'Kommen, kommen!' And he ran us up these three stories, and we got into the courtroom. There was a guide, a tour guide, he was speaking in German. The fella went up and said something to him, and he continued with his speech. Then he said something about 'hauptmann.' The hauptmann is sort of a person that's a leader, or something like that. So there were maybe 18 people there, and they all turned and looked, and I said to my daughter, 'He must have told them that I was a guard here.' So anyway, when it got done, he said to me, 'Can you wait?' He spoke English also. He said, 'Can you wait till I show this film? I'd like to talk to you.'

I said, 'Okay.' Well, I have pictures of myself in the courtroom, but I've never seen myself on the film. And I saw it that day for the first time! Of course, it was all narrated in German. Anyway, after this got over with, this Wolfgang Meyer who was in charge of this thing, came to me and he asked all kinds of questions. So we were supposed to get out of there at 4:30, he kept me there till almost 6:00 asking questions.

*

I was sweating when I got done. A lot of the questions, I couldn't answer. But what they're doing now is they had set up a museum and they wanted as much information as possible, and they had different places that were on display. He said, 'We are opening up on November 4,' of, well, let's see, that'd be a year and a half ago. And he said, 'It'd be nice if you could be here at the opening.'

And I said, 'Well jeez, if I can, I'll try.' So my daughter, my wife, and myself, we bought tickets, and then September 11 came along, so we didn't go. Yeah. This thing that they call it, I have a pamphlet at home, it was called 'Fascination and Terror,' and they were trying to tell me how they were trying to show the good and the bad. I would've liked to have gone, but I think I'm going this year. I'd like to see that, yeah. It's nice that they, rather than be mad at Americans, would show that they probably were wrong, you know? Admit it and go on from here.

When I left the service, I worked for American Bosch. I used to hand lap the inside of an injection nozzle on a diesel, you know. That was an awful job. I never went back. I didn't know what to do. Well my dad at that time was an inside crane operator. He worked an overhead crane. Of course, he was unionized. He said, 'Why don't you get into the union, and try and learn to run machines?' Stuff like that. I thought that was pretty good. So I did take an apprenticeship. I was an oiler on a crane, a helper. So I eventually got my license, and I was a crane operator, up until I retired.

*

I married in 1949, we had four daughters, and we have nine grandchildren. Like I said before, I was a happy-go-lucky kid when I went in. When I came out, I was grown up. We saw things that we don't see every day here in the States, or it wasn't totally like I was brought up. It makes me ... It made me, I should say, a little bit leery of everybody. You don't take people at face value. As a kid, anything an adult told me, that was it. But when I came back, I never trusted anybody. I think that's made me a better person. It tells you what the real world is, rather than a bowl of cherries, you know.

*

Leo DiPalma at the time of the interview, June 2002.

'*I Think About Things Like That*'

What's happening today, I think my experiences are nothing to what's going on now. I wouldn't want to be going in the service now, like our boys are doing. I hate to say this, but I have no qualms about any mistakes that we make now during the war. But I think even in that war, we didn't initiate it. It bothers me today when I read, well, we lose one guy or two guys or three guys. You know, we didn't start any of this here, so I don't feel bad when they have a problem. I do feel bad when a GI gets killed, even one.

I had a very good friend killed. When I went up, I was made a number two scout, number one scout, he had been up there a few months before me. In one little skirmish we had, he got killed. I never even saw him. That bothers me, it bothers me right now. He was one hell of a good kid. He was from Mississippi. That shouldn't be; he was married, and 21 years old, and had a child. He's gone. For what? It wasn't his fault. And there's many, many like that.

There were even, other than Clarkie, there are other guys that got killed. Older men with children, you know? Other than saying it's horrible, what else can you say? I met a guy from Boston, I remember him because when we came back to do this assault training, across the Rhine River, we were in the town of Applebee, Holland. I remember him going by, on his field jacket, he had a hub, a wheel, you know. And he had over it, 'Boston: the hub of the universe.' So hey, he's from Massachusetts, right? I'm from Massachusetts. So we got a little bit friendly and, well, he got hit with an artillery shell on that day that we crossed the Rhine River.

I think about things like that. You just can't forget it, really. It's not the way any of us in this country were ever brought up. I saw another guy die, same day, he had taken a piece of shrapnel in his leg up here, while we were in an artillery attack. Well, they had pinned us up against an elevated railroad. We managed to get back on the other side, but again, they had that position pinpointed for artillery. The German 88 was a very accurate artillery piece, and it was coming in, just clearing the railroad tracks, and getting us down below. I had gotten down into a brook, and I had dug into the brook, and dug on the bank. This other kid had actually got hit in the leg. And the medic went to him, and he said he was okay, put sulfur powder on him, bandaged the leg and covered him up for shock. He was dead in ten minutes, with just a wound in the leg.

We used to get training, of course, on shock, which I'm sure you've heard of. You believe it and you don't. As far as I'm concerned, one of President Roosevelt's sons said, I forget exactly how he put it. But [war is] an experience to go through [once], but never again. Words to that effect, I'm sure you've probably heard this. I hope it never, nobody ever has to go. I don't like war. It's too bad. But it seems like it's always necessary, isn't it?

PART FOUR

LAST THOUGHTS

Albert Tarbell later in life.

CHAPTER TWENTY-TWO

The Paratrooper V

It was time to wrap up the interview for the day, after almost three hours of non-stop testimony from a man who had an eyewitness view to some of the most important happenings of World War II in Europe, the first Mohawk paratrooper in the United States Army. He had some things to say about life after the war, and the therapeutic effects of opening up and sharing his wartime experiences.

Albert A. Tarbell

I was in Berlin until November. I think it was around November; I think I left there around November. I got orders to report to the trucking area the following morning, and a bunch of us were leaving for the States. So we had a party. We got two days' notice. They had a party for me at one of the German nightclubs. And oh, we were having a good time. At that time, that song came out, 'Sentimental Journey.' Oh, I had that band playing that over and over and over! And finally, the waiter came over, we had our own cognac with us. He said, 'There's a gentleman over there, an officer, and he'd like to join your party. He said you're having such a good time here.' It was a brigadier general from the Far East Command, on his way through, going back to the States, and he was going by the way of Berlin. He said, 'Is somebody going home?'

I said, 'Yes, sir.' I said, 'I'm going home.' Well, he sat down, and we had all kinds of drinks. Oh, we had a grand time there. Who would think a brigadier general would ask to join us regular soldiers, regular paratroopers? But he said, 'You're having such a grand time, I just had to come over and ask if I could join!'

Anyway, I ended up shipping out early in the morning, about 5:00. And who was there to meet us but General Gavin, to say goodbye to us. The last of the old guard was leaving the 82nd, coming back to the States. And he passed out Belgian fourragères to us, he handed us our Belgian fourragères.[26] He said, 'The rest of your awards will be in the mail,' and this and that. Yeah, so that was quite a send-off.

We got to Le Havre, and we got on the *SS America*, which was a luxury liner converted into the *USS West Point*, taken over by the Army in the service. And oh man, I had a couple thousand dollars in my billfold. Everybody had black market money, we had quite a bit of money. And whoa, they had some fierce card games there. I didn't even want to play [anymore], because I won over $1,000 in a poker game, American money. After that, I just didn't want to spend it, it looked so entirely different than your foreign currency you'd been getting all these years.

We had a hurricane in the middle of the Atlantic, and oh God, we were there for about two days in that storm. Oh, it seemed like a week, it seemed like a month; I thought it was never going to end. That ship would roll this way and that way and this

---

[26] *Fourragère-* award for distinguished military unit service, a braided cord worn on the left shoulder.

way. One night, it rolled, and then it stopped, and then it rolled again. And all the barracks racks came falling down. I was sleeping in the grand ballroom, right on down on the mezzanine floor, and oh, I thought we were going right over. Then it straightened back up. The ship would go right out of the water, come down, and the propellers would spin when they came out of the water. When it would hit, it would jerk! I mean, those sailors were working round the clock, those welders. And we said, 'How is this? Is this bad?'

'No, no, this is nothing!' And it seemed like the storm just died right down after that.

We finally made it back. We got back to Hampton Roads, where we left almost two years ago. And we came back to Fort Dix, and we were there just long enough for them to process us out. They wouldn't even let us keep our clothes, nothing, just a few things. I was lucky, I got through with three pistols. I had a permit for them. A sword, a couple knives, and a couple helmets; they took that. You know what I forgot to mention? That woman in the [house where we had the long R&R in France], when we were getting ready to leave there, they kissed us goodbye and shook hands. And here's this woman, come out in the other room, and she had my jacket for me. She had made a hood; she had lined the inside with fur from an old fur coat. Man, I was the envy of everyone for that! When we made that march, they thought I was a colonel or something! And she had it big enough it would fit over my helmet, it was all fur-lined—I wore that the rest of the winter, the rest of the war. I brought it back, I was going to keep it. Do you know, they took it away from me at Fort Dix? And then, they had the nerve to ask me to join the National Guard! I said, 'Well, I don't know.' I said, 'Let me think about it.' But then, I did think about it afterwards. But my wife wouldn't even let me join the Salvation Army after that, well, she was so glad to have me home. [*Laughter*]

*

I got home, I went back in the same trade that I was in, and I changed from there, I went into ironworking, [liked to be in the air]. My wife and I raised six kids and I kept working. I spent 34 years with the ironworkers, and I've been retired 18 years now.

I had a nice family. My son is a second-generation paratrooper. He's from Vietnam, and one of my daughters is an artist, so she had the Governor's Award, the first Mohawk woman to earn the Pataki Governor's Award.

*

I think [my service did change my life]. It brought me into my sphere in living; it gave me the knowledge of how to command men, too. At one time I had over 200 men and 14 foremen working for me. I think by being able to take orders and give orders and stuff like that, you know, you've got to give and take. That's one thing I learned. Our officers were some of the world's best. They ate with you. They lived with you. They fought for you.

The good thing about World War II was that we stayed as one group and the officers did not change every couple of months, like every six months you get a new batch of officers in. No, it was like this right from beginning to end, [our officers], they stayed with us. I think that made for better comradeship and I think for better soldiering, too.

'I Didn't Talk About the War'

For twenty-five years, I didn't talk about the war, just with one guy I served with. It was tough carrying that inside, I had some drinking bouts trying to drown it. That's why when my son Mike came home from Vietnam, I always got him on the side, to pump him for information, to get it out of him. The worst thing you can do is hold it inside; I had nobody to pump me for information, so I was always thinking about it. I could be driving home from work, look at the hills, and say, 'What a great place for fortification. They could have gun positions up there, and I could be ambushed, I'm wide open here.' For a long time, that kind of thing happened.

I could never sleep with my arms under the covers for many, many years—I think it had to do with that night we were counterattacked in the Den Heuvel Woods, when I was in my sleeping bag. I had nightmares; my wife would have to wake me, then I would go back to sleep. I had nightmares right up until she died; they finally went away after someone told me to sleep on the side of the bed that she slept on. After that, I only had nightmares once or twice; to this day, I don't know why. Maybe it's because I worried so much about her, and what she went through, when I was in the service.[15]

'Tell the Children that I'm a Warrior'

In September 2006, Albert returned to Nijmegen to be greeted by the Dutch people who have not forgotten the men of 1944 and their heroic deeds. At the River Waal Crossing Commemoration, as one of the few surviving first wave veterans, he recited the Lord's Prayer in the native Mohawk tongue, bringing together the generations and the spirits of the men who had passed.

Later, he sent the schoolchildren of Nijmegen an Iroquois flag, and wrote to a Dutch friend to pass on some words to them:

> Through our laws as a guiding force, and through our heroes as an ideal, the Iroquois have persisted as a people. Heroes are important—they exist, and can help you to know

who and what you are. They're like us of flesh and blood!

Tell the children that I was a warrior.[16]

Albert Tarbell passed on August 25, 2009, at the age of 86.

The bodies of former prisoners are piled in the crematorium mortuary in the newly liberated Dachau concentration camp. Dachau, Germany, April 29, 1945. National Archives, public domain. USHMM.

CHAPTER TWENTY-THREE

Dachau and the Question

As I started this book, we passed the 76th anniversary of the liberation of Dachau.

Today, if the anniversary is brought up at all, many Americans might respond with a vacant stare. More might shrug and turn away. I suppose that is to be expected. But you know me. I just think that as a nation, sometimes we allow things to slip from memory at our peril.

It was real, and it happened. And as you have read, it was American GIs who overran this camp and many others in the closing days of World War II.

The men of the 42nd and 45th Infantry Divisions arrived independently of each other, here, in southern Germany, at Dachau, on this day. A concentration camp, they were told. Their noses gave them a hint of what they were about to uncover, miles before the camp appeared in sight.

Newspaper, April 30, 1945, that hung in my classroom for years.

Read the headlines, above. Note the sub-article:

Boxcars of Dead at Dachau. 32,000 captives freed.

And so after some resistance, into the camp they entered. Life-changing events were about to unfold for the American soldiers.

For me, it's not about hero worship, or glorifying the liberator or any World War II soldier by placing him on a pedestal. Our time with them is now limited, mostly passed, but many of the liberating soldiers I knew pushed back at this, to the point of rejecting the term 'liberator'— 'It all sounds so exalted, so glamorous,' said one. But they will all accept the term 'eyewitness.'

Witnesses to the greatest crime in the history of the world.

So instead I think it is about honoring their experiences, their shock, the horror, the puking and the crying, the rage—and then, the American GIs recognizing that something had to be done. And they did suffer for it, for trying to do the right thing. Many tried to help by offering food to starving prisoners who just were not ready to handle it, only to see them drop dead. Or having to manhandle these emaciated victims who were tearing away at each other as food was being offered.

Some guys never got over it. How could you?

I have learned so much over the past few years from these guys, just through the way that they carried themselves and tried to cope with what they witnessed. In my World War II Studies and Holocaust class, we discuss these issues at length. I was so lucky to be able to teach it, to see our young people respond to learning and conserving and caring about the past. All I had to do was share my enthusiasm and expose them to the history.

Their history.

*

A few years back, I was privileged to teach a lesson to my high school seniors for NBC Learn, which was shared with other districts across the nation. Later, I stumbled upon this piece by the late author Tony Hays, who writes about his liberator father and his own encounter with the past.

Dachau Will Always Be with Us

Tony Hays

Dachau and the Question I had never been able to ask my father.

This is not so much an essay about writing as one about a writer's education, about one of those experiences that molds us, shapes us into storytellers. I read yesterday the story of Joseph C., whose father, a World War II veteran, left him with a special legacy from the war, from the hideous Nazi concentration camp at Dachau.

I feel a particular kinship with Mr. C.

My late father, Robert Hays, was the son of an alcoholic tenant farmer in rural west Tennessee. If the appellation 'dirt poor' fit anyone, it fit my grandfather's family. Daddy served in the Civilian Conservation Corps during the thirties. He and my mother, who was in the women's equivalent of the CCC, working as a nurse's aide at Western State Mental Hospital in Bolivar, Tennessee, met on a blind date in early 1940 and married in September of that year.

But just over a year later, Pearl Harbor happened. America was in the war. My father was among the first of those drafted in 1942. I won't bore you with the details, but he participated in the North African, Salerno, Anzio, and southern France invasions, saved by the luck of the draw from Normandy. But they slogged through France and on to Germany. On April 29, 1945, Allied troops liberated the Dachau concentration camp. I don't know whether he entered Dachau that day or the next, but that he was there within hours of the liberation is beyond dispute. A few months later, after more than three years overseas, he came home.

In later years, he would talk occasionally about the war, providing anecdotes that showed the chaos and random chance of battle. He spoke of driving through Kasserine Pass in North Africa just hours before the Germans killed thousands of Allied troops in a stunning attack. He spoke of a friend, defending his position from a foxhole, who was thought dead after an artillery shell landed right next to him. When the dust cleared, the friend was buried up to his neck in dirt but did not have a scratch on him. He spoke often of Anzio, where he was wounded, and of the massive German air assaults on those soldiers clinging to that tiny sliver of beach along the Italian coast.

But he never spoke of Dachau.

Ever.

When he died in 1981, we found a photo in his wallet. An old sepia-toned shot like others he had taken during the war, pictures that he kept in an old brown bag. But this one was different.

It showed a pile of naked bodies. Well, really more skeletons than not, with their skin stretched pitifully over their bones. On the back, as had been his habit, was typed simply 'Dachau.'

I was confused. Why would he keep this one photo in his wallet all of those years? Especially a photo of a place and event that he never spoke about. It obviously had some deeper meaning for him than the other photographs. If it had been a shot of the building he was in when he was wounded (hit by an artillery shell), I could have seen that. A reminder of his closest brush with death. Yeah, I could buy that. But this macabre photo? That, I couldn't see.

So, for the next fifteen years, I remained puzzled.

Until the fall of 1996. I was working in Poland, and I had some time off. I took an overnight bus from Katowice, Poland, to Munich. It was an interesting trip all in itself. We sat in a line of buses at midnight on the Polish/German border, waiting for our turn to cross, next to a cemetery, as if in some Cold War spy movie. I remember passing Nuremberg and thinking that my father had been there at the end of the war. And then there was Munich.

I spent a day or two wandering through the streets, drinking beer in the Marienplatz. I'm a historical novelist, so the short trip out to Dachau was a no-brainer. Of course it was as much my father's connection with it as anything else that spurred the visit. But I'm not sure that I was completely aware of that at the time.

Dachau literally sits just on the outskirts of the Munich metropolitan area. I looked at the sign on the train station with a sadness, wondering for how many people that had been one of the last things they saw. It was only later that I discovered there had been another depot for those passengers.

The Dachau Memorial is a place of deep emotion. In the camp proper, mostly all that are left are the foundations of the barracks. One has been reconstructed to give an idea of how horrible life must have been. The camp was originally intended to hold 6,000 inmates; when the Allies liberated Dachau in 1945, they found 30,000. The museum and exhibits are primarily in the old maintenance building. I looked with awe at life-size photos of prisoners machine-gunned, their hands torn to ribbons from the barbed wire they had tried to climb in a futile attempt at escape.

I followed the visitors—I can't call them tourists—north to where you crossed over into the crematorium area. It was there that the full brunt of what had taken place at Dachau really hit me. A simple brick complex, it seemed so peaceful on the fall day that I stood before it. But as I read the plaques and consulted my guidebook, as I stepped through the door and actually saw the 'shower' rooms where the prisoners were gassed, as I stared into the open doors of the ovens, I felt a rage unlike any I had ever known consume me.

*

That night, I went to the famous Hofbräuhaus in Munich, to wash the images of the ovens away with some beer. I hadn't been there long when an elderly American couple sat at the table. They were from Florida, a pleasant couple. He had been a young lieutenant in the American army on the push into Munich. In fact, it had been his pleasure to liberate the Hofbräuhaus from the Germans.

Of course, I asked the question. 'Were you at Dachau?'

He didn't answer for several seconds, tears glistening in the corners of his eyes as his wife's hand covered his and squeezed. Finally, he nodded, reached into a back pocket and pulled out his wallet.

With a flick of his wrist, a photo—just as wrinkled, just as bent, as the one my father had carried—landed on the table. It wasn't the same scene, but one just like it.

Here was my chance, the opportunity to ask the question I had never been able to ask my father. I pulled the photo from my own wallet and laid it next to his.

'Why? Why have you carried it so long? To remind you of the horror of Dachau, of what had been done here?'

His face carried the faintest of smiles as he shook his head.

'No, son, to remind us of the horrors that we are capable of, to remind us not to go down that road again.'

The difference was subtle, but in that moment, I learned two lessons invaluable to a writer, subtle differences are important, and when you want to know the truth, go to the source.

As I sit here now and look at that same photograph, I realize that it was my father's legacy to me, of Dachau. Joe C.'s father left him something more tangible, a reminder of the same thing for the same reason, but more forcefully stated—a tiny box of human ash from the ovens.

Dachau is still with us, and I hope the legacy left by our fathers always will be.[17]

In a subsequent communication, Tony added, 'I left out another man, actually the one that the American couple came to see. They had wanted to meet someone who might have been in the German army and had been told that a fellow came in every night and sat at the table where I was sitting. Eventually, he did, a wrinkled old guy who spoke little to no English. I knew some German, and so I translated as best I could. His name was Tony too, and he had been a teenager in the last days. He had been conscripted near the end of the war and had been taken prisoner by the Americans. He had been assigned to help clean up the hundreds of dead bodies at Dachau.

He cried as he told the story.'

The journalist and writer Tony Hays passed away in 2015.

Richard Marowitz, Al Cohen, Doug Vink
with captured souvenir,
Hudson Falls High School library, April 2000.

Richard Marowitz and Al Cohen talk to students
and display their artifacts.

Hudson Falls, NY High School, April 2001.

CHAPTER TWENTY-FOUR

War Stories

These stories were recorded around the library table after school, following the formal interview session, with just a small group of students and adults present, on April 28, 2000, just one day shy of fifty-five years to the day that the gates of Dachau were thrown open. Like with the bomber boys in Volume 3, being able to sit around a table and listen to them converse—good friends, unhindered and unscripted—was the thrill of a lifetime for all who were present. In closing, we ask you, the reader, to join us at the table one last time.

Somewhere in Germany, 1945

**Richard Marowitz
Douglas Vink
Alvin Cohen**

Rich Marowitz: The door slowly opened. There was a father, a mother, and a daughter, and they all had buckteeth. [*Laughter*]

That's not funny yet. I looked down at their little dog, and it had buckteeth! And that cracked me up. So the guys looked at me and they said, 'What the hell's the matter with you?' It's just funny. So we got them out of the way. And there's this big door in the floor that you picked up, and we picked it up and hollered downstairs, you know, in the basement. And we said to the folks, 'Is anyone down there?' And they were going like this [*makes hand motions*]. They were afraid to say so, but we knew there was someone down there, so one of the guys threw a grenade down there. And of what was left, twenty-five came out, we took them prisoner.

Now in scouting around the area, which was under sniper fire all the time, we pull in three SS troops. And the farms in Germany at the time, in the back yard they had this big square pit. This is where they put all the manure and they wet it down. It's not a healthy sight…

Doug Vink: It's not real appetizing. [*Laughter*]

Rich Marowitz: …And they wet it down and there's always a lot of flies around. There must be some system underneath where they wet it down because all this drains into a tank. And they have a tank on the back end of the wagon, and they roll it out and they can actually spray the fields and fertilize them. So we stood these SS guys in that stuff, and we said, 'When you're ready to talk, we'll talk to you.' In the meantime the Germans were still sniping at us; we kept running back and forth in front of them because they were right in the alley where the sniper fire was coming from. We figured maybe they will hit their own guys, but it didn't work. [*Laughs*]

There was a house next to us where there was some sniper on the second floor who was just raising hell with us. And finally, we got him. We didn't know who the hell it was, but we got him. And we went up and took a look, we get into the house and went up to the second floor and this kid couldn't have been more than twelve years old! And the Hitler Youth wore, you know, short pants. One of the guys, he had little kids—eleven, twelve years old—in German uniforms. And we captured a couple of them one day. One of the guys in my platoon spanked the hell out of him and told him 'Now go home.'

I said to him, 'You idiot, he could turn around and shoot you.' But that was the colonel, he was just one hell of a guy.

Doug Vink: We were on the move once and hit the fire with the big guns. The tank gun got so hot that when our loader threw a shell in it, it only went halfway and swelled up. We're out there with a big stick, they had a long stick with a comb on it, you kept trying to pound it out. Anyway, they told us to stop right where we were to stay there. It was just outside a little German town. It was Easter Sunday. Here comes the townspeople with colored eggs and getting something for us to eat. And one's saying to me, 'There's [German soldiers] in the cellar.' So three of us get out and we go up, and we got the three of them. As we're bringing them back, I get back to the tank and I'm up in the turret and I watch and there's three more of them running across the field. Now I'm a first-class machine gunner; I have citations for being a first-class machine gunner. I couldn't hit one of them in the behind going across that field. They all got away.

One of these kids was a fifteen-year-old sergeant, fifteen years old! One was sixteen years old, and the other one was in his twenties. So there we are, a tank crew, broken down, and we can't do anything. And we got those three prisoners sitting there. Now the fifteen-year-old sergeant was the toughest guy you ever wanted to meet. Every time one of those other two tried to talk to us, he'd say something, and they'd stop. So the commander said to me, 'What the hell are we going to do with them?' It's been three days now we got them.

And I said, 'Nobody will take them!' I said that because nobody's coming up. We're waiting for the tank retriever to come to pick us up. So all of a sudden, here comes an American ambulance down the road coming out right from where the battle was. I get out in the middle and I stop them. I said, 'We've got three German prisoners here and we can't hold them because they're in the way.' Well, he said, 'Are they wounded?'

I said, 'Does it make a difference?'

'Oh, yeah, we only take wounded.'

I said, 'Give me a minute.' I went up and got my submachine gun. I hit the sergeant in the head. I said, 'Is he bleeding enough?'

'Yeah, bring him down.' And there he went. Well, we gave the kid a vacation. [*Laughter*]

Rich Marowitz: I'll tell you what, I had a bad experience. We had a captain from Louisiana that took great pride in the fact that he could speak fluent French. As a result, he spoke French to everyone—Germans, Hungarians, it didn't make a difference. He just wanted to try out his French. So he came with us one time. He was assigned there, and like I said before, the girls had the little white dresses. We got into this little village in the square and the church is always in the square. And this little girl in a little white dress, he goes over to her, and he starts talking. 'This is Alsace-Lorraine,' he said, he starts talking in French, and I could tell by looking at her she wasn't quite getting what he was saying, and she started to cry like hell. Now, in

Alsace-Lorraine they speak this weird combination of German and French. Now Yiddish is a lot like German, that particular kind of German, and with a little bit of high school French, because I was still only eighteen at the time, I could make out what these people in this area were saying. So I turned around to one of my men. I said, 'That girl is going to call everyone out of church.'

He said, 'What are you talking about?'

I said, 'That kid doesn't understand what that idiot jerky captain is talking about.'

So he said, 'Are you sure?'

'Yes, I'm serious!'

Sure enough, the doors open up. It is Sunday morning, and everybody is coming out crying! They thought they were going to be shot! So someone said to me, 'Marowitz, go tell them to get back in church.' And the captain backed us up. You don't do that. There's no reason for it. War is war, but are you willing to pick on the kids and their mothers and old women?

Doug Vink: As Richard said before, you always find something funny. You had to...

This happened to us while we were in England. We were in a replacement depot waiting to be shipped over to go out where the guys got killed when they came on the beach at Normandy. And we were called as replacements, but you never sat still, even though you were in England. You figured 'oh well, I'll be going over there, let me take it easy.' No! We went on a road hike every day. Now this was the tank corps, and we still went on a hike. First, they give you infantry training before you ever become a tank man because once you lose a tank, you're definitely an infantryman. Nobody wants to lose a tank. But anyway, we were in England. So then they would take you for extra training on the tank, to make sure you're all up to date. Well, once you get to France, first thing they tell you is, 'Throw that damn book out the window! When you studied all this, forget about it—we don't do that!' You take all the tools off the tank, you buried them because you didn't want to be taking up tracks, you know, and be digging yourself out.

The funniest thing that happened to us in England, I don't know if anyone is familiar with the streets, streets are very narrow. Of course, they drive on the wrong side, but we're idiots. We don't know. We drove down the middle of the road. We got a tank—nobody is going to stop us! But then you come down to a dead end, and you got to go left or right, and there's all these little houses. We come down the hill one day, I said to the tank commander, 'I hope the driver knows we have to take a right.' Oh yeah, he knows! Forgot to turn! Right across the street, right into the house, the gun sticking over the dining room table. And the commander yells to the girl at the table, 'Would you please pass the butter!' [*Laughter*]

Rich Marowitz: We were—one day, and I don't know what the river was. It was narrow, a canal or something, and there was this barge. Well, our job is to find out what the hell is going on. So we went out and checked on the barge. And there was this huge crate. Maybe its airplane motors or something like that, we cracked open one case. Champagne! We guessed maybe there were fifty bottles of champagne, so we cracked open another crate, and guesstimated that there was another fifty bottles of champagne. We got seven jeeps and we got seven cases of champagne, and we were heading back to headquarters because we were going to go reserve for two weeks. So we loaded up and we were sitting on top of the crate while we're going back, and we get back to headquarters and we immediately crack open a case. And we're preceding to get blind, and someone runs in from regimental headquarters and said, 'There's a town about 10 miles up, we don't know whether it's ours or theirs. Go find out!' So we were 28 drunken I&R men, and we're heading up there. Now to this day when we get together the standard topic of conversation is 'How long does it take for an I&R man to get out of a jeep?' [*Laughs*]

It's never been answered because you don't wait for the jeep to stop! If something fires, you roll out! The jeep is still going. It doesn't make any difference. The helmet goes one way, you go another. But you never drop your weapon, right? And nobody asked about the driver. How the hell does he do it? The old jeeps used a choke. He was driving with a choke, that was his gas pedal. And he had a scabbard on his side of the jeep with his rifle in it, and what he did was, he would hit the break, use his foot to hit the break; the right foot to hit the break, pushed the throttle in, and peel out and grab his rifle on his way and roll out! And the jeep found a place to stop, so, actually no one ever got hurt. You have to understand combat when you're on a jeep, you never use a windshield. That's always laying down and covered with canvas. Windows folded down because you didn't want to get hit with glass and you don't want to have reflections, either.

So this is what happens, now we got fired on, and we bailed out on the way, just outside this village. And we're looking up there, and nobody is firing, and I look over. I said, 'These guys look confused!' They look more confused than we were! They were all American tanks, so they stopped shooting. Then, they were checking us over more thoroughly, and one guy had eyeglasses and they finally realized we were Americans. And so they got up, and they had machine guns, they had machine guns outside of the tanks. And they said, 'We almost destroyed you! What the hell is the matter with you guys?'

I said, 'We're drunk.' We got back in the jeeps and went back. 'The Americans are here!' [*Laughter*]

Al Cohen: We were fighting in one town, and we had half the town taken. Still fighting from door to door and the rest of the town, and lo and behold, they found a still. And a lot of these guys are from Missouri, and they're moonshiners, so they drop their rifles and packs, and they're starting the still back up again. They had one hell of a time! [*Laughter*]

Doug Vink: Well I had a job one time, when I told you about when we were stopped outside Berlin to let the Russians take it. Well, after they took over Berlin, they moved us back all the way from Berlin to Frankfurt, and they built their puptents and they stayed there for a few months until the Russians got organized enough to come. So they gave all that land back to the Russians that we had captured, the Russians got all of that. So anyway, we were in this town. Down in the town was a winemaker. So the first sergeant said to me, 'I'm gonna give you some guards, and you're gonna live at the house with the winemaker.'

He said, 'It's your job to make sure that no civilian gets more than one quart a week.' It was being rationed to the civilians, but every morning I had a jeep full to take up to the camp. So that was great, we had the best of everything there. Those were the days that you remembered, when you were having a good time.

Rich Marowitz: After the war was over, they sent us to occupy Vienna. It was an international city, and I'll explain that in a minute. They issued a Vienna pass, it was written in French, Russian, English, and something else. I don't know. Anyway, and the town was split into four. And the smart thing to do was never to go to the Russian sector because you never knew if you were going to come back. They had a lot of these Mongolian characters there. Pock-marked faces and nasty looking, and you could smell them a mile away. And every once in a while you would find one in the back of the American Red Cross. They wandered over to where they weren't supposed to be. And I get a letter from my mother from where she used to go to her favorite candy store on Utica Avenue in Brooklyn; that's where we lived temporarily for a while. The owner had a daughter in Vienna who had married a German, and he had apparently protected her all this time. And she said that the wife wants to know that if she sends you a package, could you get it to her daughter, and she would enclose the address.

So I didn't really know what the hell to say and I really didn't get a chance because all of a sudden, the package showed up with the address, and I said to one of my buddies, 'Let's take a shot, we'll go over to the Russian sector.'

So we got over there. We got chased a few times. It was kind of dark by the time we found the apartment. There were no lights in the hallway. We counted the doors and felt for the number.

It was a small apartment setup. I knocked on the door and I heard this heavy German voice. 'Who's there?' And I tried to explain who it was. So then all of a sudden, the door crept open, and the first thing I saw was a gun. He saw an American soldier, and he said, 'Come on in.' And [the German husband's wife] was hiding in the bedroom. And then we sat down. Turns out, she was Jewish, and the man has protected her all this time from Germans, and Russians, and everything else. And we gave him the package and everything, and he said, 'How are you going to get back to your sector?'

I said, 'I haven't the slightest idea, but while it's dark we're getting the hell out of here!'

We took off and we got chased again and we got fired on, but it didn't seem as bad because it was dark. By this time we were so tired, I couldn't keep my eyes open. We found this little place like a little bed and breakfast, only she wasn't serving breakfast, but the place was spotlessly clean. And in Germany they had these big beds; when you got into bed, you disappeared, totally disappeared.

She said, 'I will let you stay here tonight, but you have to take your shoes off in bed!'

I said, 'I'll guarantee you we'll take our shoes off in bed!' So she let us stay the night, and we paid her. And we slept for just a couple of hours, and we got up and we got out and we got chased again, shot at again, and I immediately wrote to my mother, and I said, 'I am not taking anything more to her daughter! Just make sure...remember that! Don't make any promises!' And that was the last time I went back in there. The Russians would shoot at anything. They don't want you over there!

Doug Vink: They weren't allies to us!

Rich Marowitz: Russians are Russians; Russians are strictly for Russians, period. If you wanted to trust a Russian, that was your problem! Let me tell you something else. These guys will verify it because I guarantee you, they heard the same thing! Every time you captured Germans, what did they say? 'We'll help you fight the Russians!'

Doug Vink: That's right. They were ready at the end of the war—they said to Patton, 'We'll take our armies and join you and we'll go against Russia.'

Rich Marowitz: I mean you cannot believe how the Russians were hated by the Germans over there.

Al Cohen: Well, they wanted to hang Patton because he said we ought to keep going through Russia.

Richard Marowitz [*to students*]: You have no idea. When some people said they were going to deal with Russians… You don't deal with Russians! You think you're dealing with Russians, but you don't. They're going to do whatever the hell they want to do, whatever you say! You think you're dealing, but you're never dealing.

Doug Vink: Your division headquarters would get orders every day, and then they would filter back down the regimental command all the way to the battalion, down the company. You'd get a map. You'd get a map that you were supposed to do that much work that day. Well, with General Patton, maps didn't mean nothing. We'd be nine days off the maps! Gone! They wouldn't know where you were. But that's the way he was, but that's the way he accomplished some things.

He was up in the oil fields when they pulled him out. We were up there, right near Berlin, and we were told to stop. We could have been in Berlin about two weeks before the Russians arrived. Nope, they made that agreement at that Yalta Conference there. [Roosevelt] gave the place away.

But anyway, speaking about the Russians, they came into this town of Raunheim and they took over for months. They came in, and they had ragbags on their feet for boots. They were the most raggedy-looking things you want to look at! They had all of our equipment and our breech blocks, which is, your blocker slides back and forth to hold your big gun. Ours was always kept clean; we had every cleaning cloth. They were always kept polished, highly polished with oil. But the Russians had painted theirs green, just like the guns. I don't know how they fired! But anyway, my buddy—I had a buddy that I went through the whole war with then—I lost track of him for 35 years, but I found him last April. We've been back together. I said, 'You got any Mickey Mouse watches?'

'Yeah, well, I got a couple.'

I said, 'Well, I've got three.' The Russians are crazy over anything like that. Mickey/Minnie Mouse watch, anything.

I said, 'We're going to be leaving tomorrow and we're told to burn everything before we go. After the fire starts in all of the tents, I said, 'I got a guy down there who wants to buy the watches.' I said, 'But when I tell you to jump in that jeep and go—you jump in that jeep and go!'

He said, 'Why?'

And I said, 'You'll find out!' We went down and sold four watches for $150 each to the Russians. So I said to him now, 'Get the engine running!'

'Why?'

'Because this one here is a special one!' I wound it up.

The Russian said, 'Yes.' Gave me $150.

'Let's get out of here!'

My buddy said, 'What was so special about it?'

I said, 'It only runs five minutes!' [*Laughter*]

Al Cohen: When I first got to war trials and I was walking the prison wall, just like you see in any prison. A brick wall. And I'm walking along, and you carry the Tommy gun, and the standard operating procedure for that was, if anybody looks out of the courthouse into the exercise yard when the prisoners are in there, wave them off. Give them two waves. If they don't go, you can open up, and boy, everyone was waiting for us to open up. But the point is, down below on the ground floor where you could look through the barred windows, you saw cases of what looked like bottles of water. And every morning they would back up a two-and-one-half-ton truck, and you know how big they are, and they would unload vodka. By the end of the week that pile in that room was down to one or two cases. This went on, week after week. The Russians—they drank that like water!

Doug Vink: What I wanted really to tell you about, when I talk about the town of Raunheim, was that I was in charge of the wine cellar. At that time, we weren't allowed to fraternize with the people. We could get court-martialed for talking to them. Of course, guys like us were too stupid to realize that, so we talked to them. We were right in town with them. So anyway, one dark morning I got up, I was changing the guard. And I said to the fella, 'What's those voices up the street?'

He said, 'I don't know. The door just opened up there,' he said. 'Some people came out. They're not supposed to be on the street. There's a curfew.'

So I jump in the jeep. I said, 'You walk down the street and I'll go down the block and I'll stop on the other block.' So all of a sudden, the voices are coming, the voices are coming up fast. They get up close to me and I flash the flashlight on, and I said, 'Halt, who goes there?'

The voice booms out, 'It's all right. It's the colonel.'

I said 'Who?'

He said, 'The colonel, your battalion commander!'

I said, 'I'm sorry, sir. I'm gonna have to take you in.'

'For what?'

I said, 'Your order. Don't fraternize!' [*Laughter*] The next morning, that order was right out the window. From now on you can talk to anybody you want to talk to. We couldn't do it, but they could.

Adult Listener: You were in tanks and there have been all sorts of things after the war about how our tanks weren't very well protected. Did you know that?

Doug Vink: In them days? Oh, we knew it. We knew for the simple reason that when we first got over there and got the tanks, the most armor we had was six inches in the front and another eight around the gun. But that moved up and down, so if the Germans had their gun up, they could shoot under there, if they were good enough. They had four on the side. You had one on the bottom and two in the back, but then where the assistant driver was there was a big rack of .75 ammunition there. Now, that wasn't much there. Next to the gunner and next to the loader were other racks, and under the floor were racks. We only had one each under there. So then they came around and welded plates on the side just where the racks were, about where you were sitting in the tank.

Rich Marowitz: On the other hand, the Germans had a thing called the Tiger tank, the King Tiger. And that was scary even to look at. When we saw these tracks this wide [*makes marks with hands about three feet wide*], we got in the jeep, turned around, and went back the other way. There was nothing you could do. It was like throwing confetti at the Empire State Building.

Doug Vink: That was an eight-man tank! They'll light up anything! They'd light right up! They would light up brighter than anything. The King Tiger had five men in the turret. That was an eight-man tank! The only way you got them was to blow the bridges out behind them and call in the Air Force.

Rich Marowitz: If you ever go to Louisville, Kentucky, Fort Knox is just outside of Louisville. Right next to Fort Knox is Patton's Armor Museum. If you want to get scared to death, go to that museum. When we went into that museum, we went around the bend and we ran into this King Tiger tank. And it scared us then and there. One side was cut away and they had plastic over it so you could see in. There was a table of four guys playing poker in there, wasn't it? [*Looking at Vink*] I mean this was a monster, a total monster. Big 88 sticking out of it.

Doug Vink: We came up on one after the Air Force knocked it out. That was coming out of Bastogne. The Air Force had hit it. The piece of the gun laying on the ground was 22 feet long, and the piece sticking out of the torque was ten feet. That's not counting what was inside the torque. Just looking at them things...

Listener: They said one of the ways we were lucky is that most of them were on the eastern front.

Doug Vink: Most of them were. There weren't too many over here.

Rich Marowitz: There was enough for me, I'll tell you that right now.

Al Cohen: We went into a little town just outside of Frankfurt, which was supposed to have been taken. Well, you don't use heavy weapons, you find a tank group to go into a town to find out if there are Germans in there. You send him in [*points at Vink, the tanker*]. So anyway, we get into this town. It's supposed to have been taken. Can't find a GI, and people are hanging out white sheets, getting ready to give up. And to make a long story short, we hear tanks running around. So one of the fellas in our squad goes down the street and it turns down into another one, and we hear a tank down there. And they used to have sandboxes on the street in case of a fire to put the fire out. So he gets back. 'What happened? Where's our tanks?'

He said, 'Tanks, hell, that's Tigers!' We didn't realize they were King Tigers when we heard them. He said, 'I had to hide in one of those sandboxes for twenty minutes until they moved away!'

Rich Marowitz: The Germans really had this thing. When our guys went across the mountains, through the Siegfried Line, the call came up for muleskinners. Where they got all these stupid-looking animals I don't know, but they got them to carry stuff up the mountains. And jeeps had a hard time getting up. We got a bunch of weasels out. A weasel is a jeep with the half-tracks, treads. The Germans figured that the Americans wouldn't go over the top. You got to be stupid to go over the top, because it's so rugged. Well, they don't know how stupid the Americans are, so they brought their men down the sides, and we went over the top. [*Laughter*] Fortunately, all of their pillboxes were not manned. I say fortunately because the Siegfried Line was built many years before we got there. And you couldn't tell a pillbox when you were standing in front of it, because trees were growing out of it, everything was growing out of it. And if you were lucky, you spotted the little tiny windows that they looked out of and were shooting out of. We got round behind one. Got in it, it was unmanned. Prior to that, we were in this field in front of it where they wanted a clear view of fire, a 'field of fire,' so they cut down all the trees, and all that was left were stumps. So, you know, we were dodging behind the stumps, running around. And then we got in behind, and we walked in and I took one look into the abandoned pillbox, and I broke into a cold sweat. They had two machine guns set up; they were set up so that they could move them in either direction, by the numbers. By each machine gun was a framed picture with every stump in the clearing, and every stump had a number. And if they took the machine gun and went by that number, you were dead on that stump, if you were behind that stump or even near it, you were dead. So this was insane—it's a good thing, these Germans were... I don't know how we won the war. To tell you the truth, I don't know how we did it. We were just very lucky, and fortunately they ran out of stuff. They had better weapons and everything else.

Doug Vink: One other thing about our tanks. They had a top speed of 35 miles per hour—downhill! [*Laughter*] Downhill. I look at one of them today and wonder how the hell we ever got home in one of those things. Lost a lot of men, too.

Listener: Did you ever really get a good night's sleep?

Rich Marowitz: I don't remember. No one ever asked me before.

Doug Vink: No, once in a while you might have the chance to be in a house with no roof.

Al Cohen: One thing I wanted to mention before...If you watch *M.A.S.H.* on TV, the operating rooms weren't like that. Believe me. I lay on one table while they were working on me. The nurse next to me, she's humming and singing and she's putting a plaster cast on me and that's as close as I ever came to that.

Rich Marowitz: I was in the hospital for a while after the war. And those second lieutenant nurses were the cutest things I ever saw, they were just so cute. And talk about drugs. The lieutenant from headquarters brought me a great radio, and I was listening to music from the United States. Great bands and everything, and it pulled in everything. It was a great radio. And there was a guy a couple of beds up from me. A real jazz nut, and he said, 'Can I listen to it?'

And I said, 'Yeah, move into the next bed if you want.' He got discharged you know, and he came back a couple of days later with a big paper bag, and in the bag was a jar. He said, 'This is for you.'

I said, 'What is it?'

He said, 'Well, open it up!' So I open it up and I took out the jar and took one look at it, and this was one jar full of marijuana ready to be rolled! So I said to him, 'What are you, some kind of maniac?' I put it back, and it scared the hell out of me. I said, 'Get the hell out. I'm surrounded by officers here—I appreciate it, pal, but don't ever come back here with that crap again!' I was close to coming home. I didn't want to mess with that.

It was nearly five o'clock; our gathering was supposed to end at 2:30. As they packed up their gear, Richard summed up the day for the high school students.

"Now look at what you've learned today. You'll never find it in a book anyplace."

B-17 commander Earl M. Morrow, World War II Memorial,
Washington, D.C., June 2016. Photo: Jessica Morrow Brand.

EPILOGUE

Americans Came To Liberate

Inscription at the World War II Memorial

"OUR DEBT TO THE HEROIC MEN AND VALIANT WOMEN IN THE SERVICE OF OUR COUNTRY CAN NEVER BE REPAID. THEY HAVE EARNED OUR UNDYING GRATITUDE. AMERICA WILL NEVER FORGET THEIR SACRIFICES."

PRESIDENT HARRY S TRUMAN
Address Broadcast to the Armed Forces, April 17, 1945

I left the early morning comfort of my hotel bed before I began my busy day in order to have some quiet time by myself. I settled into my walk in our nation's capital towards the Washington Monument.

I had been here only once before, in the sixth grade on a summer trip with my mother and her friend. We went up to the top and gazed down upon Washington, D.C. and the environs. A military helicopter went over, descending, and landed on the White House lawn. President Nixon was returning from a trip to Florida to visit his friend, Bebe Rebozo, I later learned. It was a thrill for a thirteen-year-old.

Fast-forward thirty-five years. I was in the middle of the first year of an all-expenses-paid study seminar, this first segment in the summer of 2008 a week-long introduction to becoming a 'Teacher Fellow' at the United States Holocaust Memorial

Museum. That January I was asked to apply for this exclusive teacher program when staff learned of my work with American liberators and Holocaust survivors. I submitted multiple pages of documentation, including references from soldiers, survivors, administrators, and other teachers. That April, the principal called me down to the office for a chat. Now no one, including teachers, likes to be called to the principal's office. But he came around his desk with his hand out, and told me, 'Congratulations, I just got a call from the Holocaust Museum in Washington. You're going there in July!'

It would be the most intense study of my career to that date.[27] From early morning to late at night after dinner together, thirteen other teachers from across the nation and I were tasked with lectures from world-class Holocaust historians and scholars and behind-the-scenes tours with museum staff in all departments. We were being trained to

---

[27] *the most intense study of my career to date-* this experience would be followed by more intense study and travel to the authentic sites of the Holocaust; a 2013 three-week tour with the Holocaust and Jewish Resistance Teachers Program, and a 2016 three-week residency at the International School for Holocaust Studies at Yad Vashem in Jerusalem.

be teachers of teachers, developing best practices to inform and educate others on the very complicated history behind the most horrific crime in the history of the world, a crime that our GIs would have first-hand knowledge of. But how could I return to our nation's capital, after those 35 years, and not go to the World War II Memorial showcased now right near the Washington Monument on the Mall?

The only way I would really have time to see it for myself would be if I got out of bed at the crack of dawn and walked over there from the hotel before heading across the Mall to the museum. Fifty flags fluttered in the breeze as I strolled past the Washington Monument towards my destination, the sun delivering her first rays proclaiming another hot day. I had something to see. The inscription at the base of the flagpole as I entered this national shrine read,

"AMERICANS CAME TO LIBERATE, NOT CONQUER"

The Atlantic Arch and the Pacific Arch victory pavilions flank columns of bronze and granite representing every state and U.S. territory at the time of World War II; 4,038 gold-plated silver stars on the nearby Freedom Wall symbolize the loss of a hundred servicemen and women each. On this summer morning, it is a quiet place of reflection, a place to recall the efforts and sacrifices of so many families; the only other person here at this moment was a National Park service employee cleaning coins out of the magnificent fountains. Ground was broken on the Mall shortly after the 9/11 attacks on our nation; since it formally opened in 2004, thousands of World War II veterans have been flown in to the World War II Memorial, making, in many cases, a final pilgrimage to mark the years that forged their lives. The inscription on the Freedom Wall simply reads,

~HERE WE MARK THE PRICE OF FREEDOM~

*

Nearly 70 years after the war, scholars discovered that we are only beginning to understand the extent of the Holocaust. By 2008, researchers at the United States Holocaust Memorial Museum had cataloged some 42,500 Nazi ghettos and camps throughout Europe from 1933 to 1945. The figure was "so staggering that even fellow Holocaust scholars had to make sure they had heard it correctly; the documented camps include not only 'killing centers' but also thousands of forced labor camps, where prisoners manufactured war supplies; prisoner-of-war camps; sites euphemistically named 'care' centers, where pregnant women were forced to have abortions or their babies were killed after birth; and brothels, where women were coerced into having sex with German military personnel."[18]

So much for 'but we did not know!'

*

Leo DiPalma toured Nuremberg with his daughter in 2000. Shortly thereafter, she began to record her father's stories, which became his autobiography. The book caught the attention of Eli Rosenbaum, the United States' chief law enforcement officer responsible for bringing to justice and deporting Nazi war criminals. He praised

DiPalma's efforts to remind people of the dangers of remaining silent in the face of evil. In 2009, in its replicated Nuremberg courtroom, the Virginia Holocaust Museum presented Leo with its inaugural Legacy of Nuremberg award and unveiled a wax figure of a Palace of Justice guard modeled after Leo, who then gave a riveting talk after being introduced by Rosenbaum. "When he talked to audiences about that, I think that [the idea that these crimes against humanity were perpetrated by human beings] comes through. It's easy, and it's more comforting, in a way, to think that [the perpetrators are] monsters; you know, [like], 'just be on the alert for monsters.' But that's not the message of Nuremberg."

Leo and his daughter gave talks to students and others for a few more years, until, as with so many of our veterans who offered their testimony as an example, it was just time to stop and rest. In 2018, with his wife having passed, he moved to a Massachusetts veterans nursing home, where he was loved and enjoyed the remainder of his days in the company of fellow veterans, relishing the visits from his family. In early 2020, his faculties now fading, his daughter Emily recalled, 'I just got this feeling that I needed to go see him, and I needed to go see him that day. I told him that he was a good dad and that I loved him, and I talked about our [Nuremberg] trip. And he looked up at me and he held my hand, and he smiled.'

Two weeks later, he was diagnosed with COVID-19; due to restrictions, she was unable to see her father again. 'It's kind of like a long pain that's just carried out. So, it's tough; but I knew my dad, and he wanted people to never forget what he did during World War II so that the rest of us could stay safe for the future. I feel like I need to carry that on; I'm honoring his life, not how he died.'

Leo DiPalma passed away at the age of 93 on April 8, 2020, as a result of the coronavirus outbreak at the facility.[28] Another daughter managed to see Leo a few hours before he died; she reported back to the family that a National Guardsman was posted outside of his door.

*

---

[28] The coronavirus outbreak there left at least 76 veterans dead, devastating their families and resulting in charges against the facility's administrators.

As Tony Hayes so poignantly discovered, Dachau and the memory of the experiences of our GIs—the trauma, the heartbreak, the good times, and the really, really bad times—should always be with us. One reader posted on my Facebook author page,

My father was a combat infantryman in WW II. He lived with PTSD for seventy years. I know he only told us a little of what happened, and he told us almost nothing, until the last few years of his life.

Before that, he would call his friend Paul, who was in the same unit as my father. Even after Paul died, he would drive one hundred miles to "talk to Paul" at the cemetery, because Paul was the only one he knew who understood what they had gone through. Only after Dad was unable to drive that hundred miles, did he really start telling us any significant part of what had happened.

These young men and women, caught up in the whirlwind of World War II, set the course of history by their deeds. Not all rose to the challenge, but the modest, the terrified, the sometimes bewildered-at-what-they-were-seeing young men and women slew the beast, and then tried to get on with their lives. Not everything gets packed away neatly, however, but I hope that by unlimbering their burdens to their interviewers, and now on these pages, we can return with them to the central theme of this series, to honor these lives so well-lived, and to remember their friends who did not make it home with them:

Dying for freedom isn't the worst that could happen. Being forgotten is.

Thank you for reading!

I hope you found this book interesting and informative; I sure learned a lot researching and writing it. If you liked it, you'll love the other books!

***

THE THINGS OUR FATHERS SAW ® SERIES:

VOICES OF THE PACIFIC THEATER

WAR IN THE AIR: GREAT DEPRESSION TO COMBAT

WAR IN THE AIR: COMBAT, CAPTIVITY, REUNION

UP THE BLOODY BOOT-THE WAR IN ITALY

D-DAY AND BEYOND

THE BULGE AND BEYOND

ACROSS THE RHINE

ON TO TOKYO

HOMEFRONT/WOMEN AT WAR

CHINA, BURMA, INDIA

ABOUT THE AUTHOR

Photo Credit: Joan K. Lentini; May 2017.

Matthew Rozell is an award-winning history teacher, author, speaker, and blogger on the topic of the most cataclysmic events in the history of mankind—World War II and the Holocaust. Rozell has been featured as the 'ABC World News Person of the Week' and has had his work as a teacher filmed for the CBS Evening News, NBC Learn, the Israeli Broadcast Authority, the United States Holocaust Memorial Museum, and the New York State United Teachers. He writes on the power of teaching and the importance of the study of history at TeachingHistoryMatters.com, and you can 'Like' his Facebook author page at AuthorMatthewRozell for updates.

Mr. Rozell is a sought-after speaker on World War II, the Holocaust, and history education, motivating and inspiring his audiences with the lessons of the past. Visit MatthewRozell.com for availability/details.

...And if you would like to learn more about our GIs and the Holocaust...

~SOON TO BE A MAJOR FILM~

"What healing this has given to the survivors and military men!"-Reviewer

FROM THE ABC WORLD NEWS 'PERSON OF THE WEEK'

A TRAIN NEAR MAGDEBURG

THE HOLOCAUST, AND THE REUNITING OF THE SURVIVORS AND SOLDIERS, 70 YEARS ON

–Featuring testimony from 15 American liberators and over 30 Holocaust survivors
–500 pages-extensive notes and bibliographical references

BOOK ONE—THE HOLOCAUST
BOOK TWO—THE AMERICANS
BOOK THREE—LIBERATION
BOOK FOUR—REUNION

THE HOLOCAUST *was a watershed event in history. In this book, Matthew Rozell reconstructs a lost chapter—the liberation of a 'death train' deep in the heart of Nazi Germany in the closing days of*

World War II. Drawing on never-before-published eye-witness accounts, survivor testimony, and wartime reports and letters, Rozell brings to life the incredible true stories behind the iconic 1945 liberation photographs taken by the soldiers who were there. He weaves together a chronology of the Holocaust as it unfolds across Europe, and goes back to literally retrace the steps of the survivors and the American soldiers who freed them. Rozell's work results in joyful reunions on three continents, seven decades later. He offers his unique perspective on the lessons of the Holocaust for future generations, and the impact that one person can make.

A selection of comments left by reviewers:

"**Extraordinary research** into an event which needed to be told. I have read many books about the Holocaust and visited various museums but had not heard reference to this train previously. The fact that people involved were able to connect, support and help heal each other emotionally was amazing."

"**The story of the end of the Holocaust and the Nazi regime** told from a very different and precise angle. First-hand accounts from Jewish survivors and the US soldiers that secured their freedom. Gripping."

"**Mr. Rozell travels 'back to the future'** of people who were not promised a tomorrow; neither the prisoners nor the troops knew what horrors the next moment would bring. He captures the parallel experience of soldiers fighting ruthless Nazism and the ruthless treatment of Jewish prisoners."

"**If you have any trepidation** about reading a book on the Holocaust, this review is for you. [Matthew Rozell] masterfully conveys the individual stories of those featured in the book in a manner that does not leave the reader with a sense of despair, but rather a sense of purpose."

"**Could not put this book down**--I just finished reading *A Train Near Magdeburg*. Tears fell as I read pages and I smiled through others. I wish I could articulate the emotions that accompanied me through the stories of these beautiful people."

"**Everyone should read this book**, detailing the amazing bond that formed between Holocaust survivors likely on their way to death in one last concentration camp as WWII was about to end, and a small number of American soldiers that happened upon the stopped train and liberated the victims. The lifelong friendships that resulted between the survivors and their liberators is a testament to compassion and goodness. It is amazing that the author is not Jewish but a 'reluctant' history teacher who ultimately becomes a Holocaust scholar. This is a great book."

About This Book/ Acknowledgements

*

A note on historiographical style and convention: to enhance accuracy, consistency, and readability, I corrected punctuation and spelling and sometimes even place names, but only after extensive research. I did take the liberty of occasionally condensing the speaker's voice, eliminating side tangents or incidental information not relevant to the matter at hand. Sometimes two or more interviews with the same person were combined for readability and narrative flow. All of the words of the subjects, however, are essentially their own.

Additionally, I chose to utilize footnotes and endnotes where I deemed them appropriate, directing readers who wish to learn more to my sources, notes, and side commentary. I hope that they do not detract from the flow of the narrative.

*

First, I wish to acknowledge the hundreds of students who passed through my classes and who forged the bonds with the World War II generation. I promised you these books someday, and now that many of you are yourselves parents, you can tell your children this book is for them. Who says young people are indifferent to the past? Here is evidence to the contrary.

The Hudson Falls Central School District and my former colleagues have my deep appreciation for supporting this endeavor and recognizing its significance throughout the years.

Cara Quinlan's sharp proofing and suggestions helped to clean up the original manuscript.

Naturally this work would not have been possible had it not been for the willingness of the veterans to share their stories for posterity. All of the veterans who were interviewed for this book had the foresight to complete release forms granting access to their stories, and for us to share the information with the New York State Military

Museum's Veterans Oral History Project, where copies of the original interviews reside. Wayne Clarke and Mike Russert of the NYSMMVOP were instrumental in cultivating this relationship with my classes over the years and are responsible for some of the interviews in this book as well; Lt. Col. Robert von Hasseln and Michael Aikey also conducted some of these NYSMM interviews. Please see the 'Source Notes.'

I also have decided to dedicate this volume to the memory of Tom Warner, Sr.—a Korea vet personally decorated by President Truman—and a huge fan of this series, who told me that as he received each new volume, he would read it very slowly, because he did not want it to end. Tom passed at the age of 90 as this book was going to press.

I would be remiss if I did not recall the profound influence of my late mother and father, Mary and Tony Rozell, both cutting-edge educators and proud early supporters of my career. To my younger siblings Mary, Ned, Nora, and Drew, all accomplished writers and authors, thank you for your encouragement as well. Final and deepest appreciations go to my wife Laura and our children,

Emma, Ned, and Mary. Thank you for indulging the old man as he attempted to bring to life the stories he collected as a young one.

NOTES

—THE INTERVIEWS—

Source Notes: **Nicholas F. Butrico.** Interviewed by Michael Russert and Wayne Clarke, February 3, 2003, Congers, NY. Deposited at NYS Military Museum.

Source Notes: **Albert A. Tarbell.** Interviewed by Michael Russert and Wayne Clarke, January 16, 2003. Syracuse, NY. Deposited at NYS Military Museum.

Source Notes: **Richard M. Marowitz.** Interviewed by Michael Aikey and Wayne Clarke, October 8, 2001. Latham, NY. Interviewed by Matthew Rozell, April 28, 2000, for the Hudson Falls HS World War II Living History Project, Hudson Falls, NY. Deposited at NYS Military Museum.

Source Notes: **Timothy J. Horgan.** Interviewed by Christopher Smith, December 3, 2005, for the Hudson Falls HS World War II Living History Project. Glens Falls, NY. Deposited at NYS Military Museum. Chris also contributed to this transcript and analysis.

Source Notes: **Lawrence E. Bennett.** Interviewed by Michael Russert and Wayne Clarke, January 8, 2003. Newburgh, NY. Deposited at NYS Military Museum.

Source Notes: **Augustine John DiFiore.** Interviewed by Michael Russert and Wayne Clarke, March 20, 2003. Brooklyn, NY. Deposited at NYS Military Museum. Student Reanna Rainbow contributed to this transcript and analysis.

Source Notes: **Robert C. Baldridge**. Interviewed by Michael Russert and Wayne Clarke, August 4, 2004. Lawrence, NY. Deposited at NYS Military Museum.

Source Notes: **Rudolf F. Drenick**. Interviewed by Michael Russert and Wayne Clarke, November 18, 2003. South Setauket, NY. Deposited at NYS Military Museum.

Source Notes: **Charles J. Zappo.** Interviewed by Michael Russert and Wayne Clarke, May 17,

2007. Buffalo, NY. Deposited at NYS Military Museum. Student Joseph Marine contributed to this transcript and analysis.

Source Notes: **Alvin M. Cohen.** Interviewed by Michael Aikey and Wayne Clarke, August 8, 2001. Latham, NY. Interviewed by Matthew Rozell, April 28, 2000, for the Hudson Falls HS World War II Living History Project, Hudson Falls, NY. Deposited at NYS Military Museum.

Source Notes: **Emilio J. DiPalma.** Interviewed by Michael Russert and Wayne Clarke, June 28, 2002. Cambridge, NY. Deposited at NYS Military Museum.

Source Notes: **Douglas Vink.** Interviewed by Matthew Rozell, April 28, 2000, for the Hudson Falls HS World War II Living History Project, Hudson Falls, NY. Deposited at NYS Military Museum.

---

[1] 12,500 tons a day- Hickman, Kennedy. '*World War II: Operation Market-Garden Overview.*' ThoughtCo, Aug. 28, 2020, thoughtco.com/world-war-ii-operation-market-garden-2361452.
[2] Childers, Thomas. *World War II: A Social and Military History. Part II, Lecture 20. Operation Market Garden and the Battle of the Bulge.* The Teaching Company. 1998.
[3] Miller, Donald L. *The Story of World War II.* New York: Simon & Schuster, 2001. 329.

[4] MacDonald, Charles. *A Time for Trumpets-The Untold Story of the Battle of the Bulge.* New York City: Morrow. 2002.

[5] Lippman, David. *Operation Plunder: Crossing the Rhine.* Warfare History Network. warfarehistorynetwork.com/2016/09/15/operation-plunder-crossing-the-rhine

[6] Obituary. *Alexander Drabik, 82, First G.I. To Cross Remagen Bridge in 1945.* New York Times, Oct. 2, 1993.

[7] Ludendorff Bridge. Wikipedia. en.wikipedia.org/wiki/Ludendorff_Bridge

[8] Operation Paperclip- Ossad, Steve. *The Liberation of Nordhausen Concentration Camp.* Warfare History Network. December 31, 2019. warfarehistorynetwork.com/2019/12/31/the-liberation-of-nordhausen-concentration-camp/

[9] Operation Paperclip- Ossad, Steve. *The Liberation of Nordhausen Concentration Camp.* Warfare History Network. December 31, 2019. warfarehistorynetwork.com/2019/12/31/the-liberation-of-nordhausen-concentration-camp/

[10] Van Lunteren, Frank. *Blocking Kampfgruppe Peiper: The 504th Parachute Infantry Regiment in the Battle of the Bulge.* Philadelphia and Oxford, Casemate Publishers. 2015. 192.

[11] Gavin, James M. *On To Berlin: Battles of an Airborne Commander, 1943-1946.* New York, Viking Press. 1978. 286-288.

[12] Wöbbelin. Holocaust Encyclopedia. United States Holocaust Memorial Museum. encyclopedia.ushmm.org/content/en/article/woebbelin

[13] Gavin, James M. *On To Berlin: Battles of an Airborne Commander, 1943-1946.* New York, Viking Press. 1978. 286-288.

[14] Childers, Thomas. *World War II: A Military and Social History. Part III, Lecture 28, The Race for Berlin.* The Teaching Company, 1998.

[15] Some text from final paragraphs from testimony found in Michael Takiff's *Brave Men, Gentle Heroes: American Fathers and Sons in World War II and Vietnam.* New York: HarperCollins, 2003. 258.

[16] 504th Parachute Infantry in WWII. Facebook page post, March 7, 2006. facebook.com/504thPIR

[17] Hayes, Tony. *Dachau Will Always Be with Us.* March, 2015. Accessed at getitwriteblog.wordpress.com/2015/03/12/dachau-will-always-be-with-us/

[18] Lichtblau, Eric. *The Holocaust Just Got More Shocking.* The New York Times, March 1, 2013.

www.ingramcontent.com/pod-product-compliance
Lightning Source LLC
LaVergne TN
LVHW011925070526
838202LV00054B/4501